D1757296

SHAKESPEARE
MANIPULATED

SHAKESPEARE MANIPULATED

The Use
of the Dramatic Works
of Shakespeare in *teatro di figura* in Italy

Susan Young

Madison • Teaneck
Fairleigh Dickinson University Press
London: Associated University Presses

Associated University Presses
440 Forsgate Drive
Cranbury, NJ 08512

Associated University Presses
25 Sicilian Avenue
London WC1A 2QH, England

Associated University Presses
P.O. Box 338, Port Credit
Mississauga, Ontario
Canada L5G 4L8

The paper used in this publication meets the requirements
of the American National Standard for Permanence of Paper
for Printed Library Materials Z39.48-1984.

Library of Congress Cataloging-in-Publication Data

Young, Susan, 1953 Mar. 31–
    Shakespeare manipulated : the use of the dramatic works of
Shakespeare in teatro di figura in Italy / Susan Young.
        p.   cm.
    Includes bibliographical references and index.
    ISBN 0-8386-3578-4 (alk. paper)
    1. Puppet theater—Italy.   2. Puppet plays, Italian.
3. Shakespeare, William, 1564–1616—Adaptations.   I. Title.
PN1978.I8Y68   1996
791.5'3'0945—dc20   95-21989
                                                              CIP

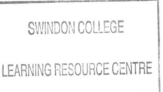

PRINTED IN THE UNITED STATES OF AMERICA

Contents

Acknowledgments

The research was conducted in Italy with the support of a much appreciated scholarship from the Italian government. I would like to acknowledge the unfailing kindness and generosity of the *marionettisti* and *burattinai* who answered my questions and allowed me access to their archives, especially Maurizio Dotti, Eugenio Monti Colla, Mariagrazia Citerbio, and all members of the Compagnia Carlo Colla e Figli, Stefania Colla of Gianni and Cosetta Colla, Signora Marta Latis, Signora Pina Ravasio and family, and Claudio Cinelli.

I am also grateful for assistance from Dott. Piervaleriano Angelini (Centro Teatro di Figura, Cervia), Dott. Remo Melloni (Civica Scuola d'Arte Drammatica, Milan) and Dott. Angione (Museo della marionetta piemontese Teatro Gianduja, Turin).

In addition, I am very much indebted to my hosts in Italy, Dott. Gianni Stecchi and Carla Mazzuoli Stecchi.

In New Zealand this undertaking has been greatly assisted by the advice of Prof. MacDonald Jackson, Shakespearean scholar and exceptional teacher. A debt of long standing is owed to Dr. Adalgisa Giorgio, Mike Hanne, and Laurence Simmons for years of encouragement.

Introduction

A connection between the greatest English dramatist and an Italian theatrical genre that many dismiss as children's entertainment, now rendered obsolete by television, may seem tenuous. However, such a link existed even during Shakespeare's lifetime. Evidence of the presence of Italian *marionettisti*[1] and *burattinai* in London in the sixteenth century is recorded by Yorick who writes of:

> una lettera del Consiglio Privato, indirizzata al Lord Mayor di Londra il 14 luglio 1573 che autorizzava, come per lo passato e fin da tempo immemorabile, i burattinai italiani a stabilire nella City le loro Strange-motions.[2]

There were several theaters established in the region by these companies; in London at Stourbridge fair, Holborn Bridge, and in Fleet Street, and also at Eltham. The letter authorizing the establishment of theaters for *marionette* and *burattini* predates by three years the construction of London's first theater, built by Burbage in Shoreditch in 1576. In fact, Thomas Dekker claims to have attended a performance of *Julius Caesar* by *marionette* before he saw it performed by actors in 1599 at the newly built Globe Theater.[3] As early as 1626 a version of *Hamlet* for *marionette* was performed in Europe; first in Dresden, then in Hamburg, Gdańsk, and Frankfurt.[4]

If Shakespeare knew Italian *marionettisti* or *burattinai*, it could have been from this acquaintance that he drew his knowledge of Italy, as suggested by Bergonzini:

> La vecchia disputa se Shakespeare avesse, o no, conosciuto di persona l'Italia Settentrionale per i riferimenti precisi a luoghi e consuetudini riportati nelle sue opere (il pozzo di San Gregorio presso Milano nel 'Due gentiluomini di Verona', Bellario come nome padovano, la messa di sera a Verona, i particolari del funerale di Giulietta in 'Giulietta e Romeo', i ricordi della Borsa di Rialto e del traghetto che congiunge Venezia con la terra ferma nel 'Mercante di Venezia' per citarne solo alcuni) potrebbe trovare una ragionevole soluzione nel fatto certo che il grande drammaturgo inglese aveva conosciuto burattinai italiani

9

(egli fa spessissimo riferimento nelle sue opere ai personaggi di legno) nei luoghi che egli stesso frequentava, come la locanda dell'Oliphant in Bankside, l'allora quartiere dei teatri. Dagli spettacoli di questi operatori è molto probabile abbia poi tratto quella conoscenza topografica e delle consuetudini del nostro paese che tanto meraviglia ed affatica gli studiosi dell'opera shakespeariana.[5]

That Shakespeare was familiar with performances by *marionettisti* and *burattinai* is evident from the many references in his works to the wooden actors.[6] The performances which Shakespeare had seen must have been staged by Italian companies because they began to perform in London more than twenty years before the arrival of their English counterparts, by which time Shakespeare had already written eighteen plays:

Nel 1573 si impiantò a Londra il primo teatrino italiano, che dovette avere spesso nel suo pubblico Gugliemo Shakespeare, così sollecito a rammentare le marionette in tanti passi delle sue opere; mentre proprio alla fine del secolo (1599) si presentò il primo burattinaio inglese, un certo Captain Pod.[7]

It could also be claimed that the *marionettisti* played a significant part in keeping alive the Elizabethan theater because in the eighteen years from 1642 during which the theaters were closed by Parliament, the wooden actors were permitted to continue their performances:

Soltanto i puppet-players si avvantaggiano di questo stato di cose: sembra che le marionette siano tollerate (al pari dei combattimenti dei tori!) come spettacolo non nocivo. Certi marionettisti di Norwich che godono fama di grande abilità sono invitati a venir a Londra. La voga delle teste di legno non cessa, col ristabilirsi della monarchia, anzi, le marionette nell'ottobre del 1662 sono chiamate a corte a divertire Carlo II e la sua famiglia, così dice Samuel Pepys. Gli attori veri sono gelosi e preoccupati e si danno da fare perché i marionettisti non facciano la parte del leone.[8]

Perhaps more than any other country, Italy can be seen to have influenced Elizabethan drama. There was a belief that Italy was a nation steeped in depravity, and the tales of a number of returning travelers reinforced this notion so that the English viewed Italy with mingled horror and fascination. In the Elizabethan drama, an Italian setting became a convention that set up certain expectations in the audience. Italians were seen as vengeful, treacherous, and lustful, and behavior of this type would automatically be expected from the characters. For such dramatists as Webster, Jonson, and Middleton, Italy was characterized by Machiavellian villains, poisoning, jealousy, feuding, luxurious but decadent courts, sexual depravity, and the pursuit of revenge. However, in the case of Shakespeare, as Praz points out:

> his Italian plays are comparatively free from the usual horrors and thrills. Horrible murders and treasons occur indeed on the Shakespearean stage but, oddly enough, not as a rule in the plays whose action takes place in Italy.[9]

In fact, a very different picture of Italy can be discerned in Shakespeare's plays, that of a sophisticated world of art, music, courtiership, education, Neoplatonic philosophy, and humanism.[10]

Much critical attention has been devoted both to the influence of Italy on English drama and to the fortunes of Shakespearean works on the Italian stage.[11] However most studies of the latter topic confine their attention to live theater. While some work has been done on Shakespeare in opera, ballet, film, or television, there has been little investigation of the use of his works in the theater of *marionette* and *burattini,* even though these theaters, especially in the late nineteenth century, were numerous, attracted large audiences, and were regarded by live theaters as serious competitors. Lombardo, Nulli, Corona, and Busi, for example, all examine the staging of Shakespeare in Italy but exclude from consideration the performances in the theater of *marionette.*[12] Hilary Gatti records seven productions using *marionette* in Milan between 1821 and 1867 in an appendix to her study *Shakespeare nei teatri milanesi dell'Ottocento* but makes no comment on them in the body of the book.[13] Perhaps this lack of attention is due to an underestimation, shared initially by the writer, of the extent to which Shakespeare featured in the repertoire of Italian theater of *marionette* and *burattini.* However, during the course of research, records have been found of some seventy productions by fifty companies dating back to 1821. These figures almost certainly represent only a small percentage of the actual performances. It is estimated that there were four hundred companies of *marionettisti* and *burattinai* in Italy in the nineteenth century[14] but for the vast majority of these we have no documented record of their history or repertoire.

Much of the early literature which dealt with the theater of *marionette* and *burattini* lacked scholarly rigor. One of the first publications devoted to the topic was *Storia dei burattini* written in 1884 by Pietro Coccoluto Ferrigni under the pseudonym of Yorick.[15] It was, for the most part, a rewriting of Magnin's *L'histoire des marionnettes en Europe*,[16] published in Paris in 1852, and attempts to valorize this theatrical genre by recording instances of illustrious personages amongst the audience but fails to document the vast amount of historical information which it contains. The next major work on the topic, Alessandro Cervellati's *Storia dei burattini e burattinai bolognesi*,[17] was not published until 1964. It is an enormously valuable record and contains much information that cannot be found elsewhere. The book includes an extensive bibliography but provides no references in the text of its primary source for specific findings. Scholarly treatment of the genre began in the late 1950s with the work of Roberto Leydi and Maria Signorelli,[18] both of whom have continued their writing and research on the topic until the present. Maria Signorelli also did extensive work in the area of the educational potential of *teatro di figura*. The most important publications to date were both catalogues of exhibitions held in 1980: *Burattini, marionette e pupi* and *Burattini e marionette in Italia dal Cinquecento ai giorni nostri*. Both works provide, for the first time, a compilation of documented factual information and avoid the romantic and somewhat patronizing approach common in writings that deal with any form of popular culture. The theater of *pupi* has received considerably more attention owing to the work of Pitrè[19] in the 1880s which dealt extensively with popular culture in Sicily. The work of Antonio Pasqualino[20] over the past twenty years is outstanding in its breadth of approach, encompassing literary, historical, anthropological, and semiotic concerns. A common feature of recent writing on the subject has been lengthy discussion of the origins of *teatro di figura*[21] in an attempt to create an illustrious pedigree for the genre.[22] While there is no doubt that *marionette* and their cousins were present in ancient civilizations, the exact lineage can only be a matter for conjecture and most discussions of it add nothing that can be proven. A further criticism of much that has been written about *teatro di figura* is that the underlying assumption is that it is an impoverished imitation of "real" theater, rather than an independent theatrical genre with its own characteristics. In addition, there has been a tendency to treat all forms of *teatro di figura* as components of a single genre, and a lack of precision in the terminology used (which can perhaps be blamed on Collodi who mistakenly described Pinocchio as a *burattino!*). For this reason, I will avoid the general term "puppet" in favor of the Italian terms which distinguish clearly between *marionette, burattini,* and *pupi.* Worthy of study, but often ignored, is the performance itself, and its status as a form of popular culture.

The topic for this study and its method of approach were decided upon only after considerable study of the literature and in response to perceived inadequacies or omissions. The observations upon which the research has been structured can be summarized as follows:

1. In the early romantic and unscholarly writing and more recent academic investigations of the nature of the genre, there is little factual information about the performers, their repertoire, dates, and places. This lack is addressed in the catalogue section which is a compilation from many sources of performance details, with the dual purpose of recording the data and providing a base for the discussion which follows.

2. Theater with *marionette, burattini,* or *pupi* is rarely based upon a published text to which reference can be made in discussion of the performance. Comparatively few of the handwritten outlines or texts which were used are extant and in many cases, all that remains is a list of the titles in the repertoire that gives no indication of the nature of the performance. For this reason, several outlines have been incorporated into the catalogue section and two manuscript texts neither of which is easily accessible, have been reproduced in the appendices.

3. The distinctions between the types of *teatro di figura* are not always clarified but they exist to such a degree that the different types cannot be treated as a single theatrical genre. For this reason, the catalogue is divided according to technique and is prefaced in this introductory section by a discussion of the differences.

4. Performances in the field of *teatro di figura* have rarely been accorded the critical attention which is given to other types of theater. Even a production such as the Colla/De Filippo *Tempest* which inaugurated the Venice Biennale and received a great deal of favorable response from the press, has been mentioned only fleetingly in the literature.[23] It will therefore be considered in greater depth in a section which follows the catalogue.

5. Much of the repertoire of the theater of *marionette, burattini,* and *pupi* is an integral part of such theater. The repertoire

has been extended however by the appropriation of works from other types of spectacle. The aim of the concluding section is to examine the outcome of such appropriation, in this case of the drama of Shakespeare, and the areas of conflict or coincidence between the two forms.

6. To date, any mention of the inclusion of a Shakespearean work in the repertoire is intended to illustrate the breadth of the repertoire and is cited as evidence of cultural worth. While this is perhaps an understandable response to the prevailing dismissive treatment of alternative theater, it has resulted in a failure to record the far more interesting question of how the work was performed, what adaptations were made, and how it was received by the audience. Yet these are the obvious aspects which would be addressed in an account of a film, ballet or operatic version of a Shakespearean work. Wherever possible in the catalogue listings these aspects have been considered but often too little is known to be able to answer these questions.

7. Throughout its history, Italian theater with *marionette* has been afflicted by a sense of inferiority with regard to live theater. The *marionettisti* responded by seeking to equal or surpass the spectacle of live theater and by imitating its repertoire, as we shall see when considering their use of Shakespearean drama. Theater with *burattini* however has always been unashamedly popular and more certain of its unique creative potential, thus its use of Shakespeare is usually a confident appropriation and transformation rather than an emulation of another genre. The extent to which *teatro di figura* is part of popular culture and the confrontation between popular and elite theatrical forms will be considered.

8. Semioticians identify a system of signs which operates in live theater and is understood by the audience. The nature of the *marionetta* or *burattino* as a sign will be compared to that of the actor and aspects of *teatro di figura* will be considered in the light of its particular system of signs.

The research began with a search of the literature for any information about the repertoire of companies of *marionettisti, burattinai,* or *pupari.* If the repertoire included Shakespearean productions, as much detail as possible about the company concerned was gathered. The bulk of the research was carried out at the Biblioteca Nazionale Centrale Firenze but work was also done in Florence at the Biblioteca Marucelliana, the Biblioteca del Gabinetto Scientifico-Letterario G. P. Vieusseux, the Biblioteca dell'Istituto Britannico and the Biblioteca Bernard Berenson at the Villa I Tatti. In addition, visits were made to the following research centers and museums: the Civica Scuola d'Arte Drammatica and the Museo Teatrale alla Scala in Milan, the Civico Museo Teatrale Casa di Goldoni and the Museo del Settecento Veneziano in Venice, the library of the Dipartimento musica e spettacolo at the University of Bologna, the Centro Teatro di Figura in Cervia, and the Centro Studi del Teatro Stabile in Turin. In the case of the more recent productions, companies were visited and *marionettisti* and *burattinai* were interviewed. Wherever possible, surviving documentation was recorded and photographs were taken. The productions range from those which are extensively documented with much surviving material (*marionette* or *burattini, copioni,* press reviews, programs, etc.) to those which are recorded only by a single, fleeting, and unsubstantiated reference. Since the aim of this research was to gather as much information as possible about the use of Shakespearean drama in Italian *teatro di figura,* even the productions of which so little is known have been included.

The material has been arranged chronologically but it has also been divided into four sections according to the technique used. Within the wider field of *teatro di figura* in Italy there are three distinct types of "figure" used and recently there have also been productions which combine "figure" and actor. A brief explanation of the terminology is contained in the glossary and each section is preceded by more detailed information. However it would be appropriate here to discuss the differences between theater with *marionette, burattini,* and *pupi.*

On a socioeconomic level, *marionettisti* and *burattinai* generally occupy quite different positions. A *burattinaio* can operate alone, or with a single assistant, and his equipment can be limited to a portable *baracca* and a dozen *burattini.* A company of *marionettisti* however requires considerably more people and a greater investment in equipment: hundreds of *marionette,* a large selection of costumes and properties, many sets, and a collection of *copioni.* Such a company is often a large scale family operation which is continued by successive generations. While a *burattinaio* is often assisted by his wife and children, he is rarely able to support an extended family and sons or daughters who wish to follow the family craft must leave and form an independent company.

The two types of theater also differ in their scenographic aims. The *burattinaio* has a style which is simplified and based on convention with minimal use of props. Very little use is made of any type of furnishing and the props most commonly used are those which can be grasped by the *burattino* such as weapons, a bag, or a letter. Special effects are limited to sound effects for the firing of guns and perhaps flames or smoke to accompany the appearance of the devil, but much is left to the imagination of the spectator. However, the traditional *marionettista* aims for a miniaturized "reality" in the appearance and movement of the *marionette* and the perspective of the backdrops. The productions were often based on those of the live theater and the audience was attracted as much by the virtuosity of the imitation as by its intrinsic value. For example, in 1881 the Teatro alla Scala presented Manzotti's ballet *Excelsior* which was a great success and had over two hundred performances. In 1884 the *marionettisti* Compagnia Carlo Colla e Figli staged a replica which was equally successful and was such a showcase for the technical expertise of the *marionettista* that it remains in the company's repertoire and continues to be performed. The range of special effects employed by the *marionettista* is extensive and the history of this form of theater has been one of constant technical innovation in an endeavor to equal or surpass the effects of live theater.

Marionettisti frequently base their performance on a written text, often their own adaptation of a literary or dramatic work. The *burattinaio* rarely uses more than a brief outline and either improvises the dialogue or supplies it from memory. It may have been drawn from previous study of a written text but may also have been acquired by oral tradition, especially prior to this century when the level of illiteracy in the south of Italy was very high.

The relationship between a *burattinaio* and the *burattino* is very close and immediate because the *burattino* becomes an extension of the body of its animator and usually speaks with his voice. The *marionetta* however is separated physically from its operator by the length of the strings, and psychologically by the slight delay in the action as it is transmitted and by the fact that it is often someone other than the *marionettista* who gives voice to the *marionetta*.

Notwithstanding the distinctions outlined above, the two theatrical forms remain closely linked. This is evident from the number of *marionettisti* who are also *burattinai*. Also, there are examples of *burattinai* who mount productions of serious drama with elaborate costumes and scenery, and *marionettisti* who produce satirical works. A common feature of the traditional forms of both types of theater is that they were destined for an adult audience, judging by the obscene or politically subversive remarks which attracted the attention of the censor to theater with *burattini*[24] and the so-phisticated themes of some theater with *marionette.*

Although *pupi* are almost identical in their construction to *marionette,* their form of theater has similarities to both of the other types. It resembles theater of *marionette* in its repertoire of serious dramatic works and the absence of satire and comedy but shares with theater of *burattini* a simplicity of staging and the use of a brief outline rather than a written text. The *pupo* is operated by means of a rod which passes through the head and is attached to the trunk and often there is a second rod attached to the right hand. These rods are stronger and shorter than the strings which control the *marionetta,* so the animation is more direct and closer to the manipulation of the *burattino* than the *marionetta.* It is this style of animation which makes possible the combat scenes, which are similar to the beatings which are a trademark of the theater of *burattini.*

The language used in the performances should be considered at this point because the natural assumption of the English speaker is that Italian theater would be performed in Italian, but in fact, for a large part of the time period under consideration, Italian did not exist as a national language. In 1860 there were very few speakers of Italian (estimates range from 2.5 percent to 12 percent of the population) and as recently as the 1950s only around 18 percent spoke Italian habitually (according to T. De Mauro and surveys by DOXA). The everyday language of most people was their regional dialect and this complex linguistic situation is reflected in the theater. We find that the major characters generally spoke Italian. It was often a formal and rather stilted official language which would have been understood by many members of the audience even though they did not themselves speak Italian. The comic characters however, usually spoke the local dialect although some, as part of their characterization, tried unsuccessfully to speak Italian and much of the humor was derived from the linguistic muddle which they created in their efforts to master the language of their betters. In the theater of the *pupi,* according to the studies of Antonio Pasqualino, the characters in the chivalric cycles invariably spoke a language which was neither Italian nor Sicilian, made up of a mixture of impressive literary phrases, Sicilian terms, colloquial Italian, and Sicilian syntax.

The sections that follow are a catalogue of all information gathered regarding the use of Shakespearean drama in Italian *teatro di figura,* concluding with an account of a notable production. The final section will discuss theoretical aspects of popular theater and the manner in which Shakespearean drama has been adapted, not in an arbitrary fashion, but in response to the essential nature of the genre.

SHAKESPEARE
MANIPULATED

Part One
Catalogue of Performance History

1

Performances with *marionette*

Marionette may be constructed from a wide variety of materials and in sizes ranging from less than thirty centimeters tall to life-size, but their two common and distinguishing features are that they are moved from above by means of strings or metal rods, and that they are full-length figures with the same body proportion as the human figure.

There are varying opinions about the etymology of the word *marionette,* but a widely accepted explanation is that it derives from the *Festa delle Marie,* a celebration in Venice that commemorated the rescue in A.D. 944 of twelve Venetian brides who were kidnapped by pirates. Originally this celebration involved a parade of twelve young Venetian women, chosen each year and given a dowry by the state. Presumably for financial reasons, the women were replaced by life-size statues, called *marione.* This annual event provided an obvious marketing opportunity and miniature versions of the statues were produced and sold as souvenirs and from these, the term *marionette* came into use. The name may thus have originated one thousand years ago, but this type of articulated, animated figure has an even longer history and was a part of the ancient civilizations of Egypt, Greece, Rome, and India. Interestingly, the Indian word for a theatrical director, *sutradhara* means "the one who controls the strings," which suggests perhaps that theater with *marionette* preceded that with human actors.

The motion of a *marionetta* under the control of a skilled operator has a magical quality and because the impulse must be transmitted through the length of the strings, it seems to become less a part of the human activity of the operator and more an expression of a life force of the *marionetta* itself, unlike the *burattino* which is always in direct contact with, and almost an extension of, the body of the *burattinaio.* Movement is an essential quality for a *marionetta* and, unlike a statue or other work of art, it is devoid of life or interest until it is moved. As a result, photography of *mario-*

Theatre for *marionette* from Casa Grimani ai Servi at Ca'Rezzonico, Venice.
Photo by the author.

Marionettes in Venice; Iago-Othello-Desdemona, from
The Mask. Reproduced courtesy of the British Institute
of Florence.

Marionetta from Casa Grimani ai Servi at Ca'Rezzonico, Venice: possibly Othello. Photo by the author.

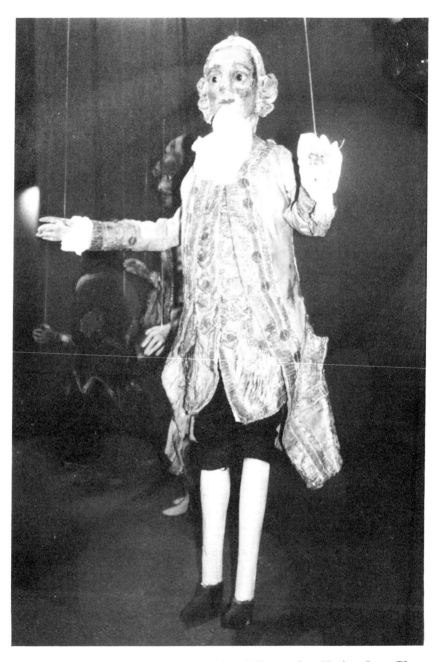

Marionetta from Casa Grimani ai Servi at Ca'Rezzonico, Venice: Iago. Photo by the author.

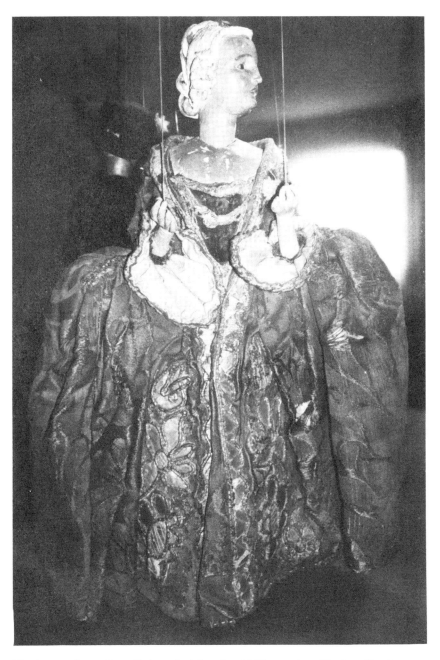

Marionetta from Casa Grimani ai Servi at Ca'Rezzonico, Venice: Desdemona.
Photo by the author.

nette is a disappointing process because even the simple motion of an operator positioning a stored *marionetta* brings it to life, but this animating force is then frozen by the camera and is absent in the resulting photograph.

In the past, the repertoire of theater of *marionette* has always followed closely that of prose theater, ballet, and opera and has sought to imitate it in miniature form. Works written specifically for the genre are comparatively rare. Theater of *marionette* also resembled the theater of actors in the separation which existed between the stage and the public, unlike the theater of *burattini* and *pupi* in which the involvement of the audience was an important element. In the seventeenth century, theater with *marionette* developed very much as a part of the theatrical and musical life of the aristocracy. A refined audience was presented with works of a religious nature, or derived from the *Commedia dell'arte,* or melodramas, none of which challenged the civil or religious authorities. The talents of architects, poets, musicians, actors, and singers were employed to enable the theater of *marionette* to compete with that of actors. In the following century the *marionette* enjoyed their golden age in which they were always closely linked to the intellectual and aristocratic world. Many small theaters were constructed within noble homes. The potential for illusion and metamorphosis and the scenographic effects were perfectly suited to the baroque taste of the time. With the opening of public theaters for *marionette* in the nineteenth century, the audience was no longer determined by social class but consisted of anyone who could afford to buy a ticket. The large companies which had established theaters, such as the Colla in Milan and the Lupi in Turin, catered to a middle-class audience and competed to achieve ever greater "realism" in miniature by means of technical innovations, the sophistication of which the smaller and touring companies could not hope to match. It was not until the second half of the nineteenth century that theater of *marionette* was taken to audiences outside the cities by touring companies. It is claimed that the touring *marionette* played a significant role in the diffusion of the Italian language in smaller centers because their theatrical works were always spoken in Italian, dialect being reserved for the characters played by the various masks.[1] The different nature of the public and the limited technical and financial resources of touring companies, usually small family operations, resulted in a change to the repertoire. Learned works were replaced by dramas of a more sensational nature, farces, stories of saints or brigands, and versions of the better known operas. Despite this widening of the social range of the audience, theater with *marionette* never became an essentially "popular" theater like that of *burattini*. Politically it always remained aligned with authority, as explained by Leydi:

> Se osserviamo la storia dei marionettisti li vediamo invece agire all'interno del sistema dell'egemonia, secondo le regole di un teatro pertinente con l'ideologia e i modelli di comportamento dalla [*sic*] classe che ne fruisce e che lo determina, lo configura, lo connota e, anche, lo controlla. Quando le marionette infrangono la regola, in realtà non propongono, con rischio, l'irruzione di una cultura 'altra' e contestativa, ma piuttosto partecipano, consapevolmente, al gioco delle contraddizioni interne del sistema dominante, proprio come il teatro 'maggiore'.[2]

The theater of *marionette*, characterized by cultivated, sophisticated drama for an adult audience has not, with a few noteworthy exceptions, survived into the twentieth century in its traditional form, but it has found a new direction owing to the possibilities which it offers to avant-garde artists, theater theoreticians, and experimental theater. The artist, Fortunato Depero, for example, staged his *I Balli Plastici* in 1918 in which for the first time, the *marionette* gave up their imitation of human reality.[3] The work of the artist, Luigi Veronesi, in collaboration with the *marionettisti*, Gianni and Cosetta Colla, also explores the expressive, non-naturalistic possibilities of theater with *marionette*.[4]

CHRONOLOGY

No.	Date	Production	Company (location)
1.	pre-1800	*Othello*	(Casa Grimani ai Servi)
2.	1821	*Romeo and Juliet*	Macchi
3.	1834	*Romeo and Juliet*	Lupi
4.	mid-1800s	*Macbeth*	Reccardini
5.	1860	*Romeo and Juliet*	Prandi
3.	1865	*Othello*	Lupi
	ca. 1868	*Hamlet*	Lupi
	?	*Antony and Cleopatra*	Lupi
6.	1866	*Macbeth*	(Teatro Silvestri)
	1867	*Romeo and Juliet*	(Teatro Silvestri)
7.	1875	*Romeo and Juliet*	Corelli
8.	1876	*Romeo and Juliet*	Dall'Acqua
9.	late-1800s	*Macbeth*	Monticelli
10.	late-1800s	*Othello*	Ajmino

11.	ca. 1900	*Othello*	Mazzatorta
12.	ca. 1900	*Romeo and Juliet*	Salici-Stignani
13.	ca. 1900	*Romeo and Juliet*	Lazzarini
14.	1906	*Macbeth*	Cagnoli
15.	1908	*Othello*	Picchi
16.	1909	*Romeo and Juliet*	Rame
17.	ca. 1915	*Hamlet*	Giacomo Colla
18.	1920–22	*Hamlet*	Zaffardi
19.	1921	*The Tempest*	Podrecca
20.	ca. 1930	*Hamlet*	Pallavicini
21.	ca. 1935	*Othello*	A. Maletti
22.	ca. 1940	*The Tempest*	Latis
23.	1959–60	*Macbeth*	G. and C. Colla
	1959–60	*The Tempest*	G. and C. Colla
24.	ca. 1965	*Hamlet*	S. Maletti
25.	1983	*A Midsummer Night's Dream*	Drammatico Vegetale
26.	1985	*The Tempest*	Carlo Colla e Figli

1. CASA GRIMANI AI SERVI—VENICE

From the situation in Venice during the eighteenth century it is apparent that the belief that *teatro di figura* has always been simply an entertainment for the masses is mistaken. At this time in Venice there was a marked distinction between the theater of *marionette* and that of *burattini*. The latter was certainly a form of popular theater, seen almost exclusively in the streets and *piazze* where improvised comedies and farces were performed. Shows with *marionette* however were performed in public theaters and in small private theaters in aristocratic homes. Here the noble audiences were entertained with performances of a more intellectual nature, either written expressly for the *marionette* or drawn from the repertoire of contemporary live theater and opera. Of the small private theaters, one of the most famous was that of Casa Grimani ai Servi, which, together with a collection of its *marionette*, is preserved today at Ca' Rezzonico, the Museum of Eighteenth Century Venice. These *marionette* and those in Bologna at the Galleria Davia-Bargellini are the only documented examples surviving from the eighteenth century. They are remarkable for the richness and elegance of the costumes.

Othello—pre-1800

The only evidence of the earliest example of the use of Shakespeare in the *teatro di figura* is the existence of *marionette* identified as Iago, Othello, and Desdemona in the Casa Grimani ai Servi collection. Nothing is known of the production itself and no *copione* has been preserved. Identification of the *marionette* is based on a woodcut by E. Thesleff with the caption "Marionettes in Venice: Iago—Othello—Desdemona" which appeared in 1908 in *The Mask*,[5] and Brissoni's illustration and comment: "*Si notano un Otello e una Desdemona in raffinati costumi settecenteschi.*"[6]

A visitor to Ca' Rezzonica can easily identify the *marionette* which match the sketches of Desdemona and Iago but the identification of Othello is less certain. The *marionetta* whose costume resembles the sketch does not have sufficiently dark skin color and further doubt is raised by the fact that earlier writers speak of a display of thirty to forty *marionette*[7] but only sixteen remain on view to the public now and Othello may no longer be included among them.

2. Antonio Macchi—Milan

The first *marionettista* in Italy known to have included a Shakespearean work in his repertoire was Antonio Macchi. In 1819 he opened a theater for his *marionette* at Santa Catarinetta at Ponte de' Fabbri near Porta Ticinese in Milan and he and his wife gave shows there until 1824.

Romeo and Juliet—1821

The first performance, on 21 March 1821, was presumably a reduction, entitled *The Tombs of Verona*. Subsequent performances of *Romeo and Juliet* took place on 4 March 1822 and 27 and 28 April 1824. This information has been gleaned from theatrical records which give no further details about the production. Given that theater of *marionette* in this period sought to align itself with live theater, it is to be expected that the repertoire would have included Shakespeare because there were many performances of his works—opera, drama, and ballet—in Milan during the nineteenth century, a total of four hundred productions in fact in the second half of the century. It has been suggested that tragic theater in Italy at this time was dominated by Shakespeare because of a lack of comparable national drama.[8] Verdi did much to create an audience for Shakespearean drama in Italy because his libretti for operatic versions of *Macbeth* and *Othello* reflected his deep knowledge of Shakespeare and were intelligent and faithful renditions. At a time when Shakespeare was penetrating the literary consciousness as a result of critical interest and the availability of translations, he was also penetrating the popular consciousness through the works of Verdi.[9] (Opera in Italy at this time was not exclusively an elite cultural form.) It was not by coincidence that more or less authentic versions of *Macbeth* were presented in Milanese theaters in 1850–51, immediately after productions of Verdi's opera. The 1866 performance of *Macbeth* with *marionette* (see chapter 1, section 6) may have been similarly inspired.

3. FAMIGLIA LUPI—TURIN

The company founded by Luigi Lupi in Torino in 1818 began with *burattini* but changed technique when it began to operate from the San Martiniano theater in 1823, and went on to become one of the greatest names in Italian theater of *marionette*. Successive generations (which one follows with difficulty as there have been seven first-born sons named Luigi and all the second-born sons are Enrico!) have continued to operate the company and Luigi Lupi VII will be followed by his son Franco Lupi.

The *marionette* of the Lupi are unrivaled in their beauty and meticulous attention to detail. The costumes and furnishings were made by skilled craftspeople and each *marionetta* possessed a complete wardrobe, including items which would never be seen by the audience. In this respect, the Lupi typify the almost obsessive quest for perfection in the staging which was a distinguishing feature of the most renowned *marionettisti*.

Romeo and Juliet—1834

Othello—1865

Hamlet—ca. 1868

Caesar in Egypt (from *Antony and Cleopatra*)—date unknown

Of the four Shakespearean productions known to have been included in the repertoire of the Lupi, the most successful was *Romeo and Juliet* which remained on the playbill of the San Martiniano theater until 1885. It appears that the others were less popular as they did not continue to be staged and little information has survived concerning them. However, the *copione* of *Hamlet* written in 1868 remains in the family collection of more than one thousand *copioni,* and much can be gleaned from this fascinating document (see appendix A). The text itself appears to be written in a different hand, but the alterations and instructions, and the separate sheets which deal with the musical accompaniment and the details of staging are written in an elderly hand, possibly that of the original Luigi Lupi. This conjecture is supported by the lists which allocate *marionette* to operators for the 1870 and 1881 productions and include "Lupi," "Luigi I," and "Luigi II" (This seems to indicate that to add to the genealogical confusion, the family head was known as "Lupi" and "Luigi I" was his son, rather than the founder as one would expect.[10]) The mask which was traditionally operated only by the original Luigi Lupi was Arlecchino. Confirmation that he was still actively involved in the productions although in his eighties is found in the lists of operators from which we see that the mask which was inserted amongst Shakespeare's characters was Luigi Lupi's Arlecchino. The following generation put aside Arlecchino in favor of Gianduja, again operated only by the current head of the company, who became the undisputed star of the performances. Gianduja appeared in every production and plots were often changed radically to allow this irrepressible mask and favorite of the audience to carry out his role as mediator between the forces of good and evil and supporter of the oppressed. However the presence of Arlecchino in the Lupi version of *Hamlet* is much less obtrusive. He appears with the players who perform *The Murder of Gonzago* and, speaking in dialect, has a brief exchange with Hamlet and later introduces the play performance. Perhaps Luigi Lupi felt that his presence was inappropriate in this tragedy because the short comic speech written for him is one of the cuts evident in the *copione.* Until the last page this version follows its source but it seems that whoever wrote the adaptation found the Shakespearean ending unbearably bleak because in this case only the usurping king dies. The curtain falls with Laertes, Gertrude, and Hamlet still alive, and a ray of light illuminates the avenged ghost of Hamlet's father.

The family collection, housed in the Museo della marionetta piemontese in Turin, holds the *copione* and the *marionetta* used for the part of Hamlet.

4. ANTONIO RECCARDINI—VENICE

Antonio Reccardini (1804–76) opened his theater for *marionette* in 1825 at the Teatro Minerva (formerly the Teatro San Moisè).

He also worked in other parts of northern Italy and in Austria and Germany. He is credited with the invention of the popular Venetian mask, Facanapa and his theater became famous and very successful. He was succeeded by his son, Leone.

Macbeth—ca. 1850

Knowledge of a performance of *Macbeth* by Reccardini that included his celebrated Facanapa comes from a single reference recounted by Pretini:

> Folchetto ascoltò una volta un Macbeth con Facanapa, scozzese fedele, 'dove dei brani autentici di Shakespeare s'alternavano coi tratti di spirito del celebre e compianto Reccardini'.[11]

5. I FRATELLI PRANDI—BRESCIA

The Fratelli Prandi toured throughout Italy with their company of *marionette*. Their repertoire included many musical and dance spectacles.

Romeo and Juliet—1860

One of the few surviving records of this company of *marionettisti* tells us that on 31 May 1860 the Fratelli Prandi were in Milan where they performed *Romeo and Juliet* at the theater at Mercato Vecchio.[12]

6. TEATRO SILVESTRI—MILAN

Macbeth—1866

Romeo and Juliet—1867

A search of theatrical records and newspaper publicity in Milan revealed that performances of *Macbeth* on 3–10 November 1866 and *Romeo and Juliet* on 13 March 1867 were given at Teatro Silvestri by a company of *marionettisti* whose name unfortunately was not recorded. One possibility is the company of Giuseppe Fiando which was one of the most important companies in Italy and a number of foreigners who visited Milan at this time mention in accounts of their travels the marvels which they had witnessed at Fiando's theater. The company operated from a permanent theater which was demolished in 1865 and, for three years, they were obliged to operate without a theater of their own before occupying the new Teatro Gerolamo, which was especially built for spectacles with *marionette* and was made famous by the Fiando company and their successors, Carlo Colla e Figli. The dates of these performances coincide with the period in which the Fiando company was "homeless" but I have been unable to confirm that they were the producers.

7. Famiglia Corelli—Naples

Nicola Corelli, active in Naples in the second half of the nineteenth century, abandoned a ballet career to set up his company of *marionette* for which he wrote his own texts based on theatrical classics and historical events of the era. His son, Vincenzo (1901–70), continued the activity and established a permanent theater in Piazza Nazionale in Naples. As a result of the closure of such public buildings during the war, the company moved to Torre Annunziata and began to operate *pupi* instead of *marionette*. The years of crisis in the '50s and '60s which saw the demise of many companies in the face of competition from television and change in the traditional audience were survived successfully by the transition to an itinerant theater. The company, with Vincenzo's brother, Amadeo, toured Puglia and Calabria. Shortly after the return to Torre Annunziata in 1970, the company suffered the double blow of the loss of most of its materials in a fire and the death of Vincenzo Corelli. His sons, Nicola and Lucio Furiati, continued to mount shows for a few years and now do so on a part-time basis, constructing their own *pupi*.

Romeo and Juliet—1875

In 1875 Nicola Corelli prepared a *copione* for his version of *Romeo and Juliet*. Until recently, it remained in the possession of the family and was the only remaining documentation of the production.

8. Giovanni Battista Dall'Acqua—Udine

Romeo and Juliet—1876

This listing is derived from a fleeting reference by Pretini:

Si trovano tracce del suo passaggio, in società con Andrea Menotti, al Teatro Nazionale di Udine nel 1876, dal 30 di settembre al 26 di ottobre. Questi erano i suoi spettacoli: 'Roberto il diavolo', 'Giulietta e Romeo', 'Facanapa custode delle donne', 'La bella e il mostro' (ballo), 'Il gigante Pantafaragaramus' (ballo); più altri pezzi classici del repertorio di allora.[13]

9. FAMIGLIA MONTICELLI—MANTUA

The theatrical enterprise of this family was begun by Ariodante Monticelli (1825–1910). His independent company of *marionette* in later years operated as part of the *Fantocci lirici di Yambo* and the *Piccoli di Podrecca*. The fifth generation of the family continues the tradition of *marionette* and has also founded a company of *burattini, Teatro del Drago*. The present day activities of the company, based in Ravenna, include a vigorous expansion of the repertoire, extensive touring throughout Europe, participation in major puppet theater festivals and work for Italian, Polish, Portuguese, and Swiss television networks.

Macbeth—late 1800s

In the second half of the nineteenth century, Ariodante Monticelli staged a production with *marionette* of *Macbeth* (subtitled *The assassin of Duncan, King of Scotland with Famiola, groom*). The *copione* was a free adaptation by Ariodante Monticelli of the Shakespearean text and it, along with the backdrops, is conserved in the family collection. The work obviously became a successful part of the repertoire because it was subsequently staged by later generations of the family—by Vittorio (1869–1926), son of Ariodante, and in turn by his nephews, Otello (1905–) and Vasco (1907–67).

10. FAMIGLIA AJMINO—TURIN

Antonio Ajmino founded a company of *marionettisti* based in Turin which performed throughout Piemonte and Liguria. He was later joined by his sons, Antonio and Luigi, and granddaughters, Clotilde and Emma.

Othello—late 1800s

The Civica Scuola d'Arte Drammatica (fondo Zaffardi) in Milan conserves a splendid late nineteenth century Othello *marionetta* which belonged to the Ajmino family.

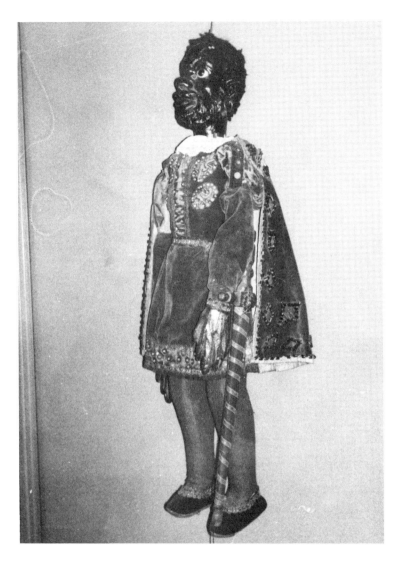

Othello *marionetta* belonging to the Ajmino family. Photo by the
author.

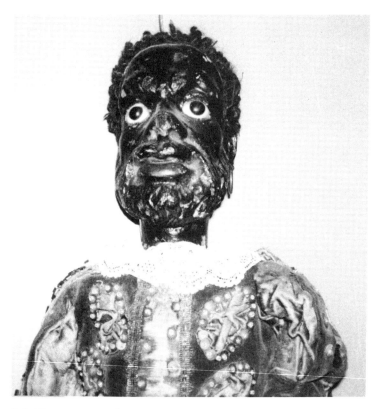

Othello *marionetta* **belonging to the Ajmino family. Photo by the author.**

11. FAMIGLIA MAZZATORTA—MILAN

The Mazzatorta were a family of traveling *marionettisti* from Milan. Capellini summarizes what is known about this company:

E' dato per certo che la famiglia Mazzatorta incominciò a dar spettacoli di marionette nel 1850. Costituitasi come compagnia di giro la sua attività si svolse in ambito lombardo, con prevalenza per il territorio milanese e le province limitrofe. Il teatro rimase nelle mani dei Mazzatorta per un secolo, venendo alimentato dai vari componenti che si susseguirono nel ciclo di generazioni. Ridottasi ormai la famiglia a soli due fratelli, la compagnia si sciolse nel 1950. Erano anni di grave crisi per tutti, marionettisti e burattinai: c'era, fortissima, la concorrenza del cinematografo ed era prossimo ormai l'arrivo della televisione, che diede il colpo di grazia ad un genere di spettacolo che da tempo andava perdendo pubblico e che non offriva più prospettive ai giovani.

Othello *marionetta* belonging to the Mazzatorta family, now held at the Civica Scuola d'Arte Drammatica in Milan. Photo by the author.

Desdemona *marionetta* belonging to the Mazzatorta family, now held at the Civica Scuola d'Arte Drammatica in Milan. Photo by the author.

Come avvenne per molte altre compagnie, alla cessazione dell'attività
seguì la graduale dispersione del materiale. Ed è stato solo grazie al
fatto che esso costituiva un patrimonio affettivo per gli ultimi due
Mazzatorta, che qualcosa si è salvato.[14]

Othello—ca. 1900

Capellini's book about the Mazzatorta contains a photograph
of the operators during a show and the *copione* which they are
using is clearly labeled *Othello*. There is no further information
about the production in the book and the author is unable to
provide a date for it. The *marionette* of Othello and Desdemona
are, however, in the collection of the Civica Scuola d'Arte Drammatica in Milan.

12. COMPAGNIA SALICI-STIGNANI—VENICE

Ferdinando Salici was a *marionettista* active in the second half of
the nineteenth century who worked in the provinces of Lombardia and Piemonte and also toured France and Switzerland.
His daughter, Luigia, chose the same career and, after marrying
Giovanni Stignani, formed a new company which operated in
Venice until ca. 1960. A close resemblance can be seen between
the *marionette* of this company and those of the Lupi family and
they were in fact produced by the same firm of wood-carvers.

Romeo and Juliet—early twentieth century

Macbeth—early twentieth century

According to an interview with Tosca Stignani (daughter of
Luigia) in July 1977, the repertoire of the company included
productions of *Macbeth* and *Romeo and Juliet*.[15] Although the date
is not known, they are likely to have formed part of the early
repertoire of the company. One often notes in repertoires which
encompass the period from the end of the nineteenth century to
the middle of the present century, the presence of two distinct
groups of works. The earlier group reflects the influence of mid-
nineteenth century taste, with reworkings of famous or classic
works. They were inserted into the repertoire of the theater of
marionette or *burattini* partly to give a cultivated tone and partly

to parallel the productions of live theater. The more recent repertoire consisted of farce, satire, and fable.

13. FAMIGLIA LAZZARINI—VENETO

Guglielmo Lazzarini (1883–1960), assisted by members of his family, operated throughout Italy, especially in the Veneto region. He later based his theater in Recoaro Terme and, at his death, the company came to an end.

Romeo and Juliet—early nineteenth century

Lazzarini had a repertoire so large that he could perform a different show every night for a month. According to Dal Pos,[16] included in this repertoire was a production of *Romeo and Juliet*.

14. ALFREDO CAGNOLI—MILAN

Alfredo Cagnoli (1881–1954) began his theatrical career as a *burattiniaio* and animated the masks of Sandrone and Fagiolino throughout Emilia-Romagna. After his marriage, he and his wife dedicated themselves to *marionette* and toured even more widely, covering Toscana, Piemonte, and Lombardia.

Macbeth—1906

When a company of *marionettisti* ceased to operate, its material was often acquired by another company and used to expand its repertoire or its stock of *marionette* and other equipment. An example of such an acquisition is the *copione* of Alfredo Cagnoli's production of *Macbeth* which was discovered in the archives of the Compagnia Carlo Colla e Figli (see Appendix B). The *copione* is the only surviving record of the production, but it is more informative than usual because it is clearly stamped with the name of the company and the cover bears not just the title of the work but the playbill of a performance. It is advertised as a "*Straordinario Spettacolo Fantastico di Prosa e Ballo*" with the title of *Macbeth ovvero l'assassinio di Duncano con Fighetto Maggiordomo e spaventato dagli Spiriti nella Caverna d'Erinni*. It must, indeed, have been an extraordinary performance as it combines the Shakespearean plot with scenes of the underworld, dance sequences, and comic episodes featuring the mask, Fighetto. The cast list is divided into historic and fantastic characters. The latter include, in addition to Shakespeare's ghosts and witches, Ostragamus (the leader of the spirits), eight dwarf witches, eight ballerina spirits, four devils, three flying dragons, a trick *marionetta* that transforms itself from a witch into various other forms, and serpents *a piacere!*

The plot follows the original closely although Macbeth's downfall is not due only to his flawed character but is plotted by Averno, king of the underworld, who instructs the witches to play upon Macbeth's ambition and relies on Lady Macbeth to complete the task. Prior to the prophecies of the witches to Macbeth and Banquo, there is a comic scene in which Fighetto, Macbeth's page whom he had sent ahead on their homeward journey, describes his encounter with the witches. Fighetto is noted for his cowardice, his insatiable appetite, his insolence towards his master, and his comic manner of speaking. He reproaches Macbeth, whom he addresses variously as Marcobetto, Martobetto, Mortobecco, or Malgobetto, for having sent him on alone, and gives a colorful description of having been used as the ball in the devils' game of football. When he hears the thunder which signals the approach of the witches, he runs away, fearing that they may be returning to finish the match. With Fighetto's departure, the tone of the performance becomes Shakespearean once more. He reappears briefly to announce to Lady Macbeth the impending arrival of Duncan, again speaking with the tone of a licensed fool (although his instruction to her to make up a bed for Duncan, and sleep in it first to warm it has been cut), but the tragedy unfolds without further interruption until the fourth act. When Macbeth decides to seek out the witches for further prophecy, he again sends Fighetto ahead and he arrives at the entrance to the underworld where the witches have left their cauldron momentarily unattended. Fighetto's terror is overcome by his greed as he is drawn closer by the odor coming from the cauldron, to the amusement of the audience who have seen the loathsome ingredients which the witches were stirring into their brew. Suddenly the trick witch appears. She is the archetypal Loathly Lady of the fairy tale—ancient and toothless—and she pursues Fighetto, proposing marriage and promising him a dozen children. He rudely rejects her and pushes her away, causing her wig to fall off, revealing her bald head. Despite his revulsion, he cannot resist the offer of a meal and takes her arm. First one arm, then the other, disappears, to Fighetto's amazement. He concludes from this that she is, indeed, a witch intent upon trapping him and attempts to strangle her. A series of transformations ensues. First, her head falls off, then she turns into a vase of flowers, then a small devil who changes size like Alice in Wonderland until the terrified Fighetto flees. With another abrupt change of tone, the tragedy returns. The dance promised on the playbill takes place after the procession of ghosts of kings has appeared to Macbeth and he has collapsed in a faint. Numerous spirits and devils appear and perform a dance around him. Act Four ends with an invocation from Ostragamus to the most evil spirits to aid in the bid for the soul of Macbeth. The cauldron transforms into a winged dragon and the stones into devils, serpents and monsters. The witches' cavern becomes an infernal abyss, which prefigures the ending of the play when the dying Macbeth consigns himself to hell, saying "*Demoni! Furie infernali! prendetemi! son vostro! son vostro!*" According to the *copione,* this dramatic scene was to have been followed by the reappearance of Fighetto, begging Malcolm for a job now that his master is dead and indulging in foolish wordplay. The bathos of this was evidently too much for Alfredo Cagnoli and his blue pencil banned Fighetto from the final scene. There seems to be a Faustian element to this portrayal of Macbeth. His character is blackened by his callous betrayal of the henchman whom he employed to kill Banquo and he consigns himself to evil and dies unrepentant.

Despite what may seem to us to be a bizarre combination of disparate elements, this was, judging from the *copione,* a serious production. The Shakespearean plot is substantially intact and the language is an elevated and slightly archaic Italian. Even Fighetto speaks Italian rather than dialect, with some comic wordplay. The transforming *marionette,* the dance scenes, and the large cast would have constituted a display of virtuoso technique on the part of the *marionettisti.*

15. FAMIGLIA PICCHI

Little is known of the *marionettisti,* Ernesto and Isidoro Picchi, other than that they were active from the second half of the nineteenth century.

Othello—1908

The *copione* for this production is conserved at the Civica Scuola d'Arte Drammatica in Milan. It is in five acts and follows Shakespeare's text closely. It is not greatly reduced in length and retains all the characters of the original and does not incorporate any of the masks of the *teatro di figura,* unlike many other versions. The source was the Italian translation by Luigi Enrico Tettoni and this *copione* for Ernesto Picchi's theater of *marionette* was produced by Sanpierdarena in October 1908.

16. Famiglia Rame—Novara

Pio Rame (1849–1921) was a traveling *marionettista* in the area of Emilia and Lombardia. His main mask was Gianduja and he later introduced Sandrone. Several members of the family collaborated with Pio Rame, including his son, Domenico (1885–1948), who introduced the acting of shows "in person" alongside the performances with *marionette.* Both he and his brother, Tommaso, also pursued careers as actors.

*Romeo and Juliet—*1909

A playbill has been preserved which advertises a performance of *The ill-starred love of Romeo and Juliet at the tombs of Verona— historic tragedy in four acts.*

17. Giacomo Colla—Milan

Giacomo Colla (1860–1948) was the head of a touring company which was very much a family operation. All eight children were involved and his wife, Francesca, had a particularly important role because she possessed the literacy that Giacomo evidently lacked, thus it was she who adapted texts for their theater and wrote out the *copioni* in her fine calligraphy.

*Hamlet—*ca. 1915

A number of *marionette* and the *copione* for this production have been preserved in the collection of Gianni Colla, son of Giacomo. The mask which was the trademark of Giacomo Colla was Famiola, created by his grandfather, Giuseppe, at the time of the Risorgimento. Famiola's costume originated as a defiant showing of the national colors at a time of Austrian domination and is an example of the use of allegorical figures by *marionettisti* and *burattinai*

LIVRAGA - ALBERGO DEL LEON D'ORO

Gran Serata d'Onore

dei fratelli

TOMASO E STELLA RAME

Mercoledì 27 Marzo 1909 alle ore 8 precise, si esparte

I DISGRAZIATI AMORI DI

ROMEO E GIULIETTA

alle tombe di Verona

Tragedia storica in 4 atti

Emozionante scena finale

LA MORTE DI GIULIETTA E ROMEO AL CIMITERO DI VERONA

Grande sfoggio di scenari e vestiari

Personaggi

Capuleto	Tomaso Rame
Giulietta (sua figlia)	Stella Rame
Romeo	Maruri, Carlo
Lorenzo (frate)	Rame Domenico
Paride	Giuseppe Marzi
Tebaldo	Biancardi Battista
Vespina	M. M.
Enrico	Antonietti Giuseppe

Terminerà lo spettacolo la farsa brillante

La consegna è di russare

Esecutori: soldato Landremol sig. D. Rame - Capitano sig. T. Rame - Irma sig. S. Rame

Carabinieri e servi

I fratelli Rame sperano nella loro serata d'onore di trovarsi come sempre onorati dal popolo di Livraga, e ne porgono i più vivi ringraziamenti.

Prezzi d'ingresso

Primi posti Cent. 40 - Secondi Cent. 25 - Terzi Cent. 15.

TIP. & PANZETTI-E COLOMBANO

Playbill for a performance by the Rame family. Photo by the author.

Hamlet *marionetta* **used by Giacomo Colla ca. 1915. Reproduced by permission of Stefania Colla.**

The ghost of Hamlet's father, used by Giacomo Colla ca. 1915. Reproduced by permission of Stefania Colla.

in order to take a political stand despite the presence of the censor. The *copione* is in poor condition and very difficult to decipher but it can be seen that all five acts of the original and the full cast are retained. Famiola, accustomed to being the protagonist, has to content himself with the role of Marcello. Naturally, he makes no attempt to play a Shakespearean role and thus Marcello has the costume, the perpetual obsession with *polenta,* and the Piedmontese dialect made famous by Famiola. The opening scene is therefore a bizarre conjunction of Marcello/Famiola, behaving as he always does, in conversation with a thoroughly Shakespearean Horatio, as if characters from two very dissimilar plays have somehow strayed onto the same stage. There is evidently further comic business for Famiola in the illegible portion of the *copione* as one of the props listed is a rope for Famiola to tie up Rosencrantz and Guildenstern. The custom of inserting the masks even into classic texts was accepted practice but it was questioned by Gianni Colla:

> la rappresentazione delle maschere tradizionali come Brighella, Gerolamo, Gianduja e Famiola, nei ruoli di testi classici, alteravano la struttura scenica con una libertà del tutto arbitraria.[17]

18. Umberto Zaffardi

The career of Umberto Zaffardi (1867–1924) encompassed forty-two years and a great variety of experience. From the age of fifteen he worked as a *marionettista* for several famous companies in the north of Italy and in Naples with a company of Sicilian *pupi.* After his marriage he was able to form his own company with the assistance of his wife and children.

Hamlet—1920–1922

Umberto Zaffardi's production of *Hamlet* was performed without the use of a *copione.* The *marionettista* had studied the text closely, adapted it for his *marionette,* and performed it from memory.

19. I Piccoli di Podrecca—Rome

Vittorio Podrecca (1883–1959) was an exception among *marionettisti,* most of whom began at an early age to acquire the skills which were part of a family tradition. For Vittorio Podrecca, the family tradition which he followed was that of the law, not the theater. It was not until he was twenty-nine that he sought, by means of *marionette,* a career which was compatible with his love of literature and music. He employed talented *marionettisti* such as Giovanni Santori and Gorno dell'Acqua and, being well known in musical and artistic circles, he was able to persuade such people as Respighi and Depero to collaborate with him. It was a time of crisis for the theater of *marionette* so Podrecca sought to revive it with the use of music as its expressive force, rather than the spoken word:

> Il successo è immediato: Podrecca aveva intuito che il rinnovamento dello spettacolo con le marionette doveva avere soprattutto basi musicali, sosteneva infatti che "le marionette sono fatte della stessa stoffa della musica, del ritmo di vita ed arte che ne emana. . . . Le marionette, anche per il fatto di essere guidate da fili arieggianti come le corde sonore, sono quasi strumenti musicali, sono intessute di musica, di sostanza melodica e sinfonica.[18]

His first productions in 1912 were *The March for Marionettes* by Gounod, *From Maid to Mistress* by Pergolesi and, for *burattini, Morgan Le Fay* by Yorick. Such was the success of the company that Respighi created his *Sleeping Beauty* for the *Teatro dei Piccoli.* In addition to his singing *marionette,* Podrecca also created dancing and acting *marionette.* Between the wars the *Piccoli* embarked upon a world tour with twenty-five people and twelve hundred *marionette* and achieved international fame over a period of fifteen years during which twenty-six thousand performances were given. After World War II, the company was based in Broadway and did not return to Italy until 1951. The years which followed were dogged by increasing financial difficulties and, four years after the death of Podrecca in 1959, the company was forced to disband. However, assistance from the regional government of Friuli–Venezia Giulia, which had not been forthcoming from the state, enabled the *marionette* of the *Teatro dei Piccoli* to return to the stage at the Teatro Stabile di Trieste, twenty years after the death of their founder.

The Tempest—1921

On 20 January 1921, Podrecca's acting *marionette* performed *The Tempest,* a noteworthy occasion because, as pointed out by Leo-

nardo Bragaglia, it was the first appearance on any Italian stage
of this major work:

> appare assurdo, inconcepibile, questo grande messaggio shakespear-
> iano, quest'opera fondamentale nella storia del pensiero umano, con-
> obbe il palcoscenico italiano, la prima volta per opera di un teatro
> di marionette.[19]

The adaption of the original text was written especially for Podrecca by Orio Vergani. The production was staged in Rome at
the Teatro Odescalchi and the actors, Vera Vergani, Cesare Dondini, Tullio Carminati, Soava Gallone, and Gino Cervi, supplied
the voices to the wooden actors. The scenery was by Caramba,
inspired by the English illustrator Rackham. The production met
with critical success, as shown by the following review:

> L'esecuzione della 'Tempesta' ci parve quello che di meglio si sarebbe
> potuto desiderare, in tutto degna del difficilissimo assunto. La messa
> in scena era una delizia degli occhi e una preziosa guida della fantasia.
> La dizione del poema che era stata affidata a ottimi attori e attrici del
> teatro e della scena muta fu una mirabile collaborazione da parte di
> tutti all'incantesimo della fiaba. Vera Vergani fu una Miranda d'una
> ingenuità e d'una dolcezza veramente squisite, Soava Gallone diede
> alla sua voce che doveva dire la parte di Ariele l'immaterialità d'un
> alito lieve e volubile; Cesare Dondini disse la parte del mite e saggio
> Prospero con quella umanità che si conveniva a questo indimenticabile
> personaggio del teatro shakespeariano, e tutti, un mirabile Calibano,
> il Calò, il Piacentini, il Brozzolari, ciascuno con una sicura e precisa
> intelligenza della sua parte, contribuirono a quella compiuta suggesti-
> one che fa dello spettacolo di ieri sera un nobile vanto di Vittorio
> Podrecca e uno degli avvenimenti più importanti della cronaca tea-
> trale di questi ultimi tempi.[20]

The critic Silvio D'Amico was similarly impressed:

> I trucchi e le trovate meccaniche di una raffinatissima semplicità ci
> hanno dato effetti deliziosi. Calibano era veramente un orrido mostro,
> Ariele volava veramente! E che tempesta e che calma visione del mare
> pacificato al ritorno![21]

In February 1923 the company produced an English version
with an abbreviated text, performed with arias by Purcell and
musical interludes by Gluck. The actors who lent their voices to
the *marionette* in this version were young English amateur actors.

20. Raffaele Pallavicini—Genoa

Raffaele Pallavicini (1874–1957) was an actor who married Clotilde, the granddaughter of the *marionettista* Antonio Ajmino (see chapter 1, section 10). She was a talented and well-known *marionettista* and actor and the couple formed their own company which toured in Liguria and Piemonte in the years between the wars. The popularity of their theater was such that they were able to stay for six or eight weeks in the larger provincial centers during which time they staged up to thirty-five productions for a predominantly adult audience. Touring companies such as this one which achieved a high artistic level brought to a popular audience a form of theater which was very similar to that which performed to middle-class audiences in the cities.

Hamlet—ca. 1930

Raffaele Pallavicini's production of *Hamlet* is described by his grandson and it is evident that his talents as an actor were a great advantage in this performance:

> C'è da dire una cosa: che non recitava solo Amleto come personaggio; ma naturalmente si faceva il Laerte, si faceva Polonio, si faceva lo Spettro, si faceva il Re, si faceva l'Amleto, si faceva tutto: il Ghildesterno, Fortebraccio, tutte quelle cose lì.[22]

We can surmise from this brief notice of the performance that it must have been a remarkably complete version because the minor characters of Guildenstern and Fortinbras were frequently omitted.

21. Alberto Maletti—Modena

It is not uncommon to find *marionettisti* who were also skilled *burattiniai*, as was Alberto Maletti (1901–52). His company had achieved great acclaim as *burattiniai* in Modena but because of the strict political censorship in that area in the immediate prewar period, they were forced to move to Genoa where they performed with both *marionette* and *burattini*.

Othello—ca. 1935

A version, reduced and adapted for *marionette,* was mounted by Alberto Maletti. No material remains from this production because, as was common practice, the *marionette* were later recycled for other shows.

22. I FRATELLI LATIS—MILAN

During the eighteenth and nineteenth centuries, in Venice especially, it was very common for aristocratic families to provide in-house entertainment for family and friends by means of elegant theaters, miniature in scale but equipped to the highest standard, set up in the home for performances of *marionette*. This custom was revived in Milan by the amateur company formed by the Latis family and friends which was active from 1939 to 1949. The *marionette* were created by Marta Latis for the company whose members were her brothers, Vito, Mario, Gustavo, cousin Giorgio, friends, Franca Valeri, Billa Pedroni Zanuso, Anna Tabet, Elio Jotta, and later, Giorgio Strehler. The company was unique with regard to both the appearance of the *marionette* and the repertoire. The *marionette* at that time were strikingly nontraditional and innovative in their appearance and even now, fifty years later, they seem surprisingly modern and are obvious precursors of the current experimental theater of animation. The construction of the *marionette* was an experimental process for Marta Latis and entirely self-taught. The sculpting of the hands and the joint articulations were done by an artisan. Initially, the *marionette* were very small and had heads constructed from *gesso* but soon acquired their distinctive appearance—still comparatively small (they are from twenty to thirty centimeters high compared to the more usual height of around seventy centimeters) but with head and body of wood and very expressionistic. Unlike many *mario-nette* of the period, no attempt was made to replicate human realism and instead colors were chosen for their symbolic value and hands were of exaggerated length, fine, and expressive. Eyes were simply and effectively suggested by a sculpted recess which acquired expression by means of the shadowing which varied as the *marionetta* moved. Each tiny wooden actor was created expressly for a particular character in the text to be performed and exists only as that character, in contrast to the temporary assumption of a succession of roles by a human actor, or the common practice amongst other companies of the reuse of *marionette*, after a change of costume, for other roles. The design of the *marionette* is clearly influenced by expressionist art and the mute agony of their faces,

Marionetta created by Marta Latis for *The Tempest*—Trinculo. Photo by the author.

Marionetta created by Marta Latis for *The Tempest*—Gonzalo.
Photo by the author.

Marionetta created by Marta Latis for *The Tempest*—Antonio. Photo by the author.

Marionetta created by Marta Latis for *The Tempest*—Sebastian. Photo by the author.

Marionetta created by Marta Latis for *The Tempest*—Prospero. Photo by the author.

particularly those made for García Lorca's *Blood Wedding* and Cocteau's *Antigone,* is reminiscent of the work of Edvard Munch.

The repertoire too was extremely innovative and culturally open, especially in the context of the fascist regime which had such a repressive effect on artistic development in Italy at that time. The first production was of *Blood Wedding* by Federico García Lorca and others included Dickens's *A Christmas Carol* (for which Giorgio Latis wrote a five act reduction of the original text, adapting it for a younger audience[23]), Jean Cocteau's *Antigone,* and *Reduce* by Ruzante. It was the belief of the company members that it is futile for theater with *marionette* to aim to approximate human actors and that it should rather exploit the symbolic and expressive qualities of the wooden figures. The company owed its formation to Vito Latis who had been an enthusiast from childhood and began to create shows for the entertainment of family and friends. The company which he later formed was strictly amateur and all members were involved with other professions such as architecture and acting. For this reason the group never became a full-time theatrical operation, although it is likely that it could have been very successful. The early performances were small private productions which therefore escaped the attention of the fascist regime but later the shows were opened to the public and took place at the Casa della cultura and the Giardini dell'Odeon. It is interesting to note that the company produced avant-garde theater for a sophisticated adult audience and that they certainly did not consider theater with *marionette* to be an entertainment for children. In other countries the theater of *marionette* has always had an adult audience, for example the *marionette* of Salzburg, the Japanese *bunraku,* and the Russian theater of Obraszov, but in Italy at precisely the time of the experimental and avant-garde theater of the Latis family, *teatro di figura* in general had begun a rapid decline into a spectacle for children. Thus the intellectually challenging and international repertoire of this small amateur theater was unique in its time and would transfer with ease to the contemporary stage, so it is to be hoped that the recently proposed restaging of *Blood Wedding* does eventuate.

The Tempest—ca. 1943

The venue for the performances was the seat of the British council in Milan. For this production, the Latis company members operated the *marionette* as usual but the parts were acted by staff of the council and the play was performed in English in its entirety. The *marionette* are conserved at the country home of Marta Latis near Como where she described, in an interview on 20 June 1992,[24] her interpretations of the characters which guided the construction of the *marionette*. A distinction is made between the colorful solidity and substance of base and earthbound characters such as Caliban and the jester, Trinculo, and the pale evanescence of characters such as Ariel, who inhabit a spirit realm. Ariel has the most delicate and slender wooden limbs imaginable, clad in a wisp of gauze, while Prospero, who moves between the two realms, has a similar delicacy in his hands and hair but is anchored to the earth by the weight of his long black cloak. Intense color is used to express the evil passions of the plotters, Sebastian and Antonio, while the subdued colors and sad expressions of Alonso and Gonzalo convey an anguish which is in fact common to all the characters, except the irrepressible Trinculo. Even the bridal couple have large, mournful eyes and a sad expression. One wonders to what extent this is a reflection of the anxieties and uncertainties of the time.

23. Gianni and Cosetta Colla—Milan

The present company is operated by Gianni, Cosetta, and Stefania Colla, the fourth, fifth, and sixth generations of the family enterprise begun by Giuseppe (1805–61). Since 1946, under the direction of Gianni Colla, this branch of the famous Colla family has pursued a more experimental path in the belief that renewal of the repertoire was a necessary response to the increasing competition for the attention of public. Turning away from the traditional repertoire of masks and melodramas they have drawn new inspiration from the texts of Pirandello, Collodi, Andersen, Shakespeare, Wilde, Tolstoy, and Stravinsky. They collaborate frequently with important artists such as Romano Rui and Coca Frigerio. Their innovations include the introduction of the human actor alongside the *marionette* and productions in which the *marionettisti* work "on view," that is, the *ponte di manovra* is visible to the public. The *marionette* and scenery are created specifically for each production, rather than the continual alteration and reuse of existing material as practiced in the past. The appearance of the *marionette* bears little resemblance to the verisimilitude of tradition. Striking in their modernity, the *marionette* of Gianni and Cosetta Colla are very much influenced by expressionistic and

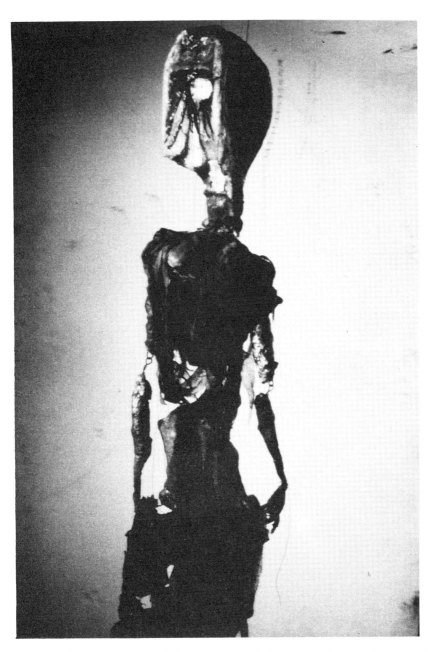

Witch *marionetta* **constructed by Romano Rui for the production by Gianni and Cosetta Colla in 1959. Reproduced by permission of Stefania Colla.**

Miranda *marionetta* **constructed by the pupils for the Scuola di Scenografia di Brera in Milan for the 1960 production of** *The Tempest*. **Reproduced by permission of Stefania Colla.**

Harpy *marionetta* **constructed by pupils for the Scuola di Scenografia di Brera in Milan for the 1960 production of** *The Tempest*. **Reproduced by permission of Stefania Colla.**

abstract art and utilize a wide variety of materials, including plastic and plexiglass, in their construction. For each show, a sound track is created using professional actors and original music.

There has been a long-standing collaboration between the company and the abstract painter, Luigi Veronesi, resulting from his project for a production of Stravinsky's *Histoire du Soldat* using *marionette*. He explains his enthusiasm for *marionette* as follows:

> Per me la marionetta è la macchina teatrale perfetta, perché può fare, nei dovuti limiti, tutto quello che un attore non potrà fare mai. È, insomma, lo strumento teatrale per eccellenza. Libera la fantasia. È il mezzo attraverso il quale si può inventare all'infinito.[25]

Macbeth—1959–1960

The Tempest—1959–1960

On 12 September 1959, a reduced version of *Macbeth* was presented in the ruins of the Roman basilica of Sant'Eufemia with the collaboration of Romano Rui, Luciana Petruccelli, and pupils of the Scuola di Scenografia dell'Accademia di Brera directed by Tito Varisco. On 10 October 1960 the version of *Macbeth* by Cino Chiarini was staged as the opening production in the Teatro dell'Arte, which was to host many productions of the company in the years to come.[26]

A second joint production with the pupils of the Scuola di Scenografia took place on 18 March 1960. It was Salvatore Quasimodo's translation of *The Tempest* and was performed at the Teatrino di Brera.[27] The *marionette* were abstract in appearance, constructed from materials such as gauze, gesso, and plastic, and relatively large, ranging from 90 to 110 centimeters in height.

24. SERGIO MALETTI—MODENA

Son of the above-mentioned Alberto, Sergio Maletti (1923–73) was known as a *burattiniaio* but, like his father, could also operate *marionette*.

Hamlet—ca. 1965

For this production, Sergio Maletti chose to use *marionette* and his Hamlet *marionetta* survives in the collection of his brother, Cesare.

25. Compagnia Drammatico Vegetale di Mezzano

Founded in 1974, this experimental company is particularly interested in the relationship between animator and object and produces shows for young audiences as well as for adults.

A Midsummer Night's Dream—1983

The directors, Giorgio Pupella and Piero Fenati, took as their departure point the underlying menace of the confusions encountered in the dream world of the lovers, and the fear that a dark side of the personality can take control of one's actions. As this production was destined for a young audience it was considered necessary to simplify the complicated multilevel plot. It was thus decided to omit the "real" world of the frame story of Theseus and Hippolyta, to reduce the role of the artisans, and to concentrate on the personalities and events of the lovers and inhabitants of the magic world. The activities of Puck, Titania, and Oberon were substantially unchanged. The text was written by Giorgio Pupella and, although it included some of the original verse, it was intended simply as a base text which could be changed during rehearsal according to the interpretation of the animators, and improvised upon during performance.

Set design is a problem for a touring company because theaters are not equipped for performances with *marionette*. For this reason, a single scenic space was designed (the woods) which, once mounted, also contained all the equipment necessary for the operation of the *marionette,* and was built in proportion to their size. The set thus became a fully equipped "container" for the performance which could be set up within the dimensions of an existing stage. It encompassed three distinct levels: the first, at stage level and close to the audience, where the actions of the lovers unfolded; the second amongst the trees, one meter higher, for the artisans' appearances; and the third, in the background at a height of one meter seventy, was the realm of the spirit creatures.

In this production, the spoken text was reduced to a minimum and emphasis was given to other languages—those of action, animation, and images—which are particularly relevant both to children and to *teatro di figura*. This is both analogous to modern culture which depends increasingly on images rather than words, and in contrast to its industrialized and mass-manufactured aspects, because the theater of *marionette* remains a world of craftsmanship and originality.

26. Carlo Colla e Figli—Milan

Giuseppe Colla (1805–61) was the founder in 1835 of a dynasty of *marionettisti* and his descendants today operate two distinct companies, both based in Milan: Carlo Colla e Figli and Gianni and Cosetta Colla. It was under the leadership of Carlo II, grandson of Giuseppe, that the Compagnia Carlo Colla e Figli became one of the most famous companies in Italy. They performed at the Teatro Gerolamo in Milan from 1906 until 1957. This theater was a rarity in Italy, being constructed specifically for *marionette*. Its reduced dimensions meant that the audience had a close view of the stage and was able to appreciate the attention to detail of the costumes and scenery and the skilled operation of the *marionette*. Having a permanent theater enabled the company to develop a very large repertoire and a great variety of costumes and scenery and it became noted for the richness of its spectacles and the excellence of its technique. In 1957 the company was ousted from the Gerolamo for a proposed redevelopment scheme which never took place. Bureaucratic difficulties have so far prevented the company from returning to the theater but at present a reopening of the Gerolamo is rumored to be a possibility. Since 1967 the company has operated under the direction of Eugenio Monti Colla and has concentrated on a revival of the old repertoire and the continuation of the traditional skills of the *marionettista*. In their laboratory in Milan, one senses immediately that each member of the company derives great satisfaction from the creativity of their work and it is an enchanting place to visit. While watching a performance from the wings, one is impressed by the speedy, silent, and utterly harmonious teamwork of the sixteen people who animate up to three hundred *marionette* and accomplish dozens of scene changes and special effects. The company tours throughout Europe, and as far away as Russia, Japan, and Australia and is even more celebrated overseas than in Italy.

The Tempest—1985

This important production, chosen to inaugurate the Biennale di Venezia in 1985, is the subject of detailed analysis in a later section.

2

Performances with *pupi*

Pupi are the traditional armed *marionette* of southern Italy and can be divided into three distinct varieties according to their area of origin—Palermo, Catania, or Naples. Their regional variations are succinctly described by Antonio Pasqualino:

> I pupi palermitani misurano ottanta centimetri circa di altezza e hanno il ginocchio articolato; oltre al ferro principale, che si aggancia al busto passando attraverso la testa, ne hanno uno per il movimento del braccio destro, cui è assicurato un filo che, passando attraverso la mano chiusa a pugno, permette di sguainare la spada e di rinfoderarla. Gli animatori li manovrano dai lati del palcoscenico, stando sullo stesso piano sul quale camminano i pupi. I pupi catanesi invece sono grandi quasi quanto un uomo, un metro e venti, hanno il ginocchio rigido e oltre al ferro principale ne hanno uno per il movimento del braccio destro la cui mano chiusa a pugno tiene sempre la spada. Vengono animati dall'alto di un ponte di manovra posto dietro il fondale. I pupi napoletani, alti circa un metro, differiscono da quelli siciliani perché non hanno ferro alla mano destra, che è aperta, ma un filo; la spada si fissa alla palma della mano, le gambe hanno il ginocchio snodato come i pupi palermitani e vengono azionati da un ponte di manovra, come i pupi catanesi.[1]

They differ from *marionette* in their appearance, method of operation, repertoire, style of performance, type of acting, and staging. The repertoire consists mainly of epic and cavalier legends, particularly from the Carolingian cycles, often serialized so that the action unfolds over a period of weeks or even months. Combat is central to the theater of *pupi* and the physical contact which it requires is a distinguishing feature of this type of theater compared to theater of *marionette*. The battle scenes are the dramatic highlights of the performances and require considerable technical expertise. Some *pupari* use special effects to heighten the drama:

> Molto curiosi sono i pupi che permettono alcuni sanguinosi 'effetti speciali': per esempio vi sono figure che a un terribile fendente dell'av-

versario si spaccano in due, o armature che vanno in pezzi, stappando contemporaneamente una bottiglietta di inchiostro rosso inserita nel torace, che innonda di 'sangue' la camicia bianca del guerriero. . . .[2]

The source from which the *pupari* drew the spectacles based on the Carolinian cycle was the *Storia dei paladini di Francia* by Giusto Lodico which was an immense prose compilation published in installments between 1858 and 1860 and reprinted many times. Lodico combined the plots of a number of chivalric works that had, in part, constituted the repertoire of the Sicilian *cantastorie,* which was subsequently taken up by the theater of *pupi.* The repertoire also included other subjects, usually presented in a single performance: tragedy, including that of Shakespeare, dramas based on the lives of saints or bandits, and historical events.

CHRONOLOGY

No.	Date	Production	Company
1.	ca. 1830	*Macbeth*	Canino
	ca. 1830	*Romeo and Juliet*	Canino
2.	1933	*Othello*	Cuticchio
	ca. 1940	*Romeo and Juliet*	Cuticchio
3.	1950	*Richard III*	Acrisio di Leo
4.	1976	*Macbeth*	Napoli
	1977	*King Lear*	Napoli
	ca. 1978	*Othello*	Napoli
5.	ca. 1981	*Coriolanus*	Amici Pupi

1. Famiglia Canino—Palermo

Alberto Canino, together with Gaetano Greco, is credited as the founder of the *opra dei pupi* in Palermo. He opened his theater in 1830 in a popular quarter of the city. A notebook which belonged to him is extant and contains five *copioni,* that are amongst the oldest examples known. The titles include two Shakespearean works, *Macbeth* and *Romeo and Juliet.* As was usual with *copioni* or *canovacci* of *opra dei pupi,* they consist, not of a written text, but of a brief description of each scene, its events, and the characters present. Using the *copione* as a guide, the *puparo* either improvised the dialogue or drew upon his memory.

Macbeth—ca. 1830

It is apparent from the *copione* (reproduced below with inconsistencies of spelling and punctuation unaltered)[3] that the complexity of the plot has been considerably reduced, becoming no more than a political power struggle. The psychological motives and consequences of Macbeth's crime are no longer central while the supernatural aspects are given ample space.

Macbet	*Macbeth*
In Quattro Atti	In Four Acts
Ridotto in tre Atti	Reduced to Three Acts
Personagi	Characters
Il Re di Scozia	The King of Scotland
Macbet	Macbeth
Banco e figlio	Banquo and son
Ladeu moglie di Macbet	Lady Macbeth
Alquanti Cavalieri	Several nobles
Il figlio del Re di Scozia	Son of the King of Scotland
Armato Chiamato	Armed man (ghost of Banquo?)
Lalcomin	Malcolm
Maghi	Witches
Diavoli	Devils
Arco per trasparizioni	Arch for apparition
Atto Primo	Act 1
Scena 1a: Bosco	Scene 1a: The woods
Le streghe annunziano Macbet Re di Scozzia, Macbet parte con Banco per andare alla città di Scozzia.	The witches proclaim Macbeth King of Scotland, Macbeth leaves with Banquo to go to the city of Scotland.
Scena 2a: Camera	Scene 2a: A room
Ladeu moglie di Macbet congiura per tentare la vita al Re. Macbet si dispone per uccidere il Re.	Lady Macbeth plots to make an attempt on the life of the king. Macbeth is prepared to kill the king.
Scena 3a: Camera letto	Scene 3a: Bedroom
Il Re di Scozzia coricato, che viene ucciso da Ladeu, non avendo questo cuore Macbet.	The King of Scotland, in bed, is killed by Lady Macbeth as Macbeth could not bring himself to do it.

Scena 4a: Camera
Macduffe e Banco, nel vedere che era tardi l'ora, vanno a risvegliare il Re. Banco e compagni entrano e vedono l'assassinato Signore.

Atto Secondo

Scena 1a: Camera
Macbet e Banco e compagni parlano dell'ucciso Re, e la fuga del figlio di Duncano Banco si dispone per partire.

Scena 2a: Camera
Macbet congiura con i suoi la morte di Banco e del figlio ancora, si disponno per assassinare quell'infelice.

Scena 3a: Bosco
Banco viene ucciso, Fleozio fugge.

Scena 4a: Camera con tavola
Macbet a tavola con i suoi, cominciano ad apparire l'ombre.

Atto Terzo

Scena 1a: Camera
Nel mezzo una pentola.
Streghe riunite tutte a voce alta gridano: Su' via? sollecitate [giarian] la pentola, arrivo di Macbet. Le streghe calano nella pentola che bolle una quantità di serpi scimie ed altri animali.
La più capa dei maghi dice queste parole:
E tu vai a cuocerti a sangue di scimia e gl'altri via discorrendo.
Cominciano ad apparire l'ombre.

Scene 4a: A room
Macduff and Banquo, seeing how late it is, go to wake the king. Banquo and companions enter and see the assassinated ruler.

Act Two

Scene 1a: A room
Macbeth, Banquo and companions talk about the slain king, and the flight of Duncan's son. Banquo prepares to leave.

Scene 2a: A room
Macbeth plots with his men to have Banquo killed as well as his son, they prepare to assassinate the victim.

Scene 3a: The woods
Banquo is killed, Fleance flees.

Scene 4a: Room with table
Macbeth is seated at the table with his men, the ghosts begin to appear.

Act Three

Scene 1a: A room
Centre stage there is a cauldron.
The witches shout in unison: Hurry up [?let's circle] the cauldron, arrival of Macbeth.
The witches drop into the boiling cauldron a quantity of serpents, monkeys and other animals.
The leader of the witches says these words:
Go and cook yourself in the blood of monkeys and other creatures, and so forth.
The ghosts begin to appear.

Scena 2a: Camera notte	Scene 2a: A room at night
Ladeu con una candela nelle mani, che contempla la morte di Doncano, Macbet la guarda che incomincia a struggersi nel pianto.	Lady Macbeth, holding a candle, contemplates the death of Duncan, Macbeth watches her as she begins to be consumed by remorse.
Scena 3a: Camera	Scene 3a: A room
Macbet ascolta gridi ci annunziano che veniva il figlio di Doncano si dispongono per l'assalto.	Macbeth hears shouts which announce that Duncan's son is coming. They prepare for the attack.
Scena 4a: Città	Scene 4a: The city
Morte di Macbet per le mani li Locamin, presa della città di Scozzia.	The death of Macbeth at the hands of Malcolm, the city of Scotland is taken.

Uccello suggests that Alberto Canino may have become acquainted with the Shakespearean tragedy through one of the famous Italian actors who performed in Palermo at that time, and decided to stage his own version.[4] Study of the *copione* supports the idea that it was based on a remembered performance rather than a written text. There are a number of small, purposeless changes which suggest memory lapses, such as the killing of Macbeth by Malcolm instead of by Macduff, the omission of the death of Lady Macbeth, and the absence of the prophecies of the witches.

Romeo and Juliet—ca. 1830

Giulietta e Romeo	*Romeo and Juliet*
In 4 Atti	In 4 acts
Personagi	Characters
Capoleto	Capulet
Romeo	Romeo
Giulietta	Juliet
Lorenzo	Lorenzo
Tibaldo	Tybalt
Paride amante di Giulietta	Paris, lover of Juliet
Isabella madre di Giulietta	Isabella, mother of Juliet
Giustina cameriera	Giustina, maid
Benvoglio	Benvolio
Mercuzio il Buffone	Mercutio the comic

Atto Primo

Scena 1a: Giardino notte
Romeo parla con Giulietta del suo
amore ma se Lorenzo si era me-
diato per la pace appare l'alba si
ritirano.
Avanza Capoleto e Lorenzo par-
lando della pace uniti ad Isabella
moglie di Capoleto, vene Giulietta
abbraccia la madre e il padre par-
lando del matrimonio di Giulietta:
Giulieta risponde che il giordino
era il suo diletto.

Scena 2a: Camera sedie
Capoleto Lorenzo, persuade che
vicino alla tomba l'uomo dovrebbe
inchinare alla pace, Capoleto decide che la figlia sarebbe sposa di
Paride.

Scena 3a: Camera
Tibaldo consapevole che Romeo si
girava nel giardino minaccia il
Montecchio della morte.

Atto Secondo

Scena 1a: Mura notte
Romeo: cercando di passare per
trovare Giulietta, Tibaldo scovre
Romeo, lo sfida questo non vuole
offenderlo per l'amore di Giulieta
ma costretto l'uccide.

Scena 2a: Camera
Capoleto chiama Giulietta dispo-
nendo, il matrimonio per lasciare
erede: voci fu portata la notizia della morte di Tibaldo, Giulietta
svene, il padre crede per l'amore di
Tibaldo, Paride giura la vendetta.

Act One

Scene 1a: A garden at night
Romeo speaks to Juliet about his
love and whether Friar Laurence
had acted as mediator for peace,
dawn approaches, they retire.
Capulet and Lorenzo enter, speaking of peace together with Isabella,
wife of Capulet. Juliet enters, em-
braces her mother and father who
are speaking of her marriage. Juliet replies that the garden is her
delight.

Scene 2a: Room with chairs
Friar Laurence persuades Capulet
that, as death approaches, man
should incline toward peace. Capulet decides that his daughter
should marry Paris.

Scene 3a: A room
Tybalt, knowing that Romeo is
wandering in the garden, threat-
ens the Montague with death.

Act Two

Scene 1a: A wall at night
Romeo, trying to get over the wall
to find Juliet, is discovered by Tybalt who challenges him. Romeo
does not want to respond because
of his love for Juliet but is forced
to and kills him.

Scene 2a: A room
Capulet calls on Juliet to prepare
herself for marriage so that there
will be heirs. News of the death of
Tybalt is brought. Juliet faints and
her father thinks that it is because
of love for Tybalt. Paris swears to
take vengeance.

Scena 3a: Camera di Lorenzo
Romeo racconta la morte di Tibaldo a Lorenzo ma sintino rumore; si nasconde Romeo, arriva Giulietta che domanda a Lorenzo di Romeo, questo lo presenta. Romeo invita Giulietta alla fuga: quella non vuole, dando le speranze a Romeo.
Questo parte per Castiglione Romeo minacciato dai Capoleti difeso dei Montecchi.

Scene 3a: Friar Laurence's cell
Romeo tells Friar Laurence of Tybalt's death, they hear noises. Romeo hides, Juliet arrives and asks Friar Laurence about Romeo, the friar presents him. Romeo invites Juliet to flee; she does not want to, places her trust in Romeo.
Romeo leaves for Castiglione, threatened by the Capulets and defended by the Montagues.

Atto Terzo

Act Three

Scena 1a: Reggia Sedie
Capoleto riceve Paride, chiama la figlia volendola sposare, mentre Romeo incolpato di tanti delitti. Questa ricusa il padre la minaccia di morte.

Scene 1a: Palace, with chairs
Capulet receives Paris and calls his daughter, wanting her to marry. Romeo is accused of many crimes. Juliet refuses and is threatened with death by her father.

Scena 2a: Camera Tavolino
Giulietta volendo la morte, Lorenzo dice di dare il sonnifero: allora Giustina prepara la veste dei sponzali, Giuletta diceva che la mettevano duopo morta.

Scene 2a: Room with small table
Juliet, wanting to die, is told by Friar Laurence to take a sleeping draught; Giustina prepares her wedding gown, Juliet says that they will put it on her after her death.

Scena 3a: Reggia
Capoleto dispone il maritaggio la notizia della morte di Giulietta fu portata.

Scene 3a: The palace
Capulet prepares for the wedding. The news of Juliet's death is brought.

Scena 4a: Camera letto
Giulietta creduta morta disponno per tumulare il cadavere.

Scene 4a: Bedroom
Believing Juliet to be dead, they prepare to bury the body.

Atto Quarto

Act Four

Scena 1a: Mura
Paride e Romeo combattino. Sentino la morte di Giulietta, cadeno le spadi delle mani.
Passa il cadavere di Giulietta.

Scene 1a: The wall
Paris and Romeo fight. They hear of Juliet's death and the swords fall from their hands.
Juliet's body is carried past.

Scena 2a: Camera
Lorenzo riceve Enrico che non
potè assicurare, se Romeo fu assalito dei capoleti, ma del scudiero di
Romeo aveva inteso che non c'era.
Capoleto senti i rimorsi per la
morte della figlia, Lorenzo piange
l'amore di Romeo e Giulieta vanno
alla tomba per avere speranze di
vedere Giulietta—via—

Scene 2a: A room
Friar Laurence receives Enrico
who could not tell him whether
Romeo had been attacked by the
Capulets, but he understood from
Romeo's servant that he was not
there.
Capulet feels remorse for his
daughter's death, Friar Laurence
weeps for the love of Romeo and
Juliet. They go to the tomb in the
hope of seeing Juliet.

Scena 3a: Tombi
Giulietta, Romeo si avvelena
credendo che Giulietta fosse veramente morta.
Giulietta si risente dell'oppio ascolta l'avvelenamento di Romeo
che si uccide con un Pugnale.
Arriva Capoleto Lorenzo e seguito
che scovrino il tutto.

Scene 3a: The tombs
Juliet, Romeo poisons himself believing that Juliet was really dead.
Juliet revives from the opium and
discovers the poisoning of Romeo,
she kills herself with a dagger.
Capulet, Friar Laurence and the
others arrive and all is discovered.

Fine della Traggedia

End of the tragedy

This *copione* is a simplified version which follows the broad outlines of the Shakespearean plot. Curiously, the secret wedding of
Romeo and Juliet does not feature. Romeo's duels with Tybalt
and Paris provide a perfect opportunity for the combat scenes
which were an essential part of the *opra dei pupi*. The tragic ending
is retained even though it was unprecedented in the repertoire
of the *pupi* for a love story to end unhappily.

2. Famiglia Cuticchio—Palermo

The family operation begun by Giacomo Cuticchio at the age
of fourteen is still active in the form of the association "Figli d'arte
Cuticchio." This group is working in three directions to ensure
the survival of their cultural heritage: the conservation of the
traditional techniques of the *puparo,* the modernization of texts,
language, and stage effects, and a vigorous program teaching the
craft to young people.

Othello—1933

Romeo and Juliet—ca. 1940

Two *copioni* exist which were rewritten from older manuscripts by Giacomo Cuticchio. From them we can glean the only information about the performance of Shakespeare by *pupi* during the century which passed between the Canino and Cuticchio productions. According to the *copione* of *Romeo and Juliet*, it was a rewriting of a version which had been staged by a *puparo* from Palermo, Giovanni Pernice, in 1912. No other record of this production survives. The copy was made on 13 December 1947 and the first page contains the following outline of the plot:

> Per domani sera si rappresenterà—Grandiosa serata veronese di Giulietta e di Romeo—Guerra fra i Montecchi e i Capuleti—Romeo uccide Paride—Romeo finto ambasciatore si presenta a Copelio—Amori notturni di Giulietta e Romeo—Morte di Tevaldo ucciso da Romeo—Morte di Giulietta e Romeo[5]

In this production the tragic love story was evidently secondary to the conflict between rival clans, a topic in keeping with the traditional material of the *pupi*. Extra battle scenes were inserted—Romeo had several encounters with Capulets and even laid siege to Verona and led his own army into battle. Giacomo Cuticchio also acquired a *cartello*,[6] painted by Rinaldi c. 1890, presumably for an earlier production of *Romeo and Juliet* of which there remains no other documentation, that he used for his own productions. It is now held in the Museo della marionetta in Palermo. The emphasis on combat which is noted in the *copione* is also evident in the *cartello*.

The second *copione* is a version of *Othello* which was rewritten on 13 July 1949 but had been in the repertoire since its first performance by Giacomo Cuticchio in 1933. This production also laid great emphasis on the battle scenes, as is evident from the summary:

> Per domani sera si rappresenterà—Otello il Moro di Venezia—Sogno che fa Basirocco—Terribile battaglia fra Turchi e Cristiani—Otello viene liberato e armato—Otello uccide Basirocco e distrugge i Turchi—Tradimento di Luigi Cassio—Terribile duello di Otello e il Generale Enrico—Morte di Enrico e Luigi Cassio—Otello viene bandito—Otello notte tempo soffoca Desdemona ma poi se ne pente e si uccide con le sue stesse mani con un pugnale[7]

It appears that the greater part of the performance consisted of battles and betrayals, the standard fare of the *opra dei pupi,* with Desdemona perhaps not appearing until the final scene, just prior to her death.

3. NICOLÒ ACRISIO DI LEO—PALERMO

Richard III—1950

Nicolò Acrisio Di Leo was a *puparo* and director active in the first half of this century. Maria Signorelli records his use of a Shakespearean text which was an unusual choice:

> Coadiuvato da Antonio Pasqualino, mette in scena un Riccardo III, recensito da Salvini come 'spettacolo veramente degno e di notevole livello artistico' (marzo 1950).[8]

4. COMPAGNIA FRATELLI NAPOLI—CATANIA

The founder of the company, in 1920, was Gaetano Napoli whose activity has been continued by his sons, Natale and Pippo. The company has operated from Catania in Sicily and has also toured within Italy and overseas. Their theater has reached a high level of professionalism and technical expertise and was awarded the Premio Erasmo in Amsterdam in 1978. The *parlatori* are Italia Chiesa, wife of Natale, and their son, Fiorenzo. The *pupi* of the Napoli are typical of the Catanese *pupi,* much taller (up to one meter fifty) and heavier (around fifty kilograms) than the *pupi* of Palermo or Napoli.

Nino Amico, member of Compagnia Fratelli Napoli, felt strongly that in order to revive Sicily's ailing *opra dei pupi* and develop its artistic capacity it was necessary to combine the traditional *pupi,* their animation technique, and their gestures with a new theatrical language, by means of the use of texts of major dramatic works. This would have the effect of giving the spoken word an importance which it had not previously had in this theatrical genre. The use of *copioni* was not unknown in the history of Sicilian puppet theater but in the vast majority of productions, the legends of the Paladins were told *a soggetto,* that is, extemporaneously. Among the first texts chosen to add to the repertoire

Sicilian *pupo* constructed for the role of Macbeth in the production staged by Fratelli Napoli, Catania. Photo by Barbara Olsen, used with permission from Barbara and Fortunato Pasqualino.

Macbeth, a Sicilian *pupo* of Nino Amico, in a performance by Fratelli Napoli of Catania. Photo by Barbara Olsen, reproduced with permission from Barbara and Fortunato Pasqualino.

Macbeth, a Sicilian *pupo* of Nino Amico, in a performance by Fratelli Napoli of Catania. Photo by Barbara Olsen, reproduced with permission from Barbara and Fortunato Pasqualino.

The witches from *Macbeth*, held by Giuseppina Trombetta Amico, a descend-
ant of one of the founders of the *opra dei pupi*. Photo by Barbara Olsen,
reproduced with permission from Barbara and Fortunato Pasqualino.

were Von Kleist's *Pentesilea,* Eliot's *Assassin in the Cathedral,* and Shakespeare's *Macbeth.*

Macbeth—1976

King Lear—1977

Othello—1981

For the production of *Macbeth* a number of modifications to the usual technique were made. Instead of the normal *pupi* which are between 110 and 130 centimeters in height, smaller versions (80 centimeters) were chosen for several reasons, such as the ease of manufacture of new costumes to replace the characteristic attire of the *pupi,* which for characters such as Orlando, Rinaldo, and Angelica is rigidly prescribed by tradition. Without regard for historical accuracy (Macbeth assumed the Scottish throne in 1040), a medieval setting was chosen. The *pupi* representing the armed characters wore armor typical of the twelfth and thirteenth centuries. More importantly, the smaller *pupi* could be constructed with flexible knees which permit a more naturalistic motion and a greater range of postures such as kneeling, sitting, sleeping with bent legs, and dancing. With the traditional large *pupo,* the rigid knees relieve the strain on the operator because, when the feet are in contact with the stage, the *pupo* supports some of its own weight. The characteristic combat scenes of these full-size *pupi* are a form of rhythmic armed dance which has become an essential component of their staging. For *Macbeth,* however, a more martial combat was desirable, and this could be achieved with *pupi* with flexible knees. Some of the traditional effects of sound and gesture were abandoned in the quest for greater naturalism. The gestures were not accompanied by the strike of wooden blocks, the marked binary rhythm of the commencement of combat was absent, and the operators were encouraged to move the *pupi* with gestures appropriate to the text rather than those dictated by convention. Thus the usual grand gestures, violent and noisy, became more gentle, balanced, and meditative and in this way the traditional *opra* aligned itself more closely with the theater of the actor. Another modification was the use of a wide range of props in comparison to traditional works in which there is little on the stage apart from the *pupi* and the backdrop.

The structure and technique of the Sicilian puppet theater imposed some limitations. There is a single, frontal plane of action,

near the back of the stage and there are no doors. The alteration
of the text had to take account of these factors and it also emphasized the function of some characters and made explicit some of
the ambiguities of the text to an audience unfamiliar with it. The
heroism or villainy of the characters was enhanced, in line with
the clear good/evil distinction found in the *opra dei pupi*. Some
reductions were made to the original text, but the performance
was still of three hours' duration. The unique feature of the Napoli productions is the use of a written text which incorporates
much of the Shakespearean original. The *copioni* used by *pupari*
usually consisted only of a brief description of the events and
setting of each scene, and the dialogue was supplied from the
memory of the *puparo*. (A typical example is included in the listing
for the Canino family, chapter 2, section 1.)

Comparison of the Shakespearean text with its adaptation for
this production reveals the changes necessary in order to overcome the limitations, and highlights the points of contact between
two very different dramatic forms:[9]

Shakespearean text	Adaptation for *pupi*
Act One	
Scene 1: The three witches.	Not represented.
Scene 2: A wounded soldier describes the battle.	The battle is represented with clashes which conclude with the surrender of Cawdor and Sweno.
Scene 3: The witches' heath. Predictions to Macbeth and Banquo.	Reduced.
Scene 4: Duncan is informed of the outcome of the conflict, he receives Macbeth and Banquo.	Reduced.
Scene 5: At Inverness, home of Macbeth, Lady Macbeth reads a letter from her husband. The arrival of Macbeth.	Reduced and united with scenes 6 and 7 to form a single scene.
Scene 6: Duncan arrives at Inverness and is received by Lady Macbeth.	

Scene 7: Lady Macbeth incites her husband to the crime.

Act Two	Reduced.

Scene 1: Inner court of Inverness castle. Meeting of Macbeth and Banquo.

Scene 2: Lady Macbeth listens to and describes the crime of her husband.	Representation of the crime. Duncan is sleeping, two armed guards are drunk and asleep. Macbeth kills them then stabs Duncan. Lady Macbeth enters and drags away her horror-struck husband.
Scene 3: Inner court of Inverness castle. The death of Duncan is discovered.	Reduced. Macduff is not present. The assassination is discovered by Lennox; Duncan's sons are advised to flee.
Scene 4: Ross and Old Man.	Reduced. The act ends with Macduff pledging rebellion and vendetta in heroic tones.

Act Three

Scene 1: Macbeth orders killing of Banquo.	Reduced and united with scene 2.

Scene 2: Lady Macbeth attempts to calm Macbeth.

Scene 3: Assassination of Banquo outside the palace gate.	Banquo killed in courtyard by a single assassin.
Scene 4: Banquet.	Reduced and united with scene 5.

Scene 5: Lennox and a noble.

Act Four

Scene 1: Macbeth visits cavern of witches.	Reduced.

Scene 2: At Fife. Killing of Lady Macduff and children.	Omitted.
Scene 3: Malcolm and Macduff in England.	Reduced and set in front of palace.

Act Five

Scene 1: Sleepwalking scene.	Reduced and united with scene 3.
Scene 2: Approach of English army and rebel soldiers.	Reduced and united with scene 4.
Scene 3: Macbeth and the doctor.	
Scene 4: Army nears Dunsinane.	
Scene 5: Macbeth hears that Birnan Wood "do come to Dunsinane."	Reduced.
Scene 6: Battlefield. Macduff kills Macbeth off stage and carries his head to Malcolm.	Battle takes place on the walls. Macduff kills Macbeth, breaking his shield and is covered with blood from Macbeth's wound. Final chorus of "Long live freedom, long live Scotland!"

The company felt confident that the two dramatic forms, Shakespearean drama and the *opra dei pupi*, were compatible because of a number of theatrical elements common to both, such as duels and battles, assassination, intrigue, vendettas, death of the wrongdoer, and the eventual reestablishment of order. The *opra dei pupi* is essentially a theater of conflict, an appropriate theatrical expression of people who have for centuries been ruled by a series of foreign oppressors, and Shakespearean works with a central conflict, such as *Macbeth,* are suitable for appropriation. Specific parallels are noted between the events of *Macbeth* and those of the traditional subject matter of the *pupi:* the scenes with the witches are comparable to the appearance of the devil or the entrance to hell; the death of the sleeping king, Duncan, to the assassination of Ruggero; and banquet scenes are a common feature. The characters of *Macbeth* would not seem totally foreign to the keen follower of the Carolingian cycles. Macbeth resembles the killers of the sleeping Pipino of France; the flight of Malcolm and Donalbain after the assassination of their father is like that of Carlotto, later to become Charlemagne; Lady Macbeth has a parallel in Soriana who persuaded Sanguino to slaughter Fiovo in his sleep; and Macduff, the noble rebel who kills Macbeth, is a figure of the avenging paladin.

It was decided that some scenes which are described in the original text but not represented, except in the imagination of the audience, would be staged by the *pupi*. The opening battle which is described to Duncan was an obvious choice for the *pupi* to portray, battles being their specialty. The staging of the killing of Duncan, while it was being recounted by Lady Macbeth, was a solution to the problem for the *pupi* of maintaining long spoken passages which the live actors can carry with their wide range of facial and vocal expression.

The success of the production can be gauged from reviews such as the following:

> i risultati sono stati più che positivi sul piano dell'esperimento (i classici con i pupi). Ne è venuto fuori uno spettacolo molto corposo, della durata di tre ore piene, che ha impegnato pupari e parlanti più del solito.[10]

The favorable reception was not surprising in a city such as Catania which has a rich and active theatrical scene, and the audience enthusiasm was such that the company subsequently mounted productions of *King Lear* and *Othello*.

The performance of a Shakespearean work in the theater of the *pupi* is not, in fact, a break with tradition because the repertoire has almost always followed closely that of the live theater. The cavalier legends were transmitted in written form, by ballad singers and traveling storytellers and were performed in the theater by human actors, *marionette,* and *burattini.* This repertoire which had become an outstanding success in other types of theater was subsequently adopted by the *pupi* and these epic tales became the foundation of the *opra dei pupi.*

5. Associazione amici dei pupi—Palermo

Coriolanus—ca. 1981

This production was mentioned briefly by Antonio Pasqualino:

un 'Coriolano' (da Shakespeare) rappresentato alcuni anni fa a cura dell'Associazione amici dei pupi.[11]

Although *Coriolanus* is not one of the better known works in the Shakespearean canon, it is an understandable choice for production in the theater of *pupi*. Its warrior hero, the vendetta with Aufidius, the threatened rebellion of the plebeians, and the battle scenes are combined with a highly formal language and rhetorical passages which have an affinity with the traditions of the *opra dei pupi*.

3
Performances with *burattini*

A *burattino* is a figure worn like a glove and moved from below by the hand of the operator. It consists of a wooden sculpted head, rudimentary arms with wooden hands, and a costume which also serves as a covering for the arm of the operator. There is no attempt at naturalism or human proportions and only rarely are there legs. The entire personality of the *burattino* is invested in the head, which may be disproportionately large, especially in the *burattini* from the Bergamo region. The appearance of *burattini* is often grotesque, deformed, or caricature-like. Usually, the index finger of the *burattinaio* is inserted into a hollow inside the head, the thumb into one sleeve, and the remaining fingers into the other. The *burattino* has a wide range of movement: he can grasp an object, gesticulate, give a slap or an embrace, bury his head in his hands, tremble, or fight and he can move about within the scenic space and come forward to address asides to the audience. The *burattino* has a much greater ability to make physical contact with other characters on the stage than is possible for a *marionetta*.

The female characters are constructed differently with a torso as well as the head sculpted from wood to ensure that they have an obviously female shape. Consequently they cannot be animated by an inserted hand and are instead supported by a rod which means that their range of movement is limited, less vigorous and expressive than their male counterparts and this limits their role in the performance. For this reason, witches in the theater of *burattini* undergo a change of gender and are played by a *burattino* of male construction so that their animation can be more energetic and fearsome. According to tradition, their part is also spoken by the *burattinaio* even when he has a female assistant. The figure of Death, on the other hand, is a *burattino* of the female type.

The *burattinaio*, in addition to animating the *burattini*, also speaks their dialogue. He must do so in a manner which gives a convincing and immediately recognizable voice to each *burattino*. This is achieved by varying not only the tone and rhythm of the voice but also by the use of different linguistic registers and dialects. A *burattinaio* usually has a repertoire of around fifteen different voices and, amongst his contemporaries, his skill is measured by his ability to change voice. The masks usually speak in dialect, although if the audience is not familiar with the dialect, they will instead speak in Italian but it will be mangled, ungrammatical, and full of malapropisms for comic effect.

CHRONOLOGY

No.	Date	Production	Company
1.	1831	*Othello*	Petrelli
2.	1862	*Hamlet*	Romagnesi
	1862	*Romeo and Juliet*	Romagnesi
3.	ca. 1885	*Romeo and Juliet*	Preti
4.	1889	*Hamlet*	Cuccoli
	?	*The Taming of the Shrew*	Cuccoli
3.	ca. 1900	*Othello*	Preti
5.	ca. 1900	*Hamlet*	Ponti
6.	1910	*The Taming of the Shrew*	Ferrari
7.	ca. 1920	*Hamlet*	Campogalliani
6.	1922	*The Taming of the Shrew*	Ferrari
8.	1923	*Hamlet*	Tirelli
	1923	*Othello*	Tirelli
9.	ca. 1930	*Hamlet*	Mandrioli
	ca. 1930	*Othello*	Mandrioli
	ca. 1930	*Romeo and Juliet*	Mandrioli
10.	ca. 1930	*Hamlet*	Pastrello
11.	1930–40	*Othello*	Sarzi
	1930–40	*Romeo and Juliet*	Sarzi
	1930–40	*The Tempest*	Sarzi
12.	1950–75	*Romeo and Juliet*	Ravasio
13.	1953	*Romeo and Juliet*	Zaffardi
14.	1955	*The Tempest*	Signorelli
	1957	*Romeo and Juliet*	Signorelli
15.	1966	*The Taming of the Shrew*	Mazzavillani
16.	?	*Macbeth*	Bertoni

1. COMPAGNIA PETRELLI—BOLOGNA

Alessandro Cervellati notes in his invaluable history of the theater of *burattini* in Bologna that the plots of many of their comedies were drawn from or influenced by Shakespeare:

Si può anzi affermare che la maggior parte delle commedie comiche o 'tutte da ridere' derivano da antichissimi canovacci e perfino da produzioni shakespeariane: così 'I due dottori' nel quale rivive lo spirito di Plauto dei 'Menaechmi' (motivo questo ripreso da Shakespeare per 'La Commedia degli equivoci') e 'Brisabella o la moglie di Fagiolino' o ancora 'La dote dei due milioni' che ricordano 'La Bisbetica domata' di Shakespeare. Del resto, il grande poeta inglese non è trascurato nè dai nostri burattinai nè da quelli stranieri: anche in Francia e nel Belgio sono in repertorio 'Amleto', 'Otello', 'Giulietta e Romeo' e perfino 'Il sogno di una notte di mezza estate', 'Macbeth' e 'Giulio Cesare'.[1]

Othello—1831

From Cervellati we learn that the Compagnia Petrelli gave a production with *burattini* of *Othello the Moor of Venice* in 1831.[2] This was an instance of the modeling of the repertoire of *burattini* on that of live theater because it had been recently performed in Bologna by actors.

2. COMPAGNIA ROMAGNESI—BOLOGNA

Hamlet—1862

Romeo and Juliet—1862

These productions are mentioned by Cervellati as further examples of the transferral of classic drama from the live stage into the *baracca*.[3]

3. FAMIGLIA PRETI—MODENA

The Preti family have a long history as *burattinai*, dating back to Carlo (1769–?) and many of the numerous offspring have continued the tradition, operating mainly in the area of Modena, Reggio Emilia, and Parma. Giulio (1804–82), son of Carlo, was the creator of the mask of Pulonia, wife of Sandrone, and Sgorghiguelo, son of Sandrone, for his son, Guglielmo (1831–1916). The family were linked with the Campogalliani family (Giulio Preti married Ermenegilda, daughter of Luigi Campogalliani) and toured the Padania area for much of the 1800s and 1900s, creating and bringing to the stage some of the most famous

Burattino of the Preti family. Photo by the author.

Burattino of the Preti family. Photo by the author.

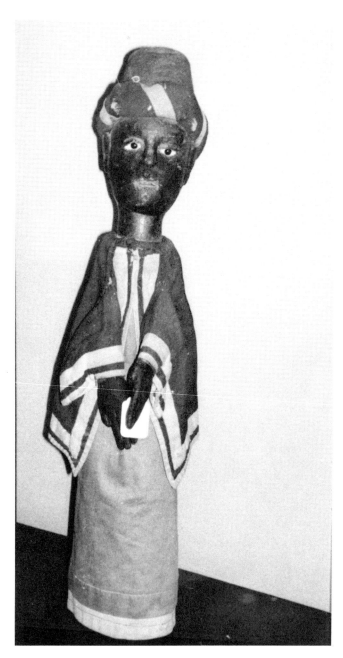

Burattino of the Preti family. Photo by the author.

characters of the theater of *burattini*. Giulio Preti refused to include the political and religious satire, the anticlericalism, the vulgarity, and the coarse humor that were almost invariably present in the repertoire of the Bolognese *burattinai*. One would imagine that without these elements the Modenese *burattinaio* would have had little public appeal but in fact his theater was enormously successful in environments ranging from the *palazzo* to the *piazza* and with both illiterate and intellectual audiences. The family repertoire included approximately two hundred works amongst which, in addition to the comedies featuring the masks, Sandrone, Sgorghiguelo, Brighella, Gioppino, Facanapa, Tartaglia, Fagiolino, and Balanzone, are many classic theatrical dramas and some of the most famous operas such as *Aida, La Traviata, Il Trovatore,* and *La Cavalleria Rusticana*. These works were presented with great care and refinement with special attention given to the scenographic effects. It was Giulio Preti who began to extend the repertoire, forging links between the theater of *burattini* and other types of spectacle, especially prose theater. His company and that of the Campogalliani succeeded in creating a public for this renewed form of their traditional theater. The shows were no longer brief performances on street corners on market and fair days. The repertoire included comedy, tragedy, and farce and a proper theatrical season could be mounted in the piazza, changing the fare every evening for two to four weeks. Many members of the family followed the theatrical tradition, giving rise to a dynasty of *burattinai* in Modena. Guilio Preti wrote many *canovacci* and texts for the *baracca*, drawing on historical fiction, prose theater, and melodrama. The popularity of the theater was such that they could sustain a long stay in each town, and thus required a sizeable repertoire to be able to vary the program each night. Sandrone and Sgorghiguelo were the undisputed stars of the *baracca* and they appeared in the main roles in all the comedies. In addition to the innovations to the repertoire, attention was also given to the scenery and staging which acquired the refinement characteristic of the theater of *marionette,* without losing its own identity. The audience continued to participate actively in the performances, voicing their approval of the heroes and disapproval of the villains.

Romeo and Juliet—ca. 1885

Towards the end of the nineteenth century, Enrico (1839–1921) and Emilio (1845–1910), sons of Giulio, brought *Romeo and Juliet* to the *baracca*. As was often the case, Shakespeare's characters shared the stage with the local masks who were interpolated into the drama to satisfy audience expectations. In this case, Sgorghiguelo and Sandrone appear in the cast list as servants of the Capulets. Sandrone, it seems, played a double role, perhaps as a reflection of his popularity with the audience, because he is also listed as a servant of Romeo. The work evidently remained in the repertoire because a *copione* rewritten in 1929 by Giuseppe Preti (1877–1961) is extant, as is a playbill for a production on 3 August 1929 presented by Medardo, Giuseppe, and Emilio. The family collection also holds a backdrop for the tomb scene and the Romeo and Juliet *burattini*.

Othello—ca. 1900

A later generation of the family, Filippo, grandson of Giulio, produced *Othello* at the beginning of the twentieth century. The *copione* is drawn from the popular romance by Mario Mariani[4] that was based on Verdi's libretto. Desdemona's handkerchief has been replaced by a lock of hair because apparently the word for handkerchief could also refer to more intimate apparel and it was feared that its use could give offence.

The entire collection of the *burattini* of the Preti family is now held by the Civica Scuola d'Arte Drammatica in Milan. The roles which a particular *burattino* played are not identified so it is not possible to be sure which was used for Desdemona, for example, but Othello must have been one of the three dark-skinned *burattini*, possibly the one with the more ornate, sequin-trimmed costume.

4. FAMIGLIA CUCCOLI—BOLOGNA

Filippo Cuccoli (1806–72) was a renowned *burattinaio* in Bologna who used the *baracca* as a vehicle for political satire against government members and others who exploited the populace. His principal mask was Sandrone who was later supplanted by Fagiolino, the mask of his son, Angelo Cuccoli (1834–1905), who worked with him. Angelo extended the repertoire greatly, drawing on legends from the literary and theatrical tradition of Italy, France, Germany, and Norway, also from antiquity, medieval, and Carolingian cycles, the history of Bologna, and politico-social satire.

Hamlet—ca. 1889

The Taming of the Shrew—date unknown

The *copione* for the production of *Hamlet* was written for Angelo Cuccoli by Pirro Gozzi (1871–1934) who reduced and adapted many works of the classic theater for the *baracca*. Gozzi's work is described by Bergonzini:

> Alla fine del secolo scorso egli ricava commedie e drammi per burattini da collane teatrali pubblicate da numerose case editrici. Tutta la sua produzione godeva i favori dei burattinai dell'areale padano, ma in particolare era adottatissima la sua stesura dell' "Amleto" che, pur tra inevitabili riduzioni, conservava integri i momenti chiave, spettacolari del dramma: il famoso monologo, il dialogo tra Amleto e Ofelia, tra il principe e la madre.[5]

Confirmation that this production was not to be dismissed as "minor" or "popular" theater comes from an eyewitness account recorded by Cervellati:

> A proposito dell' 'Amleto', recitato dai burattini di Angelo Cuccoli, lo scrittore Antonio Bruers, che aveva assistito alla rappresentazione, nella sua 'La voce di Bologna' scrisse nientemeno queste testuali parole: 'Se il casotto dei burattini fece nascere in Goethe la sublimità del "Faust", a me rivelò Shakespeare, compresi cioè, che la potenza dei suoi drammi consiste nel fatto che la sua altezza intellettuale è radicata nella più elementare umanità, per la quale le sue opere, che le menti più alte non giungono ad esaurire, sono anche drammi da arena popolare che la massa vive e comprende.'[6]

The repertoire of Angelo Cuccoli may also have included *The Taming of the Shrew* because a *copione* of this play is held in the Mazzavillani collection in Ravenna, listed as "*da una vecchia commedia di A. Cuccoli.*"[7]

5. ENRICO PONTI—BOLOGNA

Hamlet—ca. 1900

Enrico Ponti (1869–1924) performed a version of *Hamlet* which Cervellati cited as an example of the opposite extreme to the serious production of Angelo Cuccoli:

nell' 'Amleto' dato dal burattinaio Ponti, si potevano udire frasi di
questa natura, indirizzate da Sandrone a Claudio re di Danimarca:
'Sacra corona, che ti venga un cancro mastio e femmina', ed altre
squisitezze del genere.[8]

6. FAMIGLIA FERRARI—PARMA

Italo Ferrari (1877–?) worked as a *burattinaio* in conjunction
with his wife, Ebe. Their son, Giordano, continues the tradition
with his own company and has an important collection of *marionette, burattini,* and *pupi.*

The Taming of the Shrew—1910 and 1922

Both productions were adaptations, the first entitled *Convulsioni*
and the second *Contessina Fanni.* Loosely based on the Shakespearean text, the productions featured the popular masks of Fagiolino,
Colombina, Arlecchino, Brighella, and Sandrone.

7. FAMIGLIA CAMPOGALLIANI—MODENA

A dynasty of *burattinai* began with Luigi Rimini Campogalliani
(1775–1839) and operated in Modena through many generations,
only ending with the death of Francesco in 1931. Luigi Campogalliani was the creator of the *burattino,* Sandrone, who subsequently
became very famous and was adopted by many of his contemporaries. Luigi improved the scenery of the *baracca* and the characterization of the *burattini.* He also abolished improvisation and
continual recourse to the baton. He drew upon a wide range of
sources for new material for the repertoire. Francesco (1870–
1931), great-grandson of Luigi, was the most famous *burattinaio*
of his time and worked in the largest theaters in Italy, disdaining
to work in the *piazze.* His audience was mainly middle-class and
aristocratic. He was familiar with many dialects and could speak
up to fifteen different voices. According to Leydi he was :

> considerato a ragione uno dei più grandi burattinai che mai siano
> esistiti. A lui è dedicato un busto nel teatro Adriani di Mantova.[9]

Hamlet—ca. 1920

Bergonzini mentions a performance of *Hamlet* by Francesco
Campogalliani.[10]

8. Umberto Tirelli—Bologna

Tirelli was not a *burattinaio* but an artist and caricaturist who formed the Teatro Nazionale delle Teste di Legno in 1923 and employed skilled *burattinai* from Bologna to operate his creations. The heads were modelled from papier-mâché and were caricatures of many leading political and artistic figures of the period.

Hamlet, or experimental theater—1923

Tirelli's *Hamlet* was a three-act tragi-comedy preceded by a prologue by Alfredo Testoni, operated by the noted *burattinaio*, Virgilio Talli. It was performed on 6 February 1923 at the Teatro Verdi in Bologna.

Othello, or rather the beautiful . . . Moor—1923

This too was a satirical production in which Othello was a sandwich-board man who advertised a brand of chocolate. He went to Venice at a time when he was the only person prepared to volunteer to fight the Turks. As luck would have it, the Turkish army was lost at sea and Othello returned a hero. Desdemona was a coquette who moved in a circle of leading literary and theatrical personages of the time, such as D'Annunzio and Duse. She had so many affairs that Iago collected no fewer than six dozen handkerchiefs left by Desdemona in various incriminating places. However all ended happily.

9. Gualtiero Mandrioli—Bologna

Gualtiero Mandrioli worked as a *burattinaio* in Bologna in the early part of this century.

Hamlet—ca. 1930

Othello—ca. 1930

Romeo and Juliet—ca. 1930

Mandrioli was an actor of remarkable ability and his Shakespearean productions were of high quality because his talent conveyed the beauty and power of the poetry. Because of its rigidity and limited range of gesture, the *burattino* is not ideally suited to the performance of Shakespeare that is better served by the more refined movement of the *marionetta*. Nonetheless, the productions of Mandrioli brought a serious treatment of the works of the dramatist to an audience which may not otherwise have had the opportunity to hear them.

The family collection contains the *copioni* of these productions and a number of the costumes which are very elegant compared to the often rather rudimentary costume of the *burattino*.

10. BEPPE PASTRELLO—CASTELFRANCO

Most *burattinai* worked with at least an assistant animator and possibly others who helped with the construction of the *burattini* and other equipment of the theater. Beppe Pastrello (1906–) was unusual in that he worked alone and made every part of his theater himself. By using a combination of *burattini a bastone* and standard *burattini* he was able to operate up to eight characters simultaneously. Great attention was given to the finish of all parts of the theater and the total effect was considerably more refined than that of his contemporaries. He devised a number of technical innovations which allowed his *burattini* to bend from the waist, raise their hat, or even have the head detached from the body. The *burattini* were made from papier-mâché with eyes and mouth disproportionately large so that they would be effective from a distance despite the small size of the *burattini*. The lightness of these *burattini* combined with Pastrello's extraordinary skill as an animator made his dance of Arlecchino and Colombina remarkable for its grace. This item became his pièce de résistance and was inserted into every performance, whether or not it had any relevance.

Hamlet—ca. 1930

One of the oldest *copioni* in Pastrello's repertoire is his version of *Hamlet*. There are three distinct categories within his repertoire: rewritings of famous works; original short stories and tales for children; and farces. The classic works all belong to the early part of the repertoire and were later replaced by comedy and farce as tastes changed and the *baracca* began to lose its adult audience.

Comparison of Pastrello's *copione* with the original text reveals that it follows the plot in its general outline but has been heavily pruned from five acts to three. Many of the minor characters do not appear and the roles of Ophelia, Claudius, and Gertrude are considerably diminished. The major characters change not only their personality but also their names. Hamlet becomes Arlecchino, Horatio is Facanapa, and Polonius is Brighella. Nothing remains of the noble, cultivated, sensitive Hamlet of Shakespeare, he is the Arlecchino of the farces, always concerned with satisfying his needs, especially his insatiable hunger. In the final scene he does not die, but goes off to eat, saying:

> Andemo dala siora polenta. Vara che bea fritata! (indicando i morti) Pecà che no la se pol magnar.[11]

Even in a classic work such as *Hamlet,* Arlecchino continues to speak his dialect, full of everyday expressions of the peasant class. It is nowhere more evident than in the famous soliloquy if one compares the original text (*Hamlet* 3.1) and the adaptation used by Pastrello:[12]

To be, or not to be, that is the question:	Esser o no esser? Magnar o no magnar? Cantar o
Whether 'tis nobler in the mind to suffer	no cantar? Bastonar o ciapar bote? Xe
The slings and arrows of outrageous fortune,	meio darghele
Or take arms against a sea of troubles	a uno e andar in galera o ciaparle e restar
And by opposing end them. To die—to sleep,	galantomo? Robar e sgionfarse de boni boconi o
No more; and by a sleep to say we end	tignir le onge a casa e restar co'la panza svoda
The heart-ache and the thousand natural shocks	e dar una bona crepada? Crepar, e dopo? Ostrega!
That flesh is heir to: 'tis a consummation	qua sta el busilis. Co mi penso a la schizza,
Devoutly to be wish'd. To die, to sleep;	me vien la pele d'oca. Pensar che anca
To sleep, perchance to dream—ay, there's the rub:	mi,
For in that sleep of death what dreams may come,	un giorno sarò senza naso e che inveze de sti
When we have shuffled off this mortal coil,	do oci sbiseghini, gaverò do busi negri e fondi,
Must give us pause—there's the respect	fondi, brr . . . . Mi ghe pagaria la merenda a chi me savesse dir se al mondo de là se magna e se beve. Se se sta sempre a bocca suta,

that makes calamity of so long life.	mi resto
For who would bear the whips and	qua, perché, dopo morto, no vogio
scorns of time	morir de fame.
	Ah!, xe qua la bela Ofelia! Oh!,
	cara! la
	par un anzolo! solo ghe manca le
	ale. Ma quele
	se ghe le pol tacar.

The *copione* used by Pastrello was not his own adaptation but was one of a series of plays for *marionette* published by Chiopris. A copy has been conserved in the collection of the Biblioteca Nazionale Centrale in Florence.

11. FAMIGLIA SARZI—MANTUA

Francesco Sarzi (1893–1983) worked as a *burattinaio* having learned the craft from his father, Antonio (1863–1948), at an early age. He also acted in amateur theater and believed that the theater was an ideal political instrument. His son, Otello (1922–), also pursued the dual careers of actor and *burattinaio*. He kept alive the company's traditional repertoire of farces but also endeavored to regain the adult audience with a series of highly innovative productions. In 1957 he founded the Teatro Sperimentale Burattini e Marionette in Rome and was one of the first to bring classical music and literature to the *baracca* with such successful results that extensive overseas tours were undertaken. His productions included works by Brecht, Beckett, Cimarosa, Cherubini, Satie, and Kafka. Now based in Reggio Emilia, the company also holds workshops and takes the theater into the schools.

Othello—1930–1940

Romeo and Juliet—1930–1940

The Tempest—1930–1940

Francesco Sarzi's performances of Shakespeare with *burattini* were, like those of Beppe Pastrello, dialect versions in which the traditional masks appeared alongside, or in place of, the Shakespearean characters. The masks were Sandrone, Fagiolino, and Brighella.

12. Benedetto Ravasio—Bergamo

Benedetto Ravasio (1915–89) was ideally suited to the life of a touring *burattinaio* because of his love of the nomadic life and his intensely creative nature. He was determined to become a *burattinaio* but had to overcome many obstacles: parental opposition, the difficulty of obtaining his first *teste di legno,* the interruption of the war years, and the need to support the family of eight children. The strength of Benedetto Ravasio's determination and the support of his wife, Pina, were such that they gradually became successful and financially viable. However, in the late '50s, the competition from television robbed them of their audience and for two years forced Benedetto Ravasio to use his talents as a painter for survival. However, business began to improve for the *baracca* and a new success was found in Milan where, for seven years, they performed for the Circolo dei Piccoli at "Motta" in Piazza del Duomo. Benedetto Ravasio, speaking of his partnership with his wife, describes the often unsung role of the wife of a *burattinaio:*

Pina portò nel teatrino una ventata tutta femminile. Discreta, premurosa, ordinata come una formichina, con lei la baracca sembrava fiorire di boccioli di rosa. Era lei la custode delle teste di legno, che strigliava, puliva, controllava, redarguiva, quotidianamente. Era lei la sarta che disegnava, ritagliava e cuciva nuove giubbe, abiti dai colori sgargianti e cappe nere come il carbone. Ed era lei la cassiera che, con piglio casalingo, si assicurava minimi di incasso tali da coprire almeno le spese per il trasporto e per il cibo quotidiano. . . . Pina, ovvero la parte razionale, calcolatrice, della baracca. Una parte insostituibile ed indispensabile. In coppia si lavora meglio: ci sono due teste che pensano, due cuori che battono sulla medesima onda, quattro mani che si muovono sotto lo stimolo di un unico comando, due anime che si fondono. L'armonia e la serenità familiari si traducono in baracca nella perfetta sincronizzazione dei movimenti e nell'accordo totale su come animare le teste di legno. La comunione di ideali, di affetti e di sentimenti è il fluido unificante per una vita come la nostra, sempre esposta ai rischi e alle prove di un mestiere che scaraventa nel mondo degli imprevisti e dell'imponderabile.[13]

Romeo and Juliet—1950–1975

There is no written record of the production but the *burattini* remain in the collection of Signora Ravasio since the death of her husband. The following account of the production is the result of

Burattino of Benedetto Ravasio used for his production of *Romeo and Juliet*—Brighella. Photo by the author.

Burattino of Benedetto Ravasio used for his production of *Romeo and Juliet*—Gioppino. Photo by the author.

Burattino of Benedetto Ravasio used for his production of *Romeo and Juliet*—Colombina (left) and Juliet. Photo by the author.

Burattino of Benedetto Ravasio used for his production of *Romeo and Juliet—*
Arlecchino. Photo by the author.

Burattino of Benedetto Ravasio used for his production of *Romeo and Juliet*—
Romeo (now in the costume used for a later role). Photo by the author.

Burattino of Benedetto Ravasio used for his production of *Romeo and Juliet*—Juliet. Photo by the author.

Signora Ravasio with a Prince of Turkey *burattino* and, in the background photograph, Benedetto Ravasio with Gioppino. Photo by the author.

interviews conducted with Signora Ravasio at Bonate Sotto near Bergamo by the writer on 8 April and 3 July 1992.

Benedetto Ravasio based his production on his reading of the original text in translation.[14] Like many *burattinai* he often did not use a *copione* because he preferred to keep his eyes on the *burattini* and recite from memory. It was a reduced version with a smaller cast, but faithful to the plot and atmosphere of the original. The text was not drastically shortened and retained a length of two hours, which for the *burattinaio* is a physically exhausting performance as both hands are required to be held above the head for most of that time. The masks of Gioppino, Arlecchino, Colombina, and Brighella found their way into the performance but were artfully inserted. Speaking of the entry of Gioppino into plots which did not originally include him, Benedetto Ravasio said:

> Si dovevano allargargli le maglie dei canovacci per permettergli di entrare e di modellare a suo piacimento la commedia. Ma quest'ingresso forzato non doveva alterare l'originalità dell'opera.[15]

Gioppino was a servant of Romeo and Colombina was a maid who replaced Juliet's elderly, garrulous nurse. Naturally Gioppino was engaged in an amorous pursuit of Colombina but a comic subplot of a parallel pair of lovers on a lower social scale is thoroughly Shakespearean. Brighella played a servant in the house of Capulet and therefore dueled with Gioppino, again in parallel to the conflicts between Romeo and Tybalt. The masks generally spoke in dialect but, depending on the audience, they sometimes spoke in Italian, although it was an ungrammatical Italian, for comic effect. The show was widely performed and very popular and thus remained in the repertoire for many years. The female roles were spoken by Signora Ravasio. As was customary, the female *burattini* were sculpted from wood down to waist level to give them a more shapely outline. As a consequence their head and arms could not be moved by the hand of the *burattinaio* and they were instead attached to a *bastone* and moved by manipulation of the *bastone,* which permitted only a simple rotational movement. To increase their expressiveness, Benedetto Ravasio devised a spring-loaded arm joint which raised the arms. By means of a nylon thread which ran from the hands to the *bastone,* the operator could raise and lower the arms. Signora Ravasio, inside the *baracca,* supported a female *burattino* with the *bastone* in her left hand, operating the strings which move the arms with her right hand, and speaking the dialogue. The limited mobility of the traditional female *burattino* had relegated her to secondary roles, so Ravasio's innovation was of particular importance in a work such as *Romeo and Juliet* in which there is a female lead role.

13. GOTTARDO ZAFFARDI—PARMA

Son of the *marionettista* Umberto Zaffardi, Gottardo (1907–) pursued the dual career of *marionettista* and *burattinaio*. In 1929 he established his Teatro dei Piccoli at Ferrara and later moved to Parma where he operated from the Teatro Dell'Annunziata.

Romeo and Juliet—1953

The *copione* for this production was prepared by Gottardo Zaffardi and is a reduction for *burattini*.

14. Nuova opera dei burattini—Rome

Maria Signorelli (1908–92) was for many years a major figure in the field of *teatro di figura* in Italy. Her long experience in this area, her extensive research and writing, and her study of the educative value of *burattini* and *marionette* lead to her appointment to the first chair of Teatro d'Animazione[16] in 1971. In 1947 she founded the Nuova Opera dei Burattini in Rome for which she herself made more than two thousand *burattini*.

The Tempest—1955

Romeo and Juliet—1957

The Shakespearean productions form part of a repertoire which included many productions drawn from the theatrical classics of Wilde, Goldoni, García Lorca, and Gozzi.

The Tempest was presented for the first time in 1955, directed by Mario Colucci, with music of Fernando Candia and scenery by Franco Laurenti. It was followed, two years later, by a version of *Romeo and Juliet* which was a ballet with words of Shakespeare accompanied by the music of Tchaikovsky. The choreography was by Luigi Mian and the scenery by Loly Pellegrini. The *burattini* for both productions were made by Maria Signorelli.

15. Giordano Mazzavillani—Ravenna

A dentist by profession, Giordano Mazzavillani was a passionate amateur *burattinaio* and collector. He left a collection, now curated by his daughter, Cristina Muti-Mazzavillani, which is one of the largest private collections in Italy, consisting of more than four hundred items and some two hundred and fifty *copioni*.

The Taming of the Shrew—1966

The only information found regarding this production is its inclusion in a list of Mazzavillani's repertoire,[17] which indicates that the *copione* used was based on that of Angelo Cuccoli.

16. Ciro Bertoni—Bologna

Ciro Bertoni (1888–1986) was described by Alessandro Cervellati:

> Conosciutissimo a Bologna, lo è forse ancor più in tutte le città dell'alta Italia e dell'Italia centrale, dove ha dato, con vivissimo successo, un numero enorme di rappresentazioni. Parla molti dialetti ed è capace di sostenere un intero spettacolo da solo, interpretando tutti i personaggi e le maschere, ad eccezione di quelli femminili, compito questo affidato alla moglie Maria.[18]

Macbeth—date unknown

The Mazzavillani collection contains a *copione* of *Macbeth* which belonged to Ciro Bertoni,[19] but no other documentation has been found.

4

Performances with Mixed Techniques

Some of the most innovative recent productions of Shakespeare in *teatro di figura* involve the combination of various types of animated figure with human actors.

CHRONOLOGY

No.	Date	Production	Company
1.	1985	*Romeo and Juliet*	Carretto
2.	1986	*Othello*	Arcimboldo
3.	1990	*Macbeth*	Cinelli
4.	1991	*A Midsummer Night's Dream*	G. and C. Colla

1. TEATRO DEL CARRETTO—LUCCA

The Teatro Del Carretto began in 1983 with a production of *Snow White* in which the mythic qualities of the tale were presented by a technique which accorded equal importance to every scenic element: actors, *marionette*, lights, and scenery. The company places a strong emphasis on the skill of the artisan and draws its scenographic style from the minimalism of the Commedia dell'Arte and the Elizabethan stage. Meticulous attention is given to every detail of the staging so that the quality of the finish is faultless and everything operates with absolute precision.

Romeo and Juliet—1985

Director Grazia Cipriani and scenographer Graziano Gregori describe the Romeo and Juliet of this production as "mechanical actors." They are constructed from wood and papier-mâché and have the appearance of *marionette* but are moved, like *burattini a bastone*, from below the stage by means of iron rods. The vast gulf

The "mechanical" Juliet is dwarfed by the masked and expansively costumed actors who played her parents and nurse in the Teatro del Caretto's production of *Romeo and Juliet*. The set, costumes, and mechanical actors were created by Graziano Gregori. Photo supplied by Grazia Cipriani.

Juliet, her puppy, and the nurse from Teatro del Carretto's production of *Romeo and Juliet*. Photo supplied by Grazia Cipriani.

One of the swollen and deformed comic servants and the "mechanical" geese which flap about the stage desperate to avoid their fate in Teatro del Carretto's production of *Romeo and Juliet*. Photo supplied by Grazia Cipriani.

The wedding preparations in a scene from Teatro del Carretto's production of *Romeo and Juliet*. Photo supplied by Grazia Cipriani.

One of the duel scenes in Teatro del Caretto's production of *Romeo and Juliet*. The simple wooden stage set consists of a series of magic boxes that conceal the operators of the "mechanical" actors. Characters continually emerge from and retreat into the boxes. Photo supplied by Grazia Cipriani.

between the world of the young lovers and the adult world of feuding Verona is evoked by Shakespeare by means of language. In this production, the text is reduced to a minimum but the gulf is clearly rendered by the visual image. In contrast to the child-like vulnerability and beauty of the *marionette*, the masked actors who play the adult roles appear grotesque and swollen. Their power is conveyed by size and richness of costume, their entrenched beliefs by the inexpressive rigidity of the masks. In a reversal which would have pleased Gordon Craig, the *marionette*, thanks to the grace of their appearance and the skill with which they are animated, are more expressive and naturalistic than the "real" actors who move like automata. The spoken parts are combined with Bellini's music, *I Montecchi e Capuleti*, in a recorded soundtrack.

2. L'ARCIMBOLDO DEL TEATRO—FLORENCE

Patrizia Filippi operates a one-woman theater and stresses that she is an actor rather than a *burattinaia*, although she at times employs *burattini* to enrich·her solo performances.

Othello—1986

This show was designed, written, constructed, and performed by Patrizia Filippi. The text was based on a translation of Shakespeare's *Othello* and Verdi's libretto to which was added a frame story of a tailor. The performance opens with a scene in which the tailor is sewing in a chaotically disorganized workroom, which she begins to tidy in order to write in her diary a story which has been running through her mind as she stitched. A white curtain falls with a giant shadow of a writing hand projected upon it, in the manner of a film close-up. The curtain opens on Patrizia wearing a special skirt which she raises, transforming herself into a *baracca* and the performance of *Othello* begins. All the *burattini* are made exclusively from fabric and objects related to the craft of the tailor. Much thought was put into their construction so that even tiny details reflect the personality of the character. Iago is green as a symbol of his envy, Brabantio is large, silver, and highly ornamented to convey age and power. The text, although reduced to a duration of one hour, retains the plot in its entirety. The reduction is accomplished by means of the insertion of passages of commentary and explanation, by the Doge or by Emilia, leaning out of the window and gossiping with neighbors as she hangs out the laundry. Patrizia, her face always visible behind a veil at the rear of the tiny stage, donned a mask for the part of the Doge. The final scene takes place back in the tailor's workroom as she opens the ironing board, covers it with a sheet and uses it as a stage for the manipulation of the *burattini*. Throughout the performance the manipulation has been visible to the audience. The show was designed for a young audience but the result was enjoyed equally by adults.

3, Claudio Cinelli—Vinci

Claudio Cinelli works both as a *burattinaio* interested in experimental theater and as a performer of one-man shows.

Macbeth—1990

This production was a fusion of Shakespeare's play and Verdi's opera, performed by a combination of shadow theater and the manipulation and modelling technique of Japanese *bunraku*. The *marionette* are inspired by the earliest and most simple form of *bunraku*, developed in Japan in the ninth century. At this time the *marionette* were manipulated from behind by a single on-stage operator, hooded and dressed in black. By the eighteenth century, the construction of the *marionette* had become very elaborate and each one required three operators. Cinelli's *attori animati* were 120 centimeters high and weighed from five to ten kilograms. Unlike traditional *marionette,* they do not touch the stage, but are suspended above it by the operator and have a graceful, floating motion which is entirely non-naturalistic. The use of shadows and puppets expresses perfectly the show's themes of deceptive appearances, introduced by the opening words of the witches: "Fair is foul and foul is fair," and the folly of believing that any action can be complete in itself. The shadow projections give a nebulous form to thoughts, fears, and nightmares, create images of darkness and remorse, and show scenes of horror, such as the killing of Duncan. The animation was accompanied by a recording of Verdi's opera, recorded by the chorus and orchestra of La Scala, under Claudio Abbado.

Lady Macbeth from production of *Macbeth* by Claudio Cinelli. Reproduced by permission of Claudio Cinelli.

Macbeth from production of *Macbeth* by Claudio Cinelli. Reproduced by permission of Claudio Cinelli.

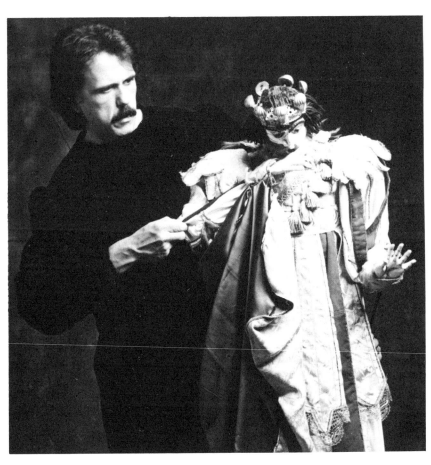

Macbeth held by Claudio Cinelli. Reproduced by permission of Claudio Cinelli.

Claudio Cinelli and other members of the theater with Macbeth, Lady Macbeth and the witches from the production of *Macbeth*. Reproduced by permission of Claudio Cinelli.

4. GIANNI AND COSETTA COLLA—MILAN

Thirty years after the above-mentioned productions (chapter 1, section 23) this company again turned to a Shakespearean work for their 1991 season.

A Midsummer Night's Dream—1991

The lyrical and dream-like music of Mendelssohn set the atmosphere of this production and was a more important element than the Shakespearean text in view of the reduced duration and the young audience. Director Stefano Vizioli chose to base his production on the fantasy world of the elves and fairies and to omit all the amorous intrigues of the world of the lovers, Demetrius, Lysander, Helena, and Hermia, but felt that the metatheatrical aspects of the "play-within-a-play" are an essential part of Shakespeare's play that had to be retained. The contrast between the concrete, fleshly world of the artisans and the ephemeral realm of the spirit creatures was highly effective in this production. Not only did Vizioli use human actors for the artisans but the forty-five *marionette* for the fairy characters were designed by Luigi Veronesi to appear totally abstract and ethereal. Veronesi, in common with Kandinsky and Schönberg, has a long-standing interest in the visualization of sounds by means of color. The white of the bodies of the *marionette* represents the light of the joy of living, of happiness, and the colors of the gauze draperies which clothe the *marionette* reflect the general atmosphere, their actions, and their state of mind. The final scene was a celebratory dance, a *bergamasca,* which united actors and *marionette* and in which each seemed to lose their material connotations so that the actors appeared to be *marionette* and the *marionette* became human.

The first series of performances began on 26 February 1991 as part of the fifth La Scala season of musical theater for young people. The show was also part of Gianni and Cosetta Colla's 1992/93 season.

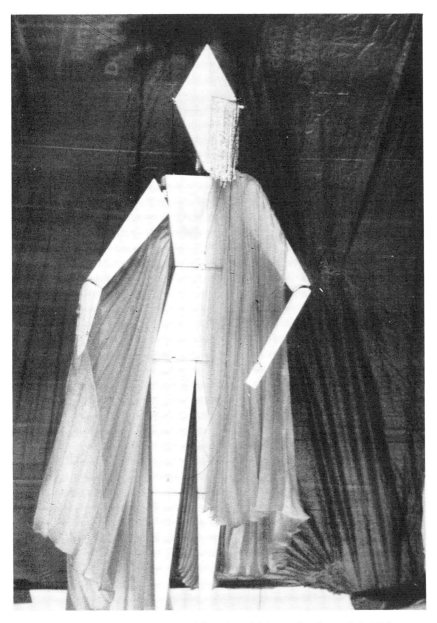

Fairy designed by Luigi Veronesi for the 1991 production of *A Midsummer Night's Dream* by Gianni and Cosetta Colla. Reproduced by permission of Stefania Colla.

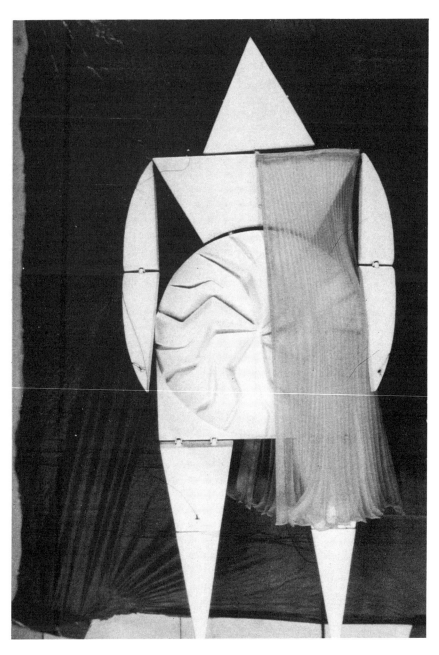

Theseus designed by Luigi Veronesi for the 1991 production of *A Midsummer Night's Dream* **by Gianni and Cosetta Colla. Reproduced by permission of Stefania Colla.**

Part Two
Commentary

5

Analysis of a Production

CARLO COLLA E FIGLI—MILAN

Having explained the nature of my research to the members of
the Compagnia Carlo Colla e Figli after a performance in Florence of their revival of the famous *Gran Ballo Excelsior* in February
1992, I was invited to visit their laboratory in Milan and gather
material from the archives of the company relating to their production of *The Tempest*. It was immediately apparent that this was
a version of considerable interest and worthy of critical attention
and documentation that it has so far not received. I returned for
two further visits and was able to assemble the following account
of the production from interviews with the producer, designer
and operators, from records kept by the company, and from
press reviews.

The Tempest—1985

> Translated and recorded by Eduardo De Filippo
> Directed by Eugenio Monti Colla
> Original music by Antonio Sinagra
> Recording edited by Luca De Filippo
> Voice of Miranda by Imma Piro

In 1983, Eduardo De Filippo, the renowned Italian actor and
author undertook a translation of Shakespeare's *The Tempest* into
the Neapolitan dialect of the seventeenth century for the Einaudi
series of *Scrittori tradotti da scrittori*. He explained his choice of this
dialect as follows:

> quanto è bello questo napoletano antico, così latino, con le sue parole
> piane, non tronche, con la sua musicalità, la sua dolcezza, l'eccezionale
> duttilità e con una possibilità di far vivere fatti e creature magici,
> misteriosi, che nessuna lingua moderna possiede più![1]

The production of *The Tempest* by Compagnia Carlo Colla e Figli: Stefano—
in storage, divested of costume and wig. Photo by the author.

The production of *The Tempest* by Compagnia Carlo Colla e Figli: *Bozzetto* for an island scene. Photo by the author.

The production of *The Tempest* by Compagnia Carlo Colla e Figli: *Bozzetto* for scene of calm sea after the tempest. Photo by the author.

The production of *The Tempest* by Compagnia Carlo Colla e Figli: *Bozzetto* for the tempest scene. Photo by the author.

The production of *The Tempest* by Compagnia Carlo Colla e Figli: *Bozzetto* for the lovers' scene. Photo by the author.

The production of *The Tempest* by Compagnia Carlo Colla e Figli: *Bozzetto* for the plotting of the fools.

The production of *The Tempest* by Compagnia Carlo Colla e Figli: *Bozzetto* for the dance of Sycorax. Photo by the author.

The production of *The Tempest* by Compagnia Carlo Colla e Figli: *Bozzetto* for the plotting of the rulers. Photo by the author.

The production of *The Tempest* **by Compagnia Carlo Colla e Figli: Ferdinand.
Photo by the author.**

The production of *The Tempest* by Compagnia Carlo Colla e Figli: Prospero.
Photo by the author.

The production of *The Tempest* by Compagnia Carlo Colla e Figli: Francisco.
Photo by the author.

The production of *The Tempest* **by Compagnia Carlo Colla e Figli: Gonzalo.**
Photo by the author.

The production of *The Tempest* by Compagnia Carlo Colla e Figli: Ariel. Photo by the author.

The production of *The Tempest* **by Compagnia Carlo Colla e Figli: Stefano.**
Photo by the author.

The production of *The Tempest* by Compagnia Carlo Colla e Figli: Antonio. Photo by the author.

The production of *The Tempest* by Compagnia Carlo Colla e Figli: Alonso.
Photo by the author.

The production of *The Tempest* by Compagnia Carlo Colla e Figli: Miranda. Photo by the author.

The production of *The Tempest* **by Compagnia Carlo Colla e Figli: Sycorax.**
Photo by the author.

**The production of *The Tempest* by Compagnia Carlo Colla e Figli: Trinculo.
Photo by the author.**

The production of *The Tempest* by Compagnia Carlo Colla e Figli: Designs for hair and beards. Photo by the author.

The production of *The Tempest* **by Compagnia Carlo Colla e Figli: Caliban. Photo by the author.**

The production of *The Tempest* by Compagnia Carlo Colla e Figli: Caliban. Photo by the author.

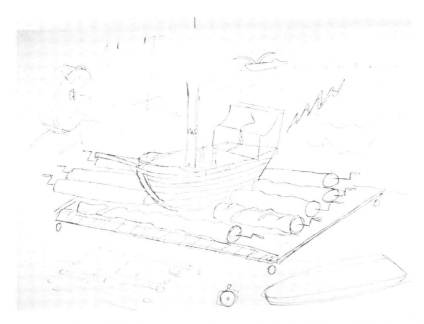

The production of *The Tempest* by Compagnia Carlo Colla e Figli: Special effects machinery used in the storm scene. Photo by the author.

His intention as translator was to be as faithful as possible to the text; however, comic passages based on dated word play that are difficult to understand even in English were rewritten, some explanatory passages were inserted, and the protective love of Prospero for Miranda was emphasized. The translation also acquired overtones of the Neapolitan background of the translator with Ariel resembling a *scugnizzo,* the infamous Neapolitan street urchin. It has the flavor of the popular fable that came from Eduardo's memories of performing in seventeenth century *féeries* as a young actor, in which all manner of supernatural beings and magical events were indiscriminately mixed. Eduardo subsequently made a sound recording of the text in which he performed all the parts himself (at the age of eighty four!), with the exception of that of Miranda. The recording was used as a teaching exercise at the Centro Teatro Ateneo, Università di Roma 'La Sapienza.' In his notes Eduardo envisaged that it could be staged by *marionette* but did not realize the project before his death. What had been Shakespeare's last drama and Prospero's final enchantment was also Eduardo's swan song.

The idea was taken up by Franco Quadri, director of the international festival of theater in Venice, who proposed to Luca, son of Eduardo, and Eugenio Monti Colla that they collaborate to produce the spectacle to inaugurate the thirty-third Biennale.

The cast of *marionette*

The production required 120 *marionette* because Shakespeare's characters were accompanied by a host of elves, sprites, birds, and animals, which were operated by twenty *marionettisti.* Monti Colla decided to populate the island landscape with a wide variety of animals, thinking of the animals which figure in medieval bestiaries, in Dante, and in Boccaccio, animals that hoax or punish humans. The creatures have a symbolic function: bats fly as plots are hatched, goslings leap over the stream during the scene of the lovers. Eduardo too had envisaged the presence of animals and had suggested that a song of Ariel be accompanied by animal noises. The inclusion of the animals was also a conscious exploitation of the possibilities of theater with *marionette.* Monti Colla directed the production with an emphasis upon the strengths of his genre of theater and awareness of its limitations. One cannot, for example, expect psychological introspection of a *marionetta,* so characterization was limited to what could be suggested by the appearance and costume, and it was left to the voice of Eduardo to develop the characterization.

The Neapolitan aspects already present in Eduardo's text owing to the dialect and the characterization of Ariel as a *scugnizzo* were further developed in the design of the *marionette*. This Ariel is no sprite but a flesh and blood street urchin. The costume and appearance of Gonzalo suggest the Neapolitan folk character of the *pazziariello*. (He also bears a striking resemblance to Eugenio Monti Colla!).

Duplicate *marionette* were required for several of the characters. To increase the illusion of depth of scene it is normal practice for *marionette* which appear in the background to be smaller in size than those in the foreground and therefore a character who is required to appear in both areas is often made in two versions, identical except for size. The nobles, for example, were made in two sizes because they are seen in the distance on the ship during the tempest scene and in the foreground when on the island. A duplicate is also required if a character is to make a complete change of costume, thus there were three Prospero *marionette;* a second one who operated tiny *marionette* in the play-within-a-play scene and a third in the costume of the leave-taking scene. Ariel's roles were so many and various that eight versions of him were required.

The greatest challenge to the Colla company was the construction of Caliban. Eduardo had described in his notes a Caliban *marionetta* who could perform a drunken dance, moving his eyebrows, ears, and stomach, and protruding his tongue, without knowing whether such a *marionetta* was technically possible. After considerable experimentation, the company produced a Caliban who answered Eduardo's description. Mechanisms were fitted inside his hollowed-out head to allow the movement of the tongue, eyebrows, and ears by means of extra strings attached externally, and his torso was articulated so that his stomach could be moved. An additional difficulty arose from the fact that most of his body was exposed, being clad only in a few leaves, therefore he had to be sculpted entirely in wood and was consequently extremely heavy. The weight was reduced to thirty-seven kilograms by hollowing out the torso. Even so, Caliban's drunken dance required three *marionettisti* who had to abandon their separate personae and "become" a single Caliban. The stature of Caliban, who dwarfed all other characters as no actor could, was an ironic contrast to his actual powerlessness. Maurizio Dotti, gifted artist and *marionettista,* describes the work of the animators:

Piegati sul proscenio, a schiena curva, vedendo solo in assoluta per-
pendicolare gli 'attori' cui diamo vita e movimento, ogni spettacolo è
una straordinaria fatica. Tra noi e la marionetta che muoviamo si crea
un rapporto di totale scambio, una magica relazione di emozioni che
solo l'applauso e lo stupore del pubblico riesce a rompere . . . fino al
prossimo spettacolo. Fino al prossimo incantesimo.[2]

For this production, the *marionettisti* worked from three *ponti di
manovra* instead of the usual one, which greatly increased the
depth of stage in which the *marionette* could perform.

The construction of the *marionette* was based on the wonderful
bozzetti of Maurizio Dotti. The heads were sculpted by Franco
Citterio and the transformation from sketch to sculpture can be
seen in the figures of the drunken Stephano. (Note that the *marionette* are stored divested of their costumes and wigs.)

The costumes are hand-sewn by members of the company, using luxurious fabrics such as velvet, silk, and brocade, often an-
tique, that catch the light and drape well but are not so bulky that
they impede the movement of the *marionette*. The wigs and beards
are made from human hair in styles based on sketches. After the
conclusion of a production, all costumes and wigs are carefully
stored and the *marionette* may be used for a different production.

Scenery

In the opening scene the spectator was faced with a city in
ruins, which could be interpreted as the human spirit, or as the
aftermath of a war, or as a devastated Naples. In the middle was
Prospero's cave, as if everything took place within his spirit. Every
so often, the rear of the cave opened up to reveal the visions of
Prospero: the wedding of Claribel in Tunisia, the dance of the
witch, Sycorax, and the wedding feast of Miranda and Ferdinand.
The opening scene in the grotto of Prospero was in total darkness
except for a light on his desk which gradually brightened to reveal
the grotto. The rear of the scene opened upon the stormy sea for
the tempest scene. The majority of the backdrops were painted
consecutively in a one-hundred-meter length that was wound onto
giant bobbins placed one at each side of the stage. As the performance progressed, the changes of scene were accomplished by the
winding of the backdrops across the stage in view of the audience,
giving the sense of a journey. Almost every scene included at least
a scrap of blue sky or sea, symbol of hope for the future.

The style of the scenic design was based on the figurative art of the late Renaissance. The large arches favored by neoclassicists and landscape painters were employed to frame the scenes. Colors were used for symbolic effect: delicate and opalescent for the declaration of love of Miranda and Ferdinand, deep and heated for the plotting of the rulers, gloomy and disquieting for the plotting of the fools, clear and tropical for the calm sea after the tempest. The wild island scenery symbolized disorder, even the trees assumed the shapes of malevolent faces. For a visual image to accompany the return to order and good government in the final scene, a delicate stencil of an ideal city scene, lit from behind, was superimposed on the rugged, ruined landscape that had framed the entire performance. Renaissance architectural ideals of order and proportion were used here to present the city as the location of civilized existence in contrast to the savagery of the island, which is a reversal of the more usual notion of the country as Arcadia.

Theatrical magic

The production consciously sought to exploit to the fullest those stage techniques that created the illusion in order to intensify the atmosphere of fantasy with which Eduardo had imbued the text, and to create effects that are possible in the theater of *marionette* but not in that of the actor. To Eugenio Monti Colla, who had previously been reluctant to stage works of Shakespeare, there was clearly common ground between Eduardo's text and the theater of *marionette:*

> La forza poetica di Eduardo De Filippo nel restituire, attraverso la ricchezza del linguaggio napoletano, la dimensione 'popolare' di un testo ormai visitato e rivisitato da interpretazioni filosofiche e intellettuali, è apparsa come il punto di raccordo più intenso e più concreto con il teatro di marionette che rende tangibile il mondo della fantasia attraverso magie e incantamenti scenici.[3]

Extensive research was done into the theatrical machinery of the seventeenth to nineteenth centuries that was then recreated for special effects such as thunder, lightning, and rain. The most dramatic scene, the shipwreck, lasted only two minutes but during that time at least fifty effects took place, culminating in the disappearance of the ship beneath the water and the appearance of a rainbow. The sea was created by a series of rollers covered in blue fabric. The front roller covered the width of the stage but those behind were in pairs with an opening in the center for the boat. The rotation of the rollers created the effect of waves with spray suggested by nylon threads that were thrown upward as the rollers turned. Lightning (a genuine electric discharge) struck the mast, which broke off, as did the prow. The boat, built from timber, was constructed so that it would collapse telescopically into itself as the storm raged until it vanished and the rollers closed over it.

Music

Even before the publication of his translation, Eduardo had begun to collaborate with a musician from Naples, Antonio Sinagra. Together they had written Caliban's song and Eduardo had recorded it. It was immediately apparent to the musician when he began to work on the project that the words and voice of Eduardo had a markedly musical quality that he sought to complement with his composition. The music for the tempest scene took the form of a frantic tarantella. The music was performed live with an eighteen-piece orchestra because it was felt that the only sound coming from "the beyond" should be that of Eduardo's voice.

Critical response

The performances at the Venice Biennale and subsequently in Milan received a great deal of critical attention. *Viva Milano* analyzed the reviews of Italy's eight major newspapers (*Il Corrierre della Sera, La Repubblica, La Stampa, L'Avvenire, L'Unità, Il Giorno, Il Giornale, Il Manifesto*) of the entire program of the Biennale.[4] *The Tempest* was the only production to receive favorable reviews from all publications.

Adaptations to performance with *marionette*

To surmount the difficulties posed by long spoken passages that are difficult for *marionette* to sustain, it was decided to represent in pantomime Prospero's account to Miranda of past events in Naples and the wedding of Claribel, daughter of Alonso, to the King of Tunisia, accompanied by Prospero's description of these events. This provided an opportunity for sumptuous costuming and exotic scenery in the staging of what appeared to be a vision, thus heightening the illusory aspects of the production and stressing the parallel between Prospero's magic and the magic of the theater. The metatheatrical aspects of the audience watching Miranda and Prospero watching the unfolding of the storm scene or the wedding procession recur when Shakespeare's masque of the goddesses is replaced by an improvised performance with *marionette* manipulated by Prospero. The performance takes place in a miniature theater that is revealed by the parting of one of the "rocks" and the *marionette* are characters from the Commedia dell'arte. This metatheatrical insertion is highly appropriate because *The Tempest,* more than any other Shakespearean work, is permeated by reflections on the nature of theater, revelations of its mechanisms, demonstration of its genres from tragedy to comedy to farce to Commedia dell'arte, a strong sense of performance, and parallels between Prospero and the theatrical director. This performance of *marionette* within a performance of *marionette* may be an echo of Depero's *I balli plastici* in which at one point the stomach of one of the *marionette,* the Great Savage, folded down to become a platform on which tiny *marionette,* representing savages, were shown dancing.[5]

The richness and charm of the production owe much to the echoes and parallels that abound: the renouncing of one's art by Prospero, Shakespeare and Eduardo; the sorcery of Prospero and the spell cast by the *marionette;* the magic of modern technology which preserves the voice of a dead man and the magic of centuries-old theatrical techniques which conjure up a violent storm. The spectacle concluded with a final parallel: the foremost curtain was raised high above the stage, revealing the *marionettisti* on the *ponte di manovra,* who, in displaying their means of producing the illusion, like Prospero, also renounce their magic.

6

Shakespeare with Strings: How the Bard Has Fared in *teatro di figura*

Attempts have been made to ennoble the theater of *burattini* and *marionette* by citing the ancient origins of animated figures or its adoption by literary or artistic figures (such as Alfred Jarry, who wrote *Ubu Roi* for *burattini*,[1] the caricaturist, Umberto Tirelli, who designed satirical *burattini*, and the futurist artist, Fortunato Depero, who created his *I Balli Plastici* for *marionette*). Often the citation of the presence in the repertoire of works by major dramatists is a claim for an elevated intellectual status. However the present study of the use of Shakespearean drama in *teatro di figura* does not seek to deny that the characteristics of the vast majority of traditional productions, especially of theater of *burattini*, are unmistakably those of popular spectacle. This is evident from the description of many of the productions recorded herein. Instead, it examines the differences between *teatro di figura* and live theater and the adaptations necessitated by a shift from one genre to another.

Before examining the alteration of Shakespearean works when performed by popular rather than traditional theater, the assertion that theater of *burattini* is a popular spectacle should be substantiated. In chapter 3 it was evident that the majority of *burattinai* have been traveling showmen, mounting their *baracca* wherever people gather, in *piazze*, in markets, and at fairs. Although their popularity and the breadth of their repertoire may have enabled them to remain in one place for an extended period, they rarely had a permanent theater, unlike the *marionettisti*. The theater of *burattini* lacks the essentials of official theater—a theatrical season, habitual performance times, and the theater itself. The patrons of "serious" theater have tended to regard the theater of *burattini* with disdain, considering it either second-rate or even scurrilous. According to Jurkowski, popular theater is an artistic or quasi artistic production addressed to the uneducated, urban public, that is generally not innovative but imitates the repertoire of the official theater.[2] If this adaptation of the repertoire is based on a limited theatrical skill, the result will have a folk flavor, which is undoubtedly true of some of the Shakespearean productions that we have considered. Popular theater with *marionette* could also be imitative, but at a highly skilled level; especially in the seventeenth century when the speech of actors was declamatory and their gestures schematic, it was possible for the theater of *marionette* to mount a perfect small-scale copy of live theater.

Theater of *burattini* has almost always been comic theater, seeking to draw from its audience what Propp describes as the ritual laugh of folklore.[3] The activities of the *burattini* in which servant outwits master, or citizen overthrows oppressor are related to Carnival popular culture. We can see influence of popular culture in the theater of *burattini* when we compare the characteristics of its masks to the nature of the same masks in theater of *marionette*. The latter, as Pasqualino points out:

> soon became refined, tending to change into symbols of urban respectability, while in the puppet shows they remained genuine peasants and retained all their original violence, their proclivity to rebellion, and disquieting traces of their descent from the demons of agrarian fertility rites.[4]

Ritual requires participation and popular theater can be distinguished from official theater in its aspects which encourage such participation. In live theater there exists a sense of "otherness": the spectator is physically separated from the stage, the performance even of a familiar work is unknown in the sense that the interpretations of the actors and director are always new, the language may well be removed from everyday speech, and oppositions are set up between actor/spectator, activity/passivity. Popular theater on the other hand has a quality of "nonotherness" which enables collective participation. It is often performed in public space and the content is known. The theater of *pupi*, for example, is designed for an audience of *conoscitori*. The costumes of all characters are rigidly codified and instantly recognizable to the audience, and the legends of the Paladins are utterly familiar. Similarly, the masks of the theater of *marionette* and *burattini* are known to the audience. Gioppino, for example, is the typical mask of the Bergamo region and he is not only known to the people of Bergamo but he represents their essential character and speaks their dialect. Emphasis in popular theater is placed not on innovation but on tradition, hence the retelling of familiar tales and the transmitting of the repertoire through the generations.

If we accept that "nonotherness" is an essential quality of popular theater we can then view the alterations made to Shakespearean works performed in the *teatro di figura* as not necessarily arbitrary or insensitive, but as a process of aligning them with the theatrical genre that has adopted them. The interpolation of the traditional masks which occurred so frequently is thus a means of making familiar the unfamiliar. The risk is that the Shakespearean work is made familiar, but is irreparably damaged in the process. The masks are least intrusive when they are introduced into a comedy or the comic subplot of a tragedy. Benedetto Ravasio, for example, successfully introduced Gioppino and Colombina to provide a comic counterpoint to the tragic love of Romeo and Juliet (*Romeo and Juliet*, chapter 3, section 12). The Lupi production of *Hamlet* included Arlecchino, also adroitly inserted into the small role of one of the traveling players (*Hamlet* chapter 1, section 3). Other more representative examples of the presence of the masks are less successful. Giacomo Colla's *Hamlet* featured the perpetually hungry Famiola as Marcello, the soldier who waits with Hamlet on the battlements for the appearance of the ghost of his father, which is an inappropriate scene for the introduction of a comic element (*Hamlet* chapter 1, section 17). However, it is when the masks replace the Shakespearean characters rather than appearing alongside them, that the drama is likely to become unrecognizable. As we have seen (chapter 3, section 10), when Hamlet is played by Arlecchino in Beppe Pastrello's version, there is very little resemblance to the play which Shakespeare wrote. These appearances of Giacomo Colla's Famiola (*marionetta*) and Pastrello's Arlecchino (*burattino*) demonstrate the different role of the masks in the two genres. In the theater of *marionette*, the masks remained important, but gradually yielded center stage to the protagonists of new works that entered the repertoire. Colla's *Hamlet* included Famiola, but in the minor role of Marcello, and Luigi Lupi's Arlecchino appeared briefly as one of the players in the production of *Hamlet*. However, the masks continued to dominate the stage in the theater of *burattini*, as Pastrello's Arlecchino did in the role of Hamlet.

The use of dialect is another characteristic of popular spectacle. In the theater of *burattini*, the local dialect lends immediacy and vigor to the performance because of its expressive power. The *burattinaio* was often an anti-authoritarian spokesman for the populace on various issues, and dialect was the appropriate language in which to express local concerns and sentiments. This aspect of the use of dialect is not relevant to the performance of Shakespeare where its use had a different function. In this case it was important in opening a largely unknown dramatic form to a new public. The improvised nature of the performance would allow the *burattinaio* to monitor the audience response[5] and, if he felt that what was being said in Italian by the major characters was not being fully understood, the comic characters speaking in dialect could add explanatory remarks. The use of dialect could be a limiting factor for a touring *burattinaio* because when he moved outside the region in which the dialect of his particular masks was understood, it was sometimes necessary for the mask to speak Italian instead. According to Signora Ravasio (chapter 3, section 12) something was lost when Gioppino, for example, spoke in Italian, because the dialect of Bergamo was an intrinsic part of his character. It is interesting that all the examples of *copioni* reproduced herein are written wholly or partly in Italian, even though some were produced before the use of the national language was widespread. It is generally agreed that the influence of television was partly responsible for the eventual spread of Italian throughout the nation and, from the evidence of these *copioni*, it would seem that the theater of *marionette, burattini,* and *pupi* played a similar role in a much earlier period.[6]

Cultivated theater is based upon the power of the word while popular theater places greater emphasis on spectacle. There is little use of a written text in traditional theater of *burattini* and *pupi;* and even theater of *marionette,* though using a text, has sought virtuosity at the expense of the dramatic power of the word. Such rejection of the word must surely be a considerable obstacle in the attempt to transfer a dramatic work from a historically word-centered genre to a genre with different values. In some cases, the productions were so loosely based upon Shakespeare that they cannot be considered a serious attempt to present his work. Instead, the rough outline of the plot was used to vary the repertoire and Shakespeare's name was used as a drawcard in the wake of successful theatrical or operatic productions of his works.

We have seen that Shakespearean productions mounted with *marionette, burattini,* or *pupi* have often profoundly altered the original plot. The Lupi *Hamlet* (chapter 1, section 3) has a greatly diminished tragic ending owing to the survival of Hamlet, Gertrude, and Laertes. Alberto Canino's versions for *pupi* of *Macbeth* and *Romeo and Juliet* (chapter 2, section 1) have reduced and simplified plots and a much greater emphasis on thrilling combat scenes. The mask Sandrone directs irreverent jibes at the king of Denmark in Enrico Ponti's *Hamlet* (chapter 3, section 5). Umberto Tirelli employed only the skeleton of the plot of *Othello* (chapter 3, section 8) as a vehicle for a satirical attack on leading literary and artistic figures. The majority of the productions listed were intended for an adult audience but those mounted especially for young people, such as Patrizia Filippi's *Othello* (chapter 4, section 2) and the Gianni and Cosetta Colla *A Midsummer Night's Dream* (chapter 4, section 4), eliminated plot complexities and accentuated fantasy and spectacle.

While those passionate about Shakespearean drama may view such alterations as acts of barbarism, one must remember that they are not unique to· *teatro di figura,* but were common practice in live theater. Italian attitudes to Shakespeare were for a long time influenced by Voltaire's criticisms of the English dramatist.[7] For this reason, the early attempts to stage Shakespeare in Italy invariably altered the works in an effort to make them more acceptable to the public. For example, one of the earliest productions was a version of *Romeo and Juliet* at the end of the eighteenth century which was:

> drawn from the French adaptation of Mercier which observed the unities, changed the tone from tragedy to sentimental comedy, and ended happily with a reconciliation of the feuding families and uniting of the young lovers.[8]

Carlson also describes a number of more faithful productions in the early nineteenth century which were unqualified disasters because of the unfavorable response of the audience and a version of *Hamlet* which was moderately successful, but had been given a happy ending.[9]

Other productions have recognized the problems involved in transferring a Shakespearean work across the double barrier posed by a foreign language and a different set of theatrical conventions, and have attempted to overcome them with a variety of approaches. The importance of the psychological dimension in Shakespearean drama poses a problem because the *marionetta* does not have the expressive tools of facial and body language which the actor employs. But the major expressive tool of the actor is the voice, and this can be given to the *marionetta* by means of the collaboration of talented actors. The productions of the Latis family (chapter 1, section 22), Vittorio Podrecca (chapter 1, section 19), and Eugenio Monti Colla (chapter 1, section 26) have responded to this difficulty by the use of a faithful text and professional actors. In doing so, they are changing the nature of their form of theater to align it with the nature of the appropriated text. The opposite approach is to alter the text to fit the strengths and conventions of the genre. At its most radical, this approach abandons almost entirely the spoken word as a means of expression. If such a performance is based upon a thorough knowledge of the text, the essence of which is then expressed by other means, the resulting production can be a successful and sensitive rendition. The *Romeo and Juliet* of the Teatro del Carretto (chapter 4, section 1), for example, conveyed the atmosphere of feuding Verona. The gulf between the corruption and power of the adult world and the purity of passion in the world of the lovers were eloquently and completely expressed by the costuming, staging, movement, and music. The amount of spoken text was minimal, but the production remained thoroughly Shakespearean because the entire text had been absorbed by the producer and her team, and then presented to the audience in a different, but equally valid, expressive language.

Other approaches utilize the qualities common to *teatro di figura* and the figurative arts, often by collaboration with artists. The body of an actor, unable to shed its corporeality, is limited in its ability to express abstract or symbolic notions. Not so the *marionetta,* and it is this figurative quality which the production by Gianni and Cosetta Colla, in conjunction with Luigi Veronesi, sought to exploit (chapter 4, section 4). The supernatural creatures which Veronesi designed for this production are free of the material constraints of the actor and are able to be demonstrably creatures from another realm. Podrecca's belief that there exists a special affinity between *marionette* and music has been supported by the many productions which reinforce the visual image with music.

The Elizabethan stage was entirely nonnaturalistic and symbolic. It made no attempt to mirror reality but sought to portray the essence of the human condition. Thus when *teatro di figura* utilizes to the full its strengths in the expression of abstract or symbolic concepts it can approach the universality of Shakespearean drama while the performance of an actor, because it is inseparable from the human form of the actor, necessarily emphasizes the individual rather than the wider implications. The performance of the actor is a barrier to the identification of the spectator with the character portrayed by the actor in that we do not see simply Othello, for example, but Olivier's Othello. The *marionetta* however has no independent existence and is thus perceived directly as the character, not as a representation of it.

The Russian ethnographer, Pëtr Bogatyrëv, was the first to adopt a semiotic approach to theater of *marionette*.[10] He maintained that this form of theater has a system of signs which is distinct from that of the theater of actors. We recognize the existence of a system of signs when we attend a theatrical performance because if we did not, we would believe that the spectacle was reality and it would seem comic or even ridiculous. If we also view the theater of *marionette* as a system of signs, we gain a better understanding of its nature and its relationship with live theater. One evident distinction between the two systems is the economy of sign which is possible in *teatro di figura*. Veltruskỳ writes:

> Here the stage figure and stage action have only such qualities as are needed to fulfill their semiotic function; in other terms, the puppet is a pure sign because all its components are intentional.[11]

The productions described in this study include examples of such economy of sign; the expressionistic *marionette* of Marta Latis (chapter 1, section 22), the abstract creations of the earlier productions by Gianni and Cosetta Colla (chapter 1, section 23), and the even more reductive designs of their collaboration with Veronesi (chapter 4, section 4). When a production combines actors and *marionette* it is necessary to maintain the distinction between the two systems by allocating different realms to each. This can be a very effective dramatic technique when used to heighten distinctions already present in the text. Thus the Teatro del Carretto production of *Romeo and Juliet* (chapter 4, section 1) emphasized the isolation of the lovers by casting them as *marionette* in a world of actors, and the Colla/Veronesi *A Midsummer Night's Dream* (chapter 4, section 4) accentuated the contrast between the artisans and the fairy creatures by using actors for the former.

A confrontation between the codes of theater with actors and with *marionette* arises with regard to the presence of the human voice in conjunction with objects which are not only inanimate but differ from humans in their size and style of movement. The confrontation can be avoided by the elimination of the vocal component as occurred in the ballet spectacles performed by *marionette*. A more common response is to distort the human voice as pointed out by Veltruskỳ:

In order to combine human speech with the inanimate object and the motion carried out by its means, the delivery is made so strange as to be perceived as inhuman when it is confronted with natural human delivery. The voice is to be perceived as the puppet's own voice and the impeded speech as its own speech, anthropomorphous rather than human.[12]

As a result, many of the characters of the theater of *marionette*, *burattini*, and *pupi* have a nonnaturalistic style of speech which is identified with the particular character, just as characters in animated film have idiosyncratic voices. In the case of Pulcinella, the distortion was obtained by the use of the swazzle (an instrument used to distort the voice) in order to endow him with a voice which was immediately distinguishable from all other characters. The distorted voices or distorted articulation also had a purely practical application for the *burattinaio*, who usually spoke all the male parts, in that it enabled him to differentiate between the characters. It is possible that the introduction of the masks into Shakespearean productions with *burattini* may have been partly motivated by the need for the *burattinaio* to distinguish vocally between the characters, because for each of the masks he would already have developed a distinctive speech style, immediately recognizable to his audience.

In the past, both *marionettisti* and *burattinai* have remained invisible during a performance but recent performances have often laid bare the mechanism of the animation. At the conclusion of the Compagnia Carlo Colla e Figli production of *The Tempest* (chapter 5) the *marionettisti* were revealed, and they operated in full view of the audience throughout Gianni and Cosetta Colla's *A Midsummer Night's Dream* (chapter 4, section 4). Not only was Patrizia Filippi visible for her entire performance of *Othello* (chapter 4, section 2), but her *burattini* were constructed in a nontraditional manner which exposes the hands of the operator. When actors share the stage with *marionette* they become part of the dramatic performance and part of the theatrical illusion. However the visible presence of the animators has a different effect, according to Green and Pepicello:

However, if human intervention takes the form of a visible, silent puppeteer who is not a part of the drama, but who merely manipulates the puppets that are part of the drama, we must see this juxtaposition of illusion and reality as a semiotic relationship that speaks to the very nature of puppetry.[13]

According to Bogatyrëv, the actor is a sign (of the character he portrays) and the *teatro di figura* operates at one remove, so that the *marionetta* is a sign of a sign. Even the most sophisticated and skillfully manipulated *marionette* are not perceived as human, rather their characteristics are metonyms of humanity. The detached and possibly distorted voice and the mobile jaw, as well as the motion and gestures are not representations of human speech and movement, but signs of them. Green and Pepicello argue that if the system of signs which constitutes *teatro di figura* is to be understood it requires human mediation:

> In the case of the visible puppeteer the mediation is subtle, so that while the human presence is discernible, it is not directly involved in the conflict of the puppet performance. Rather, the puppeteer is *almost* part of the scene, one who serves as a reminder of the base from which the performance is drawn. When human *dramatis personae* are involved, in the form of actors or interlocutors, more aggressive mediation results. Here we may view the human mediators as strongly reinforced instances of 'normalcy' whereby the various distortions of the normal semiotic system are untwisted by a human agent who thus serves to reveal himself (i.e., human beings and their conventions) as the reality signified in juxtaposition to the puppet performance.[14]

As modern theater moves further away from mimesis and makes greater use of visual imagery to express the abstract, it approaches *teatro di figura*. The success of recent productions which break down the barriers between the genres and combine the techniques shows that the future relationship between different forms of theater may be complementary rather than competitive, and that *teatro di figura* may come to be regarded as different, rather than inferior. Its role as an entertainment for the masses has been irrevocably lost to the wide range of modern leisure pursuits but at the same time its expressive potential is being increasingly adopted for avant-garde theatrical productions (which are outside the scope of this study) and experimental renditions of classical theater. This gradual shift from popular to elite is accompanied by a greater sensitivity to the dramatic potential of the text. In many of the earlier productions, the Shakespearean work was forced to take on the style of the theater with *marionette* or *burattini* at the expense of its own qualities. In recent productions, however, *teatro di figura* is employed to communicate Shakespeare's work in a manner which demonstrates the seemingly inexhaustible possibilities of his drama and the particular strengths of this type of theatrical spectacle. We have seen from the catalogue section that Italian *teatro di figura* has performed Shakespearean drama regularly for at least one hundred and seventy years, and it is likely to continue to do so because exploration of the potential for sensitive and innovative productions has only recently begun.

Appendix A

COPIONE FOR THE PRODUCTION OF HAMLET BY LUIGI LUPI

G. Lupi 1868

Amleto
Principe di Danimarca
Tragedia di Guglielmo Shakspeare

Ridotta per le scene del teatro da S. Martiniano

Con Arlecchino attore comico

La scena è in Elsinoro

To be or not be, it is the question

PERSONAGGI

3 **Amleto** Principe di Danimarca *uno con spada in mano*
ferro lungo e ventaglio alla mano
sinistra. Sotto il mantello spillato sulla
spalla sinistra

3 **Re** sposo al:

poi in nero

A transcription of the handwritten *copione,* which is held in the family collection in Turin. The spelling, punctuation, and grammar of the original have been retained. Square brackets indicate a word that is no longer legible.

3 **La Regina**
2 **Polonio, padre di**   *Bastone in mano*
                              Simile senza ferro da porre poi dietro la tenda
2 **Laerte** *poi in nero*
3 **Ofelia** *poi in bianco (simile annegata)*
   Marcello
                       Cavalieri, il 1° studente, il 2° soldato
   Orazio
   Lo spettro   *in armatura completa con velo celeste ecc.*
   Arlecchino
   1° comico
                       figure doppie (più piccole)
   2° comico
   1 Donna
   1° Seppellitore   *con zappa (ferro lungo)*
   2° Seppellitore
   Guilden paggio del Re   *non parla, piccolo*
1 **Frate**
3 **Cavalieri—Guardie**
   Corteo funebre: *4 donzelle in bianca, 2 uomini in nero, 1 comparsa in*
   nero, 2 uomini che portano la cassa sulla barella, coperta di seta bianca,
   con fili per deporla, un terzo comico che non parla.
   Luce 4 volte da sinistra

AMLETO   1881

5 atti

Per favore: I numeri indicati con sordina si suonino più che piano, pianissimo, in modo che il pubblico non senta nè ad incominciarli nè a finirli.
Se fossero troppo lunghi si farà segno da sul palco perché cessino.

Atto 1°—Sinfonia 881—poi subito il No. 1. Viva il Re—senza ritornello
parole: tazze vuotate alla salute   No. 1½
             A questa sera   2
             Vi obbedirò   3
             La vagante lucciola   4
             Sull'onore lo giuriamo   5
Atto 2°—intermezzo a piacere
parole: Sono giunti i commedianti   6
             Smarrita la ragione   7
Atto 3°—intermezzo a piacere

parole:	Cominici la rappresentazione	8
	Nè testimon vivente	9
	Un re da teatro	10
	Risparmia tua madre	11

Atto 4°—(Amleto) intermezzo a piacere

parole:	Oh è troppo vero	12
	Il non più vederlo	13
	Le voci e le mani applaudono	14
	Poca alla mia vendetta	15

Atto 5°—intermezzo a piacere, poi subito | | 16 |

parole:	Se vi piace udremo il tutto	17
	Ordina io obbedisco	18
	Muori e a Satana vado	19
	Il cui sdegno si placa	(senza il maestoso) 20

Poi ballo: *L'arbre de Noël*

Vedi in fondo per le scene

N.B. Chi fa Polonio stia attento quando è dietro la tenda e fa capolino, quando la regina grida 'Soccorso, soccorso!' dirà pur egli una volta 'Soccorso', poi corica la figura a destra, indi starà attento a gettare un gemito quando Amleto infilza la spada per ferire—e finalmente tirerà su la tenda alle parole:

Occorre:

Campana per le ore 12—Trono—2 ventagli—4 teste di morto—4 spade—1 libro con filo—Scrigno con filo e due [ ]—Barella con tappeto, biancheria e corona, 4 fili—[ ]—Placche in teatro—Tela per lanterna della fossa—Lanternino—Zappa—[ ]—Tavolo e sedie per l'atto 2°—Cassa-panca

ATTO PRIMO

Sinistra	Destra
2 Grandi	**Polonio**
Laerte *in scena*	**Regina** *in scena*
2 Guardie	**Re**
Amleto	**1 Grande** *pure in scena*
	1 Paggio
Orazio	**Ofelia**
Marcello	
2 spade, 2 mantelli per i detti	
Luce	*Da suonare le 12*
mantello e spada al 2° Amleto	
in mano	**Spettro** *dietro*
	Lastra per il vento

Sala con trono a due sedili nel Reale Castello in Elsinoro.
Re—La regina in trono a destra.
Amleto—Laerte—Polonio—Guardie

Tutti. Viva il Re!
Re. Signori grazie! La morte di un benamato fratello faceva tuttora piegare il mio capo sotto il peso del dolore. Ma oggi le vostre grida
rianimano la mia fronte e questa si rischiara ai raggi della pubblica
gioia. Io ho quindi col sorriso sulle labbra e le lagrime agli occhi scelta
colei che altre volte mi era germana in isposa. E ora che la di lei mano
alta mia è unita e dal ministro fu la nostra unione consacrata io vi
ringrazio degli evviva che mi rendete e se qualcuno di voi brama grazia
o favore si accosti e parli.
Lae. Sire . . .
Re. Laerte quale è il desir vostro?
Lae. Chieggo il vostro consenso per ritornare in Francia. Qui venni ad
inchinarvi mio re. Ora i miei voti e pensieri miei mi richiamano colà.
Re. Che ne dice il padre vostro?
Po. Egli tanto insiste che mi fu forza il cedere.
Re. Scegli dunque l'ora ed il tempo come più ti talenta e sia a te il viaggio
felice. Ora voi Amleto . . . mio parente e figlio . . .
Am. Parente troppo, figlio . . . non tanto.
Re. Perché quelle nubi sulla vostra fronte?
Am. Non vi prendete cura di me.
La R. Caro Amleto dirada quelle fosche ombre, ed il tuo occhio giri
amici sguardi sulla Danimarca. Non cercare nella polvere della tomba
il nobile tuo padre. Lo sai ogni cosa che vive quaggiù muore, e tra-
versando questo mondo passa all'eternità.
Am. È legge comune.
La R. E perché tanto sembri contristato?
Am. Non sembro no. Non è solo il nero colore di questa gramaglia,
questi caldi sospiri, questa fronte abbattuta, che ponno manifestare il
mio dolore, ma esso si nasconde qui entro di me; ed il resto non è che
un simulacro.
Re. E ben fate nell'avere pia ricordanza del padre vostro; ma il per-
severare nel pianto è segno di animo ribelle ai voleri del cielo. È destino inevitabile la morte. Confortatevi adunque rammentando che noi
sentiamo per voi amore più che fraterno.
La R. Amleto io unisco i miei voti a quelli del Re.
Am. Farò sempre ogni sforzo per obbedirvi signora.
Re. Nobile risposta. *Si alzano* Amici non più tristezza adunque. Vo' che
gioiosi brindisi sieno fatti oggi, ed abbiano per eco il tuono delle artig-
lierie! Vo' che la volta del cielo, ripetendo gli scoppi dei folgori della
terra, risuoni del plauso di tazze vuotate alla salute del Re!

Marcia Giuliva–viano tutti destra.
Am. solo—porta Polonio a sinistra. Oh potesse questa creta che mi veste
scomporsi, disfarsi come rugiada!–Come mi pare inutile ed insulsa

ogni usanza del mondo!–La vita! .. giardino incolto dove nascono
spine ed erbe selvaggie. Due mesi dacché morì; meno di due mesi!—
L'ottimo re, si tenero della madre mia ... ed ella ... Cielo e Terra!
pariva che gli si stringesse d'intorno con affetto crescente ... pure
dopo un mese ... Non vo pensarvi. Fragilità! il tuo nome è femmin-
ino! Essa sposa a mio zio, al fratello di mio padre. *Pronti Orazio e
Marcello* Sua sposa prima anche che le lagrime della vedovanza che
avevano arrossato i suoi occhi si fossero disperse! Oh vile ed infame
abbandono. Più lungo sarebbe stato il coruccio di una belva! *da sinistra
Orazio e Marcello*

Ora. Salute a vostra altezza.
Am. Che vedo ... Orazio sei tu? Dimmi che ti guido in Elsinoro?
Ora. Venni per assistere ai funerali di vostro padre.
Am. Ma che! Di piuttosto alle nozze di mia madre!
Ora. Ebbero luogo molto presto.
Am. I caldi cibi del funereo banchetto furono imbanditi tepidi al convito
nuziale. Oh Orazio, meglio sarebbe stato per me se avessi raggiunto
un mortale nemico nell'eterno regno anziché aver mirato un simile
giorno.—Padre mio! Parmi vederlo ...
Ora. Come?
Am. Cogli occhi dell'anima mia.
Ora. Era un nobile principe!
Am. Troverassi difficilmente chi lo assomigli.
Ora. Ed io lo vidi la passata notte.
Am. Chi?
Ora. Il re.
Am. Mio padre!
Ora. Vi dico il vero. Per ben due notti Bernardo e Marcello durante la
loro guardia, nel più fitto delle tenebre videro una figura maestosa
armata da capo a piedi simigliante in tutto al padre vostre. Essi mi
fecero la confidenza di questo strano caso ... ed io fui seco loro la
scorsa notte e all'ora stessa comparve.
Am. Oh! Ma dove?
Ora. Sulla piattaforma.
Am. E gli parlaste?
Ora. Si ma non rispose. Pareva volesse farlo ma si fece udire il bronzo
mattutino ed a quel suono la visione scomparve.
Am. Oh voglio ben io coi miei occhi vederla quest'apparizione. Sarò con
voi sulla piattaforma questa notte ... Se la figura del padre mio a me
si presentasse ... io gli parlerò ... dovesse l'inferno spalancando le
sue voragini impormi silenzio. Intanto vi scongiuro del segreto su ciò
che succeder possa.
Ora. Lo giuriamo.
Am. Saprò riconoscere il vostro zelo. A mezzanotte sarò con voi.
Ora. Principe ...

Am. Chiamatemi amico. A questa sera. *gli da la mano–i 2 viano—ponigli spada in mano e mantelli*

Am. solo Lo spettro di mio padre in armi! . . . Si nasconderebbe qui forse qualche delitto? Pace mio cuore . . . pace finché giunga l'ora!

Ofelia da destra

Am. vedendola, da sinistra Ofelia!

Of. per retrocedere Oh . . . perdono o principe!

Am. Perdono d'essere bella, e di rendermi pazzo d'amore? . . . dite?

Of. No . . . ma di venirvi a sturbare mentre forse . . .

Am. E quando mai gli angeli del cielo turbano la pace dei mortali?

Of. Io cercava . . .

Am. Un fortunato mortale al certo quello che voi cercate. Perché non son io!

Of. È mio fratello Laerte che volevo vedere prima che per la francia ripartisse.

Am. Egli pure ci lascia!

Of. Comprendo . . . questo vi affligge.

Am. Affliggermi io . . . quando mi è dato di specchiarmi nel vostro sembiante di paradiso.

Of. Quali parole . . . voi . . .

Am. Io dico ciò che penso, e penso ciò che dico. Oh così potessi trovar voci atte a manifestarvi l'affetto che per voi io provo . . .

Of. Debbo credervi . . .

Am. Ofelia! . . . Dubita che gli astri splendano . . . Dimmi che il folle più non appar; dimmi che il vero mente e sa fingere . . . Ma deh . . . che io t'ami non dubitar. *via sinistra*

Of. È dunque vero! *Laerte da destra*

La. E che sorella?

Of. Laerte! *spada a Amleto*

Dimmi chi ratto da te si parte allor che io giungo?

Of. Amleto.

La. E che ti diceva?

Of. D'amarmi!

La. E tu credi?

Of. L'aurora crede al giorno e la donna all'amore.

La. Rifletti . . . egli è principe e come tale non può disporre di sé e di suoi affetti. E se tu troppo creduta a suoi seducenti discorsi incauta ti arrendessi alle sue focose importunità . . . faresti perduta! . . Oh guai a lui allora . . . benché mio signore e di sangue regale saprei . . .

Of. Laerte . . .

Polonio da sinistra

Pol. Qui ancora o figlio? . . Al mare . . . al mare. Il vento gonfia i fianchi delle vele e sei aspettato. Ricevi la mia benedizione e parti.

Lae. Vengo o genitore. Vi raccomando mia sorella. Le folli premure d'Amleto per lei . . .

Pol. Già le ho osservate . . . ma spero cesseranno . . .

Of. I suoi giuramenti d'amore . . .

Pol. Reti insidiose. Quando il sangue bolle, il cuore prodiga giuramenti alla lingua. Sono lampi che danno più luce che calore, ed in un attimo si estinguono. Come padre e come amico non voglio che t'intrattenga seco mai più.

Of. Vi obbedirò . . .

Pol. Laerte . . . andiamo. *viano tutti—Mutazione, è notte—La piattaforma del Castello—Amleto—Orazio—Marcello*

Am. Il freddo è acuto . . . Sentite come sibila il vento. Che or'è?

Ora. Poco manca a mezzanotte!

Am. S'avvicina dunque il momento in cui lo spettro usa vagare?

Ora. Tosto che sia battuto l'ultimo tocco. *Vento*

Am. Oh come vorrei affrettare gli istanti! *Suonano le 12*

Ora. Ecco! . . Ora apparirà senza dubbio . . .

Am. Un fremito insolito le mia membra invade . . .

Comparisce lo spettro dietro, da destra

Ora. Miratelo o Principe!

Am. Che! . . Dove? . .

Ora. Là . . . là!

Am. guarda Angeli e ministri di grazia difendeteci! . . E tu spirito benefico o pur infernale . . . vomitato dagli abissi o sceso dal cielo . . . Tu vieni sotto forma si sacra per me che io voglio parlarti. Ti chiamerò Amleto . . . padre . . . Re dei danesi . . . ma rispondimi . . . Dimmi— Perché le tue ossa sepolte squarciarono il funereo lenzuolo? A quale oggetto ne vieni? . . . Parla . . . e ne scongiuro.

Spe. fa cenno che gli altri si ritirino

Ora. Pare che accenni volervi parlare da solo.

Am. Ebbene, lasciatemi!

Ora. Oh no principe . . .

Am. Perché? . . Qual timore vi prende! La mia vita mi è da meno di un obolo e niun danno potrà accadere alla mia anima immortale come la sua. D'altronde il destino mi chiama e rende ogni piccola fibra del mio corpo robusta come i muscoli d'un Leone! . . Lasciatemi. *i 2 viano sinistra*

Am. Siam soli.

Spe. Guardami.

Am. Ti veggo.

Spe. Io sono l'anima di tuo padre condannata ad errare la notte e a rimanere prigioniera delle fiamme il giorno, finché il mio fine impenitente non sia purificato dal fuoco. Se amasti tuo padre vendica a Amleto il suo assassinio.

Am. Assassinio!

Spe. Orribile . . . inumano.

Am. Palesato e con ali rapide quanto il pensiero dell'amore, volerò alla vendetta!

Spe. Crede ognuno che dormendo io nel giardino un serpe velenoso

mortalmente mi pungesse. Favola! . . . Menzogna! Il serpe che tolse
di vita tuo padre, porta oggi la sua corona.

Am. Oh profetica anima mia! . . tuo fratello! . .

Spe. Si, colui seppe con arte iniqua cativarsi il cuore della mia sposa . . .
Oh quale abisso ella cadde!—Ignaro del tradimento ordito io riposavo
nel giardino . . . quando di sopiatto venne tuo zio colla coppa del
veleno di cui alcune goccie versò nel mio orecchio. In un baleno il
corpo mi si copri di lebbra e perdetti e vita e sposa e regno, trovan-
domi al cospetto dell'eterno giudice nella pienezza de miei peccati,
senza le preghiere implorante dalla squilla de moribondi. Orribile
cosa! . . Oh non lasciare che il letto reale della Danimarca sia più oltre
polluto. E però non macchinar nulla contro tua madre . . . Abbando-
nala alle spine che le accerchiano il cuore. Ora addio. La vagante
lucciola annunzia il vegnente mattino a la sua vana favilla impal-
lidisce—figlio sovvengati di me! *sparisce*

Am. Oh! . . anima mia raffrenati! E voi muscoli del mio corpo rinvigor-
ite e sostenete il mio peso sopra la terra. Che io mi sovvenga di te,
ombra adorata?—Si . . . finché resti memoria di questo reo mondo!
Oh donna colpevole . . . Oh maledetto scellerato. *Orazio e Marcello*

Ora. Principe . . .

Am. Venite . . . venite!

Ora. Che fu?

Am. Orrende cose!

Ora. Dite.

Am. Non posso—Ognuno vada ove lo chiamano le sue bisogna. Ma
prima vi leghi a me un giuramento.

Ora. E quale?

Am. Che niuna parola di quanto avenne vi sfuggirà!

Ora. Sull'onore lo giuriamo.

Am. Giurate sulla mia spada!

Ora. Né vi basta? . .

Am. Su questo ferro vi dico! *voce dello spettro* Giurate!

Am. L'udite voi?

Ora. Oh meraviglioso prodigio!

Am. Sulla mia spada adunque! Giurate.

Tutti. Giuriamo!

Quadro e Sipario

Atto Secondo

Sinistra	Destra
Ofelia *con ventaglio in mano*	**Polonio**
Orazio	**Re**
1° comico	**Regina**
Arlecchino	

Donna
2 comici
Amleto   *con libro, legge*
Mobilio in scena
Libro con filo in mano a Amleto
Scrigno da deporre sul tavolo

Polonio (destra) incontrando Ofelia (sinistra) turbata

Sala regia—tavolini e sedili

Of. Padre . . . padre mio! . . *confusa*
Pol. A che così turbata?
Of. Oh se sapeste!
Pol. Parla.
Of. Siamo noi soli? *guardano*
Pol. Ma si. Che ti avvenne?
Of. Sola poi anzi io me ne stavo nella mia stanza . . . quando pallido più dell'usato, capelli sparsi . . . vesti scomposte . . . lo sguardo stranamente fisso, Amleto improvviso mi si parò d'innnanzi.
Pol. Pazzo d'amore per te.
Of. Non so . . . Paura mi prese . . . E lui la mano mi stringe e poi senza far motto mi guarda in volto e analizza i miei tratti come chi volesse disegnarli.
Pol. E poi?
Of. Un sospiro . . . un gemito escì dal suo cuore e lentamente con sovrumana marcia senza guardar l'uscita, sola mi lasciò compresa da turbamento, ritirandosi a quel modo.
Pol. Il suo amore per te è dunque reale . . . e io a torto ti consigliai di respingerlo . . . di non ascoltarlo. Il re appunto s'accosta . . . a lui nulla tacere io devo . . . va o figlia e spera come me in quest'istante la tua felicità e il ritorno d'Amleto all'usata pace. *Ofelia inchina e via sinistra, ponite lo scrigno*

Re e La regina, da destra
Re. Polonio?
Pol. Sire, gli ambasciatori di Norvegia sono tornati.
Re. Tu sei sempre apportatore di liete novelle.
Pol. Né è ciò tutto. Fidanza ho ormai di aver rinvenuta la fonte della pazzia d'Amleto.
Re. Dici tu il vero?
Pol. Voi conoscete mia figlia . . . incapace di mentire, di nascondere segreto alcuno al padre. Ofelia adunque mi palesò come reiterate volte d'un ardente amore Amleto le parlasse . . .
Re. Che sento!
Lae. E come accolse ella queste dichiarazioni?
Pol. Da uomo onorato e fedele, io disse a mia figlia che Amleto era

troppo al di sopra di lei e le imposi di starsene rinchiusa e di non ricevere né lettere né doni. Mia figlia obbediente così fece, ed il principe vistosi non curato si diè in preda alla melanconia, e da questa al delirio che ci fa tutti accuorati.

Re. Credete che la sia così?

Pol. Io credo non aver mentito giammai. Per poco che le circostanze mi favoriscano scoprirò ove si cela la verità, fosse nascosta nel centro della terra.

Re. Come farlo?

Pol. Sapete che il principe spesso passeggia in questa galleria.

Lae. Ebbene?

Pol. Quand'egli vi sarà farò venir qui mia figlia e noi celati assisteremo al loro colloquio.

Re. Stabene.

Lae. Eccolo! . . Sventurato! Si avanza leggendo.

Pol. Vi prego . . . allontanatevi. Io gli parlerò. *i 2 escono destra—Amleto con libro da sinistra*

Pol. Come state o mio principe?

Am. Bene per bontà di Dio.

Pol. Mi riconoscete signore?

Am. Si . . . tu sei un pescivendolo.

Pol. V'ingannate signore.

Am. Vorrei almeno che tu fossi onesto come lui.

Pol. Onesto!

Am. Si l'essere onesto, come va il mondo è difficile d'assai, e se n'ha uno ogni diecimila.

Pol. È vero.

Am. Avete voi una figlia?

Pol. Si mio signore.

Am. Non la lasciate uscire di mezzodì. Siate cauto amico.

Pol. (Fu certo l'amore che gli sconvolse la mente!) Che leggete o signore?

Am. Parole, parole.

Pol. Ma . . . che cosa dice quel libro?

Am. Calunnie. Dice che i vecchi hanno la barba grigia, che il loro volto e aggrinzito, che han poco cervello e sono deboli in ogni fibra. Quantunque io pure sappia tali cose, dico però poco onesto chi le scrive!

Pol. Avete ragione.

Am. Che ne sapete voi? *in collera*

Pol. Io . . .

Am. calmandosi Ah . . . Già, è vero, da qualche po sono corrucciato, sono fatto tanto melanconico che né la vita né l'uomo non han più allettamenti per me.

Pol. Se l'uomo più non vi alletta saranno male accolti i commedianti che mandaste a chiamare.

Am. Chi farà le parti di re sarà bene accolto, e S. Sl. avrà il mio ossequio e il mio tributo, l'amoroso non sospirerà gratis, il buffone farà la sua parte in pace. E chi sono?

Pol. Gli attori di città. Diconsi eccellenti. Seneca e Plauto sono loro familiari. Sono atti al fantastico come al drammatico.

Am. declama "Oh Jefte, oh d'Israele. Giudice sommo, qual tesoro avevi!"

Pol. Quale? . . *pronto Orazio*

Am. "Una figlia eletta e bella
Ch'egli amò d'immenso amor"

Pol. (Siamo da capo con mia figlia.)

Am. Non ho ragione vecchio Jefte?

Pol. Datemi pur tal nome se vi aggrada, io ho una figlia che amo assai.

Am. Aspetta . . . "L'uom propone e Dio dispone . . . Ogni cosa di quaggiù. . Qual doveva tal sempre fu!" La prima linea della canzone del Natale vi dirà il resto . . . Oh le figlie!

Orazio

Ora. Principe, sono giunti i commedianti.

Am. Benvenuti alfine . . . vediamoli. *Arlecchino—Donna e i 2 comici*

Am. Buoni amici vi saluto.

Tutti. Principe . . . Altezza *inchinano*

Am. al 1° comico Oh! . . ti sei fatto vecchio tu . . . e voi signora più bella

La. Mi raccomando a voi quest'oggi. D'una certa importanza sarà la recita per cui vi ho fatti venire. Procurate che la vostra voce non resti svergognata, come una moneta falsa nel crogiuolo. *guarda Arlecchino* E questa gotica figura che mi è nuova . . . cos'è?

1.Co. È il buffo che prese il posto del povero Alaso che è morto.

Am. Mi piace il viso di costui e spero non ci lascierà si presto come ha fatto il suo compagno. Di un po è un pezzo che fai il comico?

Arl. Sior no, sior no . . . l'è poco tempo.

Am. E che facevi tu prima?

Arl. El barbier per servirve.

Am. Capisco, dopo aver detto male del prossimo in bottega imparasti a far lo stesso sulle scene. Quale professione intanto trovi migliore?

Arl. Ma ve dirò . . . come Comico lavoro più poco, ma magno anca più de magro e se no se trova da far dei debiti no se magna del tutto.

Am. Povera arte! . . A che sei ridotta!

Arl. Ma mi . . .

Am. Non è a stupire però; se il barbiere è atto a fare il comico!

Arl. Ve ciamo perdon ma se gho fatto il barbier per qualche tempo, mio pare l'era professor de filosofia e sotto le sue lezioni . . .

Am. Avrai imparato a dubitare di tutto e a ragionare coi piedi.

Arl. Sior no . . . sior no . . . No steme a far sto torto.

Am. Sono curioso d'udire un saggio de tuoi filosofici intendimenti. Duolmi però che stasera, nella commedia che desidero esponiate, il buffone non avrà parte.

Arl. Fasso miga solamente la parti buffe salo. S'ingignemo in un modo e nell'altro . . .

Am. E questo è male. Misero quel comico che oggi fa il padre, domani l'amante giovine e apassionato. Sono due parti che farà male tutte e due. Avrei qualche consiglio a darvi.

1.Co. È per noi un onore . . .

Am. L'Erode del teatro non sia più furioso dell'Erode della storia. L'intelligenza vi serva di guida. Comparate l'azione al discorso badando di non variare i limiti della decenza e della verità. Vi sia cara la censura dei giudiziosi più degli applausi della moltitudine; mostrate la virtù colle sue vere sembianze, il vizio colle sue turpi imagini, conservando ad ogni tempo, ad ogni secolo la sua impronta.—Ditemi potreste voi rappresentarmi *L'assassinio di Gonzago?*

Pol. Non è questo troppo lungo?

Am. Altrettanto direbbe qui il barbiere dei peli della tua barba!

1.Co. Quando vogliate o principe.

Am. E potresti aggiungere alla recita quindici o venti dei miei versi?

1.Co. Si o signore.

Am. Sta bene . . . io te li scriverò. A rivederci stassera. Polonio ite con essi a far loro apprestare riposo e quanto gli può abbisognare. Non manchino di nulla. Voi seguitelo e se è possibile non ridete di lui.

Pol. (Misero . . . ha affatto smarrita la ragione) *via*

Arl. Sior prinsipe i miei rispetti . . . *viano*

Am. Andate . . . andate. *Amleto e Orazio soli*

Am. *a Orazio* Ora io posso a mia voglia parlarti.

Ora. Mio principe . . .

Am. Amico ascolta. Avrà luogo una rappresentazione stassera innanzi al re. Vi è una scena che riproduce molte circostanze della morte di mio padre. Quando vedrai quell'atto, risveglia tutta la penetrazione dell'anima tua e leggi nel cuore di mio zio.

Ora. Lo farò.

Am. Se a un tal punto del dramma il suo delitto non esce dalle labbra dell'anima sua dove sta nascosto, la visione comparsa fu uno schemo di Satana, e tutte le mie presunzioni son nere come le fucine di Vulcano. Non ti sfugga un motto però . . . non un batter di ciglio.

Ora. Contate o principe sulla mia fedeltà.

Am. Ci credo . . . Vanne. *Orazio via*

Am. Riprendi la tua maschera o Amleto, istrione per vendetta, compi la parte che ti affida lo spettro di tuo padre . . . Essere o non essere! . . Ecco il problema!—È più nobile all'anima patire i colpi dell'ingiusta fortuna o ribellandosi contro tanti mali opporsi al torrente e col morire finirli? Morire? . . Dormire! . . Dormire? . . e se al sonno eguale fosse la morte? . . Se l'immagine di ciò che fa orribile questo mondo ci seguisse anche nella tomba! . . Oh dubbio crudele! . . L'ignoto . . . oh quanto è temuto, poiché l'uomo non osa d'un colpo troncare le sofferenze di questa vita, le ingiustizie, gli oltraggi dei superbi, le torture dell'amor disprezzato. Chi viene! La vaga Ofelia! Oh vergine, nelle tue orazioni sovvengati de miei peccati. *Ofelia, con scrigno*

Of. Mio buon principe, come viveste in questi giorni?

Am. Vi ringrazio . . . bene.

Of. Io ho qui molti vostri doni che da qualche tempo bramo restituirvi. Vi prego, riceveteli ora.

Am. Io? . . Io non v'ho mai dato nulla.

Of. Oh mio signore . . . So bene che li ebbi da voi e ognuno era accompagnato da dolci parole che ne accrescevano il prezzo. Io mi credevo felice . . . ero insensata. Il mio amore oggi vi è importuno . . . Questi doni non hanno più nessun valore per me . . . riprendeteli.

Am. Ah! . . Siete onesta voi?

Of. Signore . . . *con subito ripentimento*

Am. E anche bella . . .

Of. Che intende vostra altezza?

Am. Dico che non vidi mai fin'ora tanti pregi uniti! Un tempo vi amai . . .

Of. Almeno me lo faceste credere.

Am. Non dovevate credermi. Io non vi ho mai amata!

Of. Oh!

Am. Vuoi un consiglio! . . Entra in un convento. *Pronto il sipario*

Of. In un convento! . . e perché signore?

Am. Perché vorresti divenir madre di altri peccatori? Io pure sono alquanto onesto e nullameno potrei accusarmi di colpe abbastanza gravi per desiderare che mia madre non mi avesse mai messo al mondo; . . orgolioso . . . ambizioso . . . vendicativo . . . ecco che cosa sono io! . . Tutto il mondo mi assomiglia . . . Povera giovine . . . non credere a noi . . . Va' . . . vatti a far monaca! *si avvia*

Of. (La sua ragione è perduta! . . non v'ha più speranza.)

Am. ritornando Oh se tu tieni veramente al sposa un pazzo sai . . . che i savi fanno già qual destino loro prepariate . . . *ride* Ah! ah! ah! . . Vatti a far monaca! . . Va' a farti monaca! . . *via*

Of. Potenze celesti! . . restituitegli il senso! *s'inginocchia*

Sipario

ATTO TERZO

Sinistra	Destra
Ofelia *con ventaglio nella destra*	**Regina**
Polonio	**Re**
Grande e Paggio *sulla quinta*	**2 Grandi** *[ ] sulla quinta*
Amleto *ferro lungo/ [ ] / ventaglio nella sinistra e mantello [ ] senza spada*	
Orazio	**Polonio** *senza ferro*
dietro:	
Arlecchino *piccolo*	**Spettro**
Re	
Regina	*Sasso dietro*

Luce
Amleto *senza mantello né spada*
Luciano *con coppa*
Spada
Notte

Pronti a far notte
Tam-tam

Lampada accesa appesa

Sala con teatro chiuso da cortine. Due seggio
Soni a destra e Taboret—tre taboret a sinistra
Re—La Regina a destra
Polonio e Ofelia a sinistra

Re. Ho deciso. Se il suo deliro continua i mestieri che egli parta per l'Inghilterra. Orazio e Gilisterno suoi migliori amici lo accompagneranno. Non si può senza pericolo lasciar più oltre libero il campo alla sua follia.

La R. Facciamoci animo . . . Prossegua Ofelia coi dolci modi ad accarezzar quel cuore. La dolorosa metamorfosi speriamo che alfine scompaia ed egli diverrà quel di prima per tutti.

Pol. Eccolo che viene per la rappresentazione cui ci ha chiamati.

Re. Non una parola che possa alterare i di lui sensi. Secondarlo è miglior partito.

La R. Quanto è diverso da quel di prima. Povero figlio mio!

Amleto

Re. Come sta Amleto questa sera?

Am. Bene assai. Pari al camaleonte io vivo d'aria. *Passa in mezzo*

Re. Voi parlate in enigma e io non v'intendo.

Am. Neppur io . . . *a Polonio* Mi diceste altra volta d'aver recitato voi pure.

Pol. Si e fui detto per la tragedia abile attore.

Am. Comprendo ora perché siete buon cortigiano. E in quali parti vi distingueste?

Pol. La mia favorita era quella di Brutto nella morte di Cesare.

Orazio

Am. Oh . . . ebbene signori?

Ora. Non si attende per incominciare che un vostro cenno.

Am. Prendete dunque posto o signori. *eseguiscono Re, Regina destra Ofelia a sinistra e Polonio alla di lei sinistra a destra resti un sedile libero a proscenio*

La R. seduta Avvicinati a me Amleto. Siedi al mio fianco.

Am. No madre . . . *indica Ofelia* Qui vi è calamita più attraente. Permettete *a Ofelia* che io mi adagi ai vostri piedi? *Si sdraia*

Of. Principe . . .

Am. È si dolce coricarsi ai piedi di una fanciulla! *Scioglie il mantello*

Of. Siete ilare oggi.

Am. L'uomo deve essere gaio e gioviale. Alirate come è gioconda mia madre, eppure non son due ore che mio padre è morto. *Pronta la musica*

Of. Son già due mesi.

Am. Ah . . . è vero . . . converrà adunque che io pure gitti questi abiti di lutto .. Piangere più di due mesi uno sposo ... un padre! .. ma vi par? .. La è follia! Muoia chi vuol, e duri la sua ricordanza come quella del Carnevale di cui si legge nell'epitaffio. Del carnevale quest'ultim'ora. Nei colmi [ ] s'alloghi e mora.—Cominci la rappresentazione. *Musica sul palco poi si apre la tenda. La scena figurerà un Giardino con sedile a destra.*

Of. Qual dramma si rappresenta?

Am. Nol so ... ma ce lo dirà il prologo. I comici non ponno serbar segreti.

Arlecchino sul palco—inchini

Arl. Per nu, per la tragedia, imploriam clemenza. Ci accordi amico orecchio la vostra gran pazienza. *via*

Of. È breve assai il prologo.

Am. Come l'amor di donna. *1 Comico e Donna—vestiari teatrali alla reale con corona ecc.*

1 Co. Già lunghi anni abbiam vissuto insieme o dolce sposa mia, e l'astro del giorno e la splendente luna già trenta volte all'ampia terra volsero intorno, dacché le nostre destre stringeano Imene e Amore e fean con santi nodi dei nostri cuori un cuore.

Do. Cosí la luna e il sole possan compir gli stessi celesti giri innanzi che l'amor nostro cessi. Ma aimè da qualche tempo voi siete conturbato. Straniero ad ogni gioia; da quel dí pria mutato. *Amleto scherza col ventaglio*

1.Co. Mio dolce amor, lasciarti fra poco, aimè degg'io, che più non basta il nerbo vitale al viver mio; ma tu onorata, amata dopo me vivrai. Su questa lieta terra, tu forse alcuno avrai che a te più dolce sposo ...

Do. Oh ... se amassi ancor, sciagura l'amor saria, delitto dell'anima spergiura. Stè il cielo maledica, se bramo altro consorte. Chi nuovo sposo accoglie trasse il primiero a morte. *Polonio si alza e siede al proscenio*

Am. Udite?

Do. Chi nuove nozze anela, segue un pensier che figlio è di vil brama avara, non già d'amor consiglio.

1.Co. Io credo all'alma vostra concordi le parole, ma sovente s'infrange quanto per noi si vuole. Ora, ti credi avversa di un altro imene al rito, ma tuoi pensier morranno col primo tuo marito.

Do. Luce a me nieghi il sole, la terra nutrimento, né dí né notte io trovi pace mai più e contento. Di qua, di là, vendetta sempre mi tenda un laccio se, vedova, corressi d'altro marito in braccio.

Am. *a Ofelia* Guai se infrange i suoi giuramenti.

1.Co. Solenni giuri!—Intanto o dolce sposa mia, mi si aggrava lo spirito, che d'ingannar desia le tarde ore col sonno. *siede e si addormenta*

Do. Rintegra i sensi tuoi, né mai sciagura alcuna si ponga in mezzo a noi. *lo abbraccia e parte*

Am. *alla Regina* Come vi piace il dramma signora?

La R. Mi pare che la regina prometta troppo.

Am. E perché? Essa saprà mantenere a quanto s'impegna.

Re. Conoscete voi questo dramma? .. non vi è nulla che possa offendere?

Am. Oh nulla! *si alza*

Re. E come s'intitola?

Am. La rete dei topi. Rappresenta un omicidio. Gonzaga è il nome del re. Battista quello della sua sposa. Vedrete fra poco. Egli è un intrico d'inferno. Ma che ne cale di ciò? Alla maestà vostra, ed a noi puri di coscienza, tal cosa non interessa. I perversi ne rimangano commossi; noi rideremo.

2° Comico con coppa entra guardino sulla scena

Am. Ah ... ecco Luciano ... il fratello del Re ... udite. *entra un momento e cambialo*

2.Co. Negri pensier, man pronta ... veleno possente ... ora e luogo propizio ... né testimon vivent. L'opra si compia—questa d'erbe letal mistura tolga di vita una inutile, debole creatura. *va a versare il veleno nell'orecchio del Re dormente*

Am. Ecco ... lo avvelena per carpirli lo stato! Vedremo poi come l'assassino si cattivi l'amore della moglie dell'ucciso ... e ...

Re. fuori di sé alzandosi Oh! .. Basta! ..

Of. Che ha il re?

Am. Onde tale spavento?

Re. Lasciatemi ... lasciatemi ... oh, è orribile! .. Cessate! .. Via, via di qui .. *Cadono le tende. Il Re via e tutti lo seguono a destra. Spegni i lumi dietro—Amleto e Orazio soli*

Am. Ah! .. è vero! Oh padre mio! .. Lo spettro non mentiva. Vedesti? Oh iniquo ... e cinge la corona! .. S'infuochi sul tuo capo. Le punte del rimorso l'accerchino, e si configgano nelle sacrileghe tempia! *Polonio*

Pol. Principe ...

Am. Che si vuole?

Pol. La regina mi manda. La vostra condotta l'ha empita di sorpresa e di duolo.

Am. Venga. Son pronto. Ma dimmi tu, che vuole essa da me? Vuol che io le rappresenti un dramma? Tu vecchio Jefte dammene l'argomento e sia di utile a chi lo udrà! Si tratta di uccidere traditori, maledire agli adulteri e ai ... *scoppio di risa* Ah! Ah! Sei pur buffone!

Pol. La regina ...

Am. L'aspetto!

Pol. Sta bene. *via destra*

Am. Oh ... via questa larva di pazzo, che abbrutisce il mio volto ... Si apra l'anima mia al pensiero della vendetta!

Notte

Pronti a mettere la spada a Amleto

Ora. Prudenza o mio signore.

Am. Amico, non temere! Son padrone di me ... lasciami. *Orazio via*

Ecco l'ora della notte consacrata ai neri malefizi, ecco l'ora in cui i sepolcri si spalancano, in cui l'inferno soffia i suoi veleni nel mondo. Ora potrei bere sangue fumante, e commettere atti si orribili che il giorno puro e santo frenerebbe di vedere! Verrà mia madre. Oh mio cuore non smarrire la tua naturale bontà, non lasciar entrare nel mio seno l'anima di Nerone. Ch'io sia crudele e non snaturato. La lingua e l'anima dissimulino a la di lei sentenza tuoni nella mia voce, senza che la mia volontà consenta ad eseguirla.

Regina e Polonio

Pol. piano Parlategli con fermezza . . . io veglierò lì dietro quelle tende. *via*

pronto altro Polonio dietro

Am. Ecco

La. Ebbene madre, che volete?

La R. Amleto tu hai molto offeso tuo padre!

Am. Regina . . . voi offendeste il padre mio!

La R. Non mi rispondete cose che suonano su lingua vana.

Am. Né voi parlatemi con lingua malvagia.

La R. Che vuoi dire Amleto?

Am. Io, nulla!

La R. Scordasti chi sono? *Polonio fa capolino dietro le tende*

Am. No. Voi siete regina, siete la moglie del fratello del vostro sposo . . . E così non fosse! . . oh madre! . . (Non m'inganno è lui che ci spia dietro quella tenda . . . Dov'è la mia spada . . .) Ah . . . ora vengo! . . *Entra, ponigli subito la spada sinistra*

La R. Chi lo comprende! . . oh labirinto crudele . . . È vana ogni speranza! *si avvia*

Am. con spada la ferma Non vi muoverete, prima che io non v'abbia posto d'innanzi agli occhi uno specchio fedele in cui possiate contemplarvi!

La R. Che intendi di fare! Non vorrai già uccidermi? . . Soccorso . . . soccorso.

Pol. di dietro Soccorso? . .

Am. Per l'inferno . . . costa v'è un topo; scommetto d'ucciderlo. *vibra il colpo nella tenda*

Pol. grido e muore Ah! . . Dio! . .

La R. Che facesti!

Am. Era forse il re?

La R. Oh atto crudele e sanguinario! . .

Am. Sanguinoso si, e quasi tanto come lo è uccidere un re per sposarne il fratello!

La R. Uccidere un re!

Am. Si . . . Ho detto . . . Ed ora . . . *alza le tende*

Che! . . Polonio! . . Ah io sono pur maledetto! La vittima della mia follia sarà sempre Ofelia! Ofelia! . . Perdonatemi o signore quest'omicidio! E tu *a Polonio* infelice . . . tu pazzo che volevi intrometterti negli affari altrui subisci la tua condanna. *alla regina* E voi cessate di meravigliare e lasciate che io denudi il vostro cuore per vedere se egli è affatto indurato nel delitto!

La R. Ma che feci per udire da te parole così feroci!

Am. Essa lo ignora! . . un azione vile e infame che fa chiamare ipocrisia la virtù e che ha svegliata l'ira del cielo e costernata la terra come nel dì del giudizio del mondo.

La R. Ma qual è quest'azione di cui mi accusi?

Am. Oh modestia! Dov'è il tuo rossore? Inferno, se puoi accendere tanta passione nel cuore della vecchiezza la virtù dovrà fondersi come cera ai fuochi della gioventù, e conviene assolvere da ogni delitto il giovane che segue l'impulso del suo ardore . . . poiché lo stesso ghiaccio arde di tanto fuoco, e la ragione prostituisce il senso!

La R. Amleto cessa per pietà; tu rivolgi i miei occhi sull'anima mia e m'indichi in essa macchie nere e feroci che non si cancelleranno giammai.

Am. Voi vivete in seno alla corruzione, e prodigaste i più teneri baci dell'amore sovra una bocca impudica e perversa.

La R. con terrore Ah cessa . . . cessa!

Am. Un vile . . . uno scellerato, uno che non vale la centesima parte del vostro sposo! Un tagliaborse! Un ladro. Si un ladro! . . che s'accosta allo scrigno reale e ruba la corona e se la pone in [ ].

Am. Un re da teatro . . . *tam-tam si presenta lo Spettro*

Am. vedendolo Ah! . . Salvatemi angeli celesti . . . proteggetemi . . . che vuole la larva?

La R. Figlio!

Am. Vieni forse a rimproverarmi poiché fui lento nell'eseguire i tuoi cenni . . . perché il dubbio mi ratenne? *Luce a sinistra*

Spet. Figlio, il terrore opprime tua madre. Ponti fra lei e la commozione dell'anima sua. Parlate Amleto.

Am. Ebbene signora, a che pensate?

La R. Tu stesso dimmi, che pensi? . . A chi rivolgi la parola? su chi fissi lo sguardo?

Am. Su lui . . . su lui! Mirate quali fuochi ci vibra! . . Oh cessa di affiggere in me i tuoi sguardi . . . Il tuo aspetto potrebbe sconcertare i miei tremendi propositi . . . Non mi fissare!

Spet. Risparmia tua madre . . .

Am. Oh si obbedirò! . .

La R. Ma a chi favelli?

Am. Non lo vedete?

La R. Io nulla vedo! . .

Am. Ma guardate . . . Mio padre! . . sotto le stesse vesti che portò in vita. *via Spettro lentamente*

Ecco . . . sparisce . . . È svanito!

La R. È una larva creata dalla tua fantasia . . . Effetto del delirio che provi.

Am. Quel che dissi non è delirio. Ponetemi alla prova lo ripeterò. La follia non ha simile linguaggio. Oh . . . madre! era lui! . . il vostro primo sposo, il padre mio! Egli intercedeva per voi! per voi che lo scordaste si presto, per voi che sul suo funebre lenzuolo vi coricaste a nozze d'obbrobrio! Oh pentitevi del passato, evitate l'avvenire che si avanza, e non gettate su putrida canna un fetido frammento che ne aumenterebbe la pestifera effervescenza.

La R. Amleto tu mi trai squarciato il cuore!

Am. Gittatene lungi da voi la parte corotta, vivete innocente coll'altra. Oh abbiate la forza del bene e quando vi crederete degna della benedizione del cielo io vi domanderò la vostra.

La R. Che debbo fare?

Am. È me lo chiedęte? Oh madre! . . Badate! . . La morte è in cammino! *Sipario*

ATTO QUARTO

Sinistra	**Destra**
Amleto *mantello, piccolo*	**Re**
Regina	**Ofelia** *morta con testa avanti—fiori in grembo, portata da 2 fili*
Orazio	
Ofelia *con fiori in testa e nella veste che tiene con filo*	
Marcello	
Laerte	

Al finale cambia scena. 2 sedili di pietra.
Atrio reale—in fondo luogo ridente con verzura e onde del lago
Re a destra.

Re Polonio ucciso! . . E pertanto che aveva egli fatto? Misero vecchio! Il suo fine mi ricorda il mio delitto! Ovunque io ne trovo l'impronta fatale . . . l'omicidio di un fratello! *da sinistra la regina affannata*

La R. Oh sire . . . l'avete voi veduto?

Re Chi?

La R. Mio figlio! . . Son pochi istanti che qui fu veduto dirigersi colla spada in pugno.

Re Oh . . . E con quale disegno?

La R. Dio solo lo sa! Amleto da ieri sera, che l'omicidio fatale di Polonio s'aggiunse a disperarlo . . . si nasconde . . . fugge lo stesso Orazio sui intimo amico . . . non ascolta voce nè consiglio! . . Oh proteggetelo!

Re. Proteggerlo? . . Egli minaccia la mia corona e la mia vita . . . Se ieri io fossi stato là sarei estinto. Ma non è tutto . . . l'invidia imputa a noi il suo delitto. E ora che Laerte ritorna che non sarà per vendicare la morte del padre!

La R. Si solleciti dunque la partenza di Amleto per l'Inghilterra.

Orazio

Ora. La giovine Ofelia chiede di voi Regina.

La R. Non voglio vederla.

Re. E perché?

La R. Oh voi non lo sapete dunque o Claudio, la misera saputo il fine del padre suo impazzo!

Re. Infelice!

La R. Incessantemente chiede di lui, e si dispera e piange della sua tardanza.

Re. E Amleto è causa di tutto ciò! Guai s'egli non obbedisce al mio volere.

La R. Non più vederlo! ..

Re. È l'unico mezzo per stornare dal nostro capo mali irreparabili. Siete madre o Geltrude, ma siete anche sposa e regina, pensateci. Orazio conducete qui Ofelia ... Sarà bene parlarle, perché i malevoli che l'odono potrebbero scendere a troppo sinistre congetture.

Ora. Obbedisco. *via*

La R. Poi anzi io già l'incontrai! .. Ma ... quanto è cambiata! .. Si percuote il petto, calpesta i fiori del terreno e pronuncia parole quasi senza senno! .. Dio! ..

Re. Coraggio ...

La R. Non posso! Alla mia anima inferma la più lieve circostanza sembra il presagio di qualche gran disastro, tanto una coscienza colpevole è piena di sospetti.

Re. Oh è troppo vero! La coscienza col lungo temere d'esser tradita si tradisce da sé!

Ofelia in bianca con corona e fiori nella veste che tiene con una mano.

Orazio

Of. Egli è partito, è morto. O mesta! Morto, partito, non torna più! L'erba è cresciuta sulla sua testa, il freddo sasso vi poggia su. Ah! Ah! *ride*

La R. Buona fanciulla, che vonno dire questi versi?

Of. Zitta ... zitta ... *canta*
  Questo è il giorno di S. Valentino
  Sorgon tutti col primo mattino
  Del mio amante al balcon volerò
  Sua fedel Valentina sarò!
  Egli sorge, s'abbiglia festante
  La sua porta dischiude all'amante
  Ma colei, che zitella a lui va,
  Se ritorna Zitella chi il sa?

Re. Povera Ofelia!

Of. Povera io? .. perché? .. vedete la terra che mi sorride ... udite l'olezzo di questi fiori ... al suolo li spargo ... ai miei piedi li getto *eseguisce* e voglio che ovunque la gioia ... il diletto ... Ma! .. il padre? .. il padre dov'è? ..

La R. Fa cuore figlia mia . . . ascolta . . .

Of. Ascoltare . . . che mai? . . Questo è ramerino . . . l'erba del ricordo . . . Oh ve ne prego amate e ricordate! Vorrei pur darvi una viola . . . ma aimè . . . Sulla scoverta bara recarono il padre mio . . . egli non è più! . . . non è più! *piange singhiozzando forte*

La R. Oh dolore!

Re. Potessi colle ricchezze di cui abbonda il mio regno assisterla!

Of. Ora è tempo di gioia! . . *ride e cade in ginocchio* Ah ah! . . mettetelo in terra . . . e quindi cantate . . . cantate, che esulta il mio cuor . . . Ma! . . E il non più vederlo! . . più mai! . . mai! . . *piange forte* Ah . . . ah . . . Tutto è finito . . . il canto e la gioia più non udrai.

La R. Ah più non reggo alla desolante scena! *passa a destra*

Of. si alza Ma! . . È lui che viene . . . No . . . non m'inganno . . . m'ascolta m'aspetta . . . vengo . . . vengo tosto con te! . . *via a destra*

Re. Oh seguitela Orazio . . . non l'abbandonate un istante. Vegliate su lei. *Orazio via*

Re. Ah trista verità! Quando i dolori vengono, vengono a legioni, non ad uno ad uno come i delatori . . .

Voci. Morte al Re—Viva Laerte!

Re. Quali grida sono queste! . . Una nuova sciagura . . .

Marcello

Mar. Oh . . . Sire . . . salvatevi! . . Una sommossa popolare minaccia queste mura . . . Il giovine Laerte è alla loro testa . . . egli nell'eccesso del suo delirio urta e rovescia i vostri ufficiali. I rivoltosi lo acclamano re, le voci e le mani applaudono a quel grido!

Re. Oh insensati! Guai a loro! Stolti Danesi . . . vedremo chi è il più forte!

Laerte

Lae. Dov'è il re? *furente*

Re. Qui, suddito ribelle, qui.

La. Rendimi il padre . . .

La R. Laerte calmatevi!

Lae. Se una sola goccia del mio sangue fosse calma, essa disonorebbe la memoria di mio padre!

Re. Per qual cagione incitare tanta rivolta? Perché sei tanto inasprito? Favella!

Lae. Dov'è mio padre?

Re. È morto.

Lae. Chi l'uccise?

Re. Se desiderate conoscere la verità sulla morte di vostro padre, dovrà per questo la vostra vendetta come cieco uragano, strascinar seco l'amico ed il nemico, l'innocente ed il colpevole senza distinzione?

Lae. I soli nemici.

Re. Chiaro vedrete come io sia innocente di questa morte.

Lae. Desidero che il siate; non mi nascondete cosa alcuna.

La R. Laerte perdonate a chi vi priva di padre, e il vostro perdono sarà castigo a chi gli tolse la vita.

Re. Io pure a ciò vi esorto. Il colpevole è troppo amato da sua madre e dal volgo. Ciò mi vietò vendicarmi e su me così cadde il sospetto.

Lae. Fu dunque Amleto?

Re. Si; ma il colpo che tolse di vita il buon Polonio era a me diretto! Oh Laerte . . . quanto mi costo essere seco lui clemente, pure dopo matura riflessione . . .

Lae. Dovrò dunque perdere così la sorella e il padre, nè vendicarli? Mio re qualsiasi cosa che dalla mia fede chiediate l'avrete, ma in ciò non mi è dato l'obbedirvi! Dov'è Amleto? . . dov'è?

Re. alla regina Raggiungete Ofelia—E voi, ritiratevi *a Marcello che parte* Ed ora che siamo soli Laerte . . . un buon consiglio . . . se tu vorrai seguirlo . . .

Lae. Non mi consiglierete la pace, io spero . . .

Re. No . . . no! . . guerra invece.

Lae. E guerra mortale!

Re. Siete disposto a tutto per vendicare la germana . . . il padre?

Lae. Lo sono . . . E determinato a segno, da trafiggere il cuore al suo uccisore fors'anche a piè degli altari!

Re. Il luogo santo è conveniente all omicidio espiatorio. Ma meglio è che un duello agli occhi di tutti le apparenze salvi . . . e insieme il fine del colpevole decida! . . Sfidato da voi il principe per orgoglio si limit-erà alla difesa . . . voi però nel colpirlo dovette esser certo che la sua ferita sia mortale. A tal uopo io tengo un veleno in cui basterà che sia tinta la punta della vostra spada perché la più piccola graffiatura rechi la morte con sè.

Lae. L'atto è infame, ma nulla mi trattiene dall'eseguirlo contro colui che tanto lo ha meritato.

Re. È dunque deciso?

Lae. Reca il liquido velenoso . . . quindi cerchiamo di lui!

Re. Andiam . . . *guarda* Ma a che così spaventata, corre verso di noi la regina?

Regina

La R. Oh sventura! . . sventura!

Re. Che fu! . . Parla!

La R. Ofelia . . . la misera Ofelia nelle onde del lago lasciò miseramente la vita! . .

Lae. Gran Dio! . . mia sorella! . .

La R. Essa non è più!

Lae. Ah . . . è troppo! . . è troppo . . .

Re. piano a Laerte Morta anche lei per Amleto! . .

Lae. Amleto! . . Oh io voglio che questo braccio d'un colpo solo si ven-dichi entrambi! Avesse egli mille vite! . . che una è poca alla mia ven-detta! *via*

Mutazione—si vede il lago illuminato dalla luna. Fra le canne il cadavere di Ofelia—Amleto poi viene avanti—disperato s'inginocchia
Sipario

ATTO QUINTO

Destra	**Sinistra**
Becchino *nel buco*	**Becchino** *che parla*
Amleto *mantello da levarsi*	
Cranio [ ]	*Cranio di morto e ossa in scena*
Orazio	
2 con torcia	
2 con barella che depongono	*Campana*
4 donzelle in bianco	*musica in orchestra*
*1 nero***Marcello**	
Re *e*	
Regina *in nero*	*spada per Amleto*
Laerte *con spada a filo [ ] in nero*	*Luce*
Spettro *dietro*	

Un cimitero—Notte. Chiaro di luna. Due seppellitori scavano una fossa attorno a cui sono ossa di morti. Passano dietro Orazio e Amleto.

1° Se. Dico io. Da quando si permette la sepoltura in luogo sacro a una persona che si è suicidata?

2° Se. È l'ordine del Coroner . . . scava la tua fossa e non cercar altro.

1° Se. Capisco, perché è una fanciulla nobile hanno trovato modo di far credere che involontariamente si è annegata.

2° Se. Tira dritto e abbi pazienza.

1° Se. Pazienza? O si è cristiani o non lo si è! Nobili, gentiluomini lo siamo tutti a questo mondo! Ed ecco la mia zappa che rappresenta il mio blasone.

2° Se. Cioè?

1° Se. Cioè il primo gentiluomo fu un giardiniere.

2° Se. Giardiniere?

1° Se. Si . . . Adamo—non potrai negarmi che egli sia il nostra avo comune. E la sua arma gentilizia, non era la zappa? Di un po?

2° Se. Verissimo.

1° Se. Un altra domanda.

2° Se. E quale?

1° Se. Senti un poco. Quale abitazione dura più d'una casa, d'un palazzo?

2° Se. Bel mistero! Un patibolo. Può servire a mille e più locatori.

1° Se. Vedo che tu hai tendenze per quell'abitazione. Ma non hai colto a segna.

2° Se. Dunque . . . secondo te?

1° Se. A parer mio la più sicura e capace abitazione è l'opera nostra—una fossa! Il giudizio finale soltanto viene a turbarne la tranquillità. Di qui a allora . . .

2° Se. Chi vivrà vedrà, vuoi dire? Sei curioso davvero quest'oggi. Basta ora puoi finire da te la bisogna . . . Io vado a cena poi ritorno per colmare la fossa. *via destra*

1° Se. Fai presto. *canta lavorando* Oh . . . Bella Rita, di questo cuore *Amleto e Orazio in mantello*

Dolce speme vita ed amore

Vienine a me che ti dirò

Quanto che t'ami e t'amerò . . .

La la . . . lara . . . la la lara . . .

Am. Vedi un po Orazio quell'allegro seppellitore. Egli canta l'amore scavando una fossa!

Ora. Effetto d'abitudine.

Am. È vero . . . *urtando col piede in un cranio* Cos'è questo?

Ora. *guarda* Oh . . . il cranio d'un morto.

Am. E dire che questo cranio ebbe pure una lingua e cantava forse come canta costui che indifferente alla morte, le ride così dapresso!

Ora. *guardando* Eccone un altro . . . ma meglio conservato a quanto sembra . . . vi pare?

Am. Sarà la testa d'un cortigiano avvezzo a subire con indifferenza la disgrazia di chi cade; e pronto soltanto a piegare il flessibile dorso e strisciare attorno a chi è al potere e può mantenerlo negli ozi e conferirgli titoli e onorificenze.

Ora. È anche probabile.

Am. Ed ora il verme della terra ha in sua balia questo volto rosichiato . . . sfracellato dalla marra del seppellitore. Appunto *al seppellitore* tu che sembri vecchio di questo mestiere mi sai dire quanto può restare il carcame d'un uomo sotto terra prima d'infracidirsi?

1° Se. Anzi tutto bisognerebbe vedere se il carcame non è fracido prima che morto; poiché sono molti i corpi che trovansi in cancrena. In media si può mettere dai tre ai nove anni. Per esempio un conciatore si conserva nove anni.

Am. Un conciatore? E perché dura egli tanto tempo?

1° Se. Perché la sua pelle si rende impermeabile in conseguenza del suo lavoro, così l'umidità più difficilmente viene a guastarlo. *guarda nella buca* Oh signore . . . se volete vedere una testa strana . . . guardate qui . . .

Am. *guarda* Chi è questi?

1° Se. Indovinate . . . il buffone del Re—Yorik di lieta memoria.

Am. Lui! . . Come s'è fatto brutto! Povero Yorik—egli che mi faceva ridere ora fa schifo! Orazio . . . sii sincero, credi tu che Alessandro nella sua tomba sia divenuto simile a questo cranio?

Ora. Si certo . . .

Am. Oh umana superbia! . . fallaci grandezze . . . Vedete ove si finisce?

Dalla terra si esce . . . e la più eletta creatura terra ritorna! *guarda—campana funebre* Ma io non m'inganno . . . Un funebre convoglio viene verso di noi . . . Lo accompagnano il Re . . . la Regina! . . Vedi! . . con mano violenta pose fine a suoi giorni quello che recano qui . . . poiché la croce non precede il corteo!

Ora. Teniamci là in disparte se vi piace, udremo il tutto.

Am. Dici bene . . . viene *si ritirano a destra, leva il mantello e [ ]lo solo in dorso da cadere, e spada in mano*

Marcia funebre—Cavalieri—Regina—Re—Frate—2 uomini colla bara con corona ecc. ecc.—Laerte—Marcello e seguito.

Lae. al frate Nè altre pietose cerimonie vi è dato di rendere alla misera salma?

Fra. No! La di lei morte è sospetta. Si fece anche molto ponendo sulla bara la corona delle vergini e accordandole il suono dei sacri bronzi del tempio.

Lae. Tutto finisce così?

Fra. Sarebbe profanare il servizio dei morti quando si volesse cantare il requiem per questa creatura che troppe circostanze segnano violenta contro se stessa.

Lae. Sia . . Io confido con quest'ultimo saluto il suo corpo alla terra, la di lei anima a Dio! Ofelia, noi ci rivedremo in un mondo migliore! *piange*

Am. in ascolto Ofelia! . . Signore eterno, che sento!

Lae. Oh . . . anatema e sventura sul vile assassino che fu causa della sua follia! *piange* Oh sorella io non so dividermi da te! . . Interrate me pure con lei . . Sia minor duolo a questo cuore affranto un subitaneo fine!

Am. si avanza E chi sei tu che con accenti di duolo inveisci e insulti al mio nome? . . Amleto io sono!

Lae. snuda la spada Che l'inferno s'abbia l'anima tua! *la regina li frappone* Ah!

Am. La preghiera è empia . . . Nel fodero quella lama! e ritiratevi da me! So frenare la mia collera . . . ma è più prudente per voi il tenervi in guardia . .

La R. Amleto!

Lae. Assassino . . .

Am. Disgraziato . . .

Tutti. Signori . . . calma . . . signori . . . pace.

La R. Figlio mio *è sempre in mezzo*

Am. Volete voi dunque lottare assieme per questa causa fino a che i nostri occhi sieno chiusi e per sempre?

La R. Per quale causa? *Amleto passa in mezzo*

Am. Per lei! . . Io l'amava . . . ed io eguaglio in amore . . . cento . . . mille fratelli!

La R. Calmati o Amleto per amor di tua madre . . . Egli è pazzo . . . Laerte risparmiatelo per Iddio!

Am. Dimmi! . . Che faresti tu dunque per lei? Temere come una fanciullo . . . piangere come una femmina? . . Ma questo è troppo comune!

Combattere sulla di lei tomba agli occhi degli spettatori? . . ritirarci ciascuno in un chiostro austero, ove ad ogni istante si scambiano quelle parole: Bisogna morire? . . O finalmente preferisci che la stessa fossa e noi e lei estinta rinserri? . . Vediamo! . . Io non esito! Fallo ed io lo farò? . . Vuoi di più? . . Ordina, io obbedisco! Parla Amleto è pronto!

Lae. Incrocia il tuo ferro col mio, altro non ti chiedo!

Am. Lo vuoi? . . Sia . . .

La R. Ah no . . . *comparisce lo Spettro in fondo*

Spe. T'arresta!

Am. Ancora la larva!

Spe. Laerte non è il colpevole! . . l'amore di figlio, di fratello, lo accieca . . . La punta della sua spada è avvelenata . . . ma chi l'asperse di veleno è il solo che tu devi colpire.

Am. Che intendo!

Lae. Io aspetto . . .

Am. Ma voi dunque non lo vedete? Voi non lo udiste? *agli astanti*

Lae. Infine . . . che più indugi?

Am. Eccomi . . . Ma apprendi da questo colpo quanto valga il mio braccio . . . *colla spada disarma Laerte*

Lae. Maledizione . . . la spada . . .

Am. Non è nulla, prendi la mia!

Re (Inferno!)

Lae. La vostra . . .

Am. Si . . . facciamo cambio . . .

Lae. (Sono perduto)

Am. A che impallidire così? . . prendi! . . Dio, palesa il tradimento! . . Oh Giustizia! L'assassino riceva ora il suo castigo . . . Laerte . . . il tuo dolore ti assolve . . . questo braccio questa lama onorata vendichi ora il padre mio!

Re. Guai detti!

Am. Rettile velenoso . . . Cagione d'ogni sciagura . . . impenitente muori . . . e a Satana vada l'anima tua! *trafigge il Re*

Luce a destra

Re. Oh! . . . Dannazione! . . Ah . . . l'infer . . . no . . . *spira*

La R. Oh il mio sposo! . . *piangente*

Am. Madre . . . non dare tal nome a quel mostro orrendo d'ipocrisia e di delitto! . . Vedi l'ombra del tuo primo consorte il cui sdegno si placa . . . la cui fronte si rasserena! . . Le mie preghiere . . . il tuo pentimento, ottengano dalla clemenza suprema la parola del perdono!

Un raggio di luce illumina lo spettro e con quadro cala il sipario.

Fine

Scene

Atto 1°: Salone gotico con finestrone—a destra trono con due seggioloni (che va via a vista). Mutazione—fondale castello provinciali—rompimento di tela a laterali [ ]

Atto 2°: Sala baronale dell'Inghilterra—tavolo e sedie di legno—cassa-panca a destra

Atto 3°: Il teatro (dietro l'appoggio) suo piano all'altezza di 20 cen-timetri—6 lumini accesi formano ribalta—2 placche (non di cristallo, una con stemma) sono accese ed attaccate alle [ ]—lateralmente al piccolo proscenio—Fondino di giardino e sasso a destra contro il detto fondino. 2 piccoli laterali
1 rompimento di tela e 2 tende ordite per chiudersi poi a suo tempo.
N.B. Quando le tende si chiudono si devono rapidamente spegnere tutti i lumi dietro—poi si toglie il palcoscenico e si porta subito indietro lo scenario che forma proscenio contro quello di fondino di Giardino.
Quando muore Polonio lo si corica dietro la tenda a destra e si scopre poi quella, che sta pure aperta perché possa vedersi lo spettro. Avanti vi sono due laterali e una lampada in mezzo, accesa con fiamma a benzina che dura tutto l'atto.
2 seggioloni [ ] e 4 taboretti—i seggioloni a destra e un taboretto al proscenio gli altri 3 taboretti a sinistra.
Un cuscino a sinistra quasi in mezzo per Amleto. Luce da sinistra.

Atto 4°: Giardino di [ ]—faggiami—sedili di pietra.
Al finale dell'atto si fa un po di scuro—musica—si alza la scena e si vede il lago a sfondo [ ] con due rompimenti di verdura e le onde poste inclinatamente—avanti rompimento di tela
Avanti alle onde, tre gruppi di canne—Le tre onde sono per metà di garza con lama d'argento, perché si veda parte del corpo sott'acqua di Ofelia galleggiante, coi fiori in grembo che passa da destra a sinistra, testa avanti.
Dette onde sono illuminate sotto il palco—un raggio di luce elettrica scende da sinistra.

Atto 5°: Cimitero—a sfondo
N.B. riportandosi al luogo e all'epoca, anzichè monumentale questo cim-itero dovrebbe essere collina con cipressi e cumoli. In lontano la città di Elsinoro illuminata dagli ultim' raggi del sole che trammonta.
Una buca a destra alla scena con tela dipinta inchiodata sul palco che figura la terra scavata dal becchino. (Il teschio si getta poi nella buca)
Barella con cassa coperta di seta bianca, da deporre in mezzo.
Luce da destra, spettro a sinistra.

Appendix B

COPIONE FOR THE PRODUCTION OF *MACBETH*
BY ALFREDO CAGNOLI

PENUL'ULTIMA RECITA

TRATTORIA AL RELLEGRINO

Questa sera Sabato 22 Settembre 1906

esporrà lo

Straordinario Spettacolo Fantastico di prosa e Ballo

dal titolo

MACBETH

Ovvero

L'ASSASSINIO di DUNCANO

Con

FIGHETTO

Maggiordomo e spaventato dagli

SPIRITI nella CAVERNA d'ERINNI

Azione Coreografica in 5 atti e 8 quadri

PREZZI SOLITI

A transcription of the handwritten *copione,* which is held in the archives of the Compagnia Carlo Colla e figli in Milan. The spelling, punctuation, and grammar of the original have been retained.

Divisione delle Parti

I
La Selva Incantata
I Vaticini

II
Il Regicidio

III
Ambizione e Rimorso
L'Ombra di Banco

IV
L'evocazione Infernale

V
I Profughi Scozzesi
La Morte di Macbeth
Il Trionfo di Malcolmo

Personaggi

Storici

Duncano, Re di Scozia
Macbetto, Generale
Banco, idem
Lady Macbeth
Malcolmo, figlio di Re Duncano
Macduffo, Nobile Scozzese
Fleanzio, figlio di Banco
Dama di Lady Macbeth
Medico

Fighetto, paggio—scudiero

Nobili di corte (4)
1 Capitano
1 Armigero
Riccardo, Sicario
Profughi Scozzesi

Soldati Scozzesi
Servi con Fiaccole
Soldati Inglesi
Musicanti

Fantastici

Ombra di Banco
Ostragamus, Re Stregone
Streghe, Apparizioni (3)
Streghe, Maggiori
Oltre Streghe, Nane (8)
Spiriti, Ballerini (8)
Diavoli, (4)
Le tre Apparizioni:
1—Un Capo coperto d'Elmo
2—Un Fanciullo insanguinato
3—Un Fanciullo coronato con un arboscello in mano

Gli Otto Re, apparizioni
3 Draghi volanti
Strega, truccata per la trasformazione

Serpenti a piacere

Atto Primo

L'Harmuir—Provincia di Moray—Luogo Deserto, interminabile, sparso di dirupi—È Notte con Luna.

Scena I

Ostragamus nel mezzo, circondato dalle Streghe.

Ostra. Donne, che tali all'apparenza siete . . . ma germi invece di diabolico seme sul mondo sparse, atte a contaminare coll'alito vostro l'immenso creato. Che faceste? . . dite su!

1ª Stre. Ho sgozzato un Verro.

Ostra. E tu? . .

2ª Stre. Al Sire di Nairn, rapii un figlio.

Ostra. E tu? . .

3ª Stre. Di Williams la sposa, che mi oltraggiò, la confinai sulla spiaggia del mare, sopra uno scoglio seminuda.

Ostra. Bene! Or dunque, voi figlie dell'Erebo, destinate a fare nel mondo il maggior male possibile . . . fide ministre del regno buio di Pluto . . . oggi egli affida, alla vostra sagacità un'importante missione. Egli è per ciò che qui vo' radunate, onde parteciparvi i tenebrosi suoi segreti.

1ª Stre. Parla . . . rendi a noi palese il volere del Re d'Averno nostro signore . .

Ostra. Udite adunque. Oggi riede fastoso del Campo, Macbetto, il prode Duce di Duncano, vincitore delle armi ribelli, e del Re di Norvegia. Carico di gloria, egli corre a cogliere gli allori che il Re gli prepara in premio del suo trionfo. Ma gonfio di sé, non si appaga degli onori che il Re gli comparte, ma, vanitoso assai, egli aspira di salir più in alto. L'Averno vuole secondare la sua ambizione, che trascinarlo dovrà agli Abbissi. La vaghezza di vedere questi luoghi rinomati, e forse anco il pensiero di trarne proffitto, lo fece deviare dal retto cammino; e fra breve, egli col solo Banco, altro glorioso Duce, sarà qui di passaggio. Doveva precederlo un suo Scudiero, ma io lo feci smarrire dal suo cammino, lo consegnai ad Astarotte, affinché il racconto de'suoi timori non lo induca a retrocedere. Ed ora gli tengono compagnia oltre Astarotte, anche Bistary . . . Cok-nên-crò . . . e Belzebù. Egli è faceto, e quegli Spiriti, vorranno certo divertirsi a sue spese. Ordinai loro però che non le venga fatto alcun male, e tosto sarà rimesso in libertà. Or dunque, fra poco Macbetto sarà qui, voi vi presenterete ad esso, e gli predirete il suo avvenire che troverete nell'oscuro Libro del Fato. Questa è la vostra missione. Sua moglie, di lui più ancora ambiziosa, compirà il resto. Udiste ora il cenno di Pluto, apparecchiatevi con tutta l'energia vostra ad eseguirlo.

1ª Stre. Nulla verrà da noi ommesso, onde avviluparlo in quella rete che l'Averno gli tende.

2ª Stre. Non potrà di certo sottrarsi alle arti nostre insidiose.

3ª Stre. Sconvolgerò gli Elementi tutti a suo danno, si mai restio fosse ai desideri nostri.

1ª Stre. Dovrà cadere! . .

2ª Stre. Si cadrà! . .

3ª Stre. E con noi per sempre perduto! *Tuoni*

Tutte. Che fu? . .

Ostra. Questo motto, annuncia di Macbetto l'arrivo. Amiche, io vi lascio . . . ritiratevi voi pure, ed apparecchiatevi tosto a compire la grande opra.

Tuoni e Lampi. Viano.

Scena II

Macbeth e Banco

Macb. Credilo amico, giorno non vidi io mai di questo più fiero, e bello! . .

Ban. Ne tanto glorioso! . .

Macb. Il superbo nemico ha dovuto mordere rabbioso la polvere, ove credeva di ergere la orgogliosa sua fronte.

Ban. E bene gli sta! Dalla ricevuta lezione, impari lo stolto a cimentare le armi nostre. Ma, . . permettimi, o Macbetto, che io t'interroghi, per quale motivo hai voluto recarti in questo tenebroso luogo, e ritardare il tuo arrivo in Iscozia, ove ti attendono il Re, i Grandi, ed il popolo tutto, onde tributarti tutti gli onori, e gli applausi ben dovuti al tuo coraggio e valore . . .

Macb. La Scozia non tarderà molto a vedermi; ma prima voglio appagare un mio strano desiderio che da lungo tempo mi stimola, e che ora mi si rende irresistibile. La fama dei prodigi che accadono in questi luoghi, di cui tanto me parlano i Vati, in cui abitano delle Fattucchiere che leggono nell'avvenire, e sanno predire la sorte futura, a chi ardito osa qui innoltrarsi, ha stimolato la mia curiosità di venire io pure in traccia di questi Esseri portentosi. Ecco il motivo per cui abbandonando il mio marziale Corteggio, volli venire colla tua sola scorta in queste fatate selve, onde vedere si posso incontrarmi in esse, ed udire il mio vegnente vaticinio.

Ban. Quale strano capriccio! Ti dirò che molto ne intesi parlare io pure. Però, io non presterò mai fede alle autenticità del vero, e dei fatti che qui si narrano, se non resto pienamente convinto co'miei occhi.

Macb. Sarà follia, ne convengo teco . . . ma non posso resistere a quell'impeto di curiosità che tanto punge il desiderio mio. Daltr'onde, questa dimora non ritarderà di molto il mio arrivo in Iscozia . . . ed i miei corrieri avranno di già recato il mio annunzio al Re. Ho pure qui spedito innanzi il mio scudiero Fighetto, perché investigasse questi luoghi, ma temo che la sua pusillaminità non lo renda capace a tale impresa.

Ban. Ridendo Poveraccio! . . Se vede non uno Spirito, ma un vivente qualunque; l'apprensione della paura che egli ha viaggiando solo, e di notte, un'ombra sola, lo farà morire di spavento.

Scena III

Fighetto e detti
Figh. di dentro Aiuto! . . misericordia! . . Ah! povero me! . . Ah signori, dirin—din . . . don—don . . . dan—dan . . . Brocoli . . . Cavoli . . . cioè, no . . . Diavoli! . . vi prego . . . vi scongiuro . . . abbiate un poco compassione di me povero uomo!
Ban. Quale voce si è questa?
Macb. Sembra appunto Fighetto.
Ban. Che gli sia accorso qualche sinistro evento?
Macb. Andiamo tosto a vedere.
Dall'alto cade Fighetto—e rimane seduto per terra
Figh. Oh! me povera creatura! . . Io sono bell'e morto! Non ho più nean-che un mezzo quintale di fiato nelle *mie budelle!* . . Tanta fatica che ha fatto la mamma, per mettermi assieme queste quattro ossa . . . e quelle canaglie di quei diavoli, mi hanno sconquassato in una maniera, che mi sento tutta la macchina Fighettoria in convulsione! . .
Ban. Fighetto? . .
Figh. Balzando dalla paura Ah! misericordia! . . degli altri Dia-voli? . . ah! . . sono morto! . . sono morto! . . *cade*
Macb. Alzati . . . non vedi che siamo noi.
Figh. E chi sono questi noi?
Macb. Come, non mi conosci più? Sono il tuo padrone Macbetto.
Figh. Si alza Siete proprio voi!? . . lasciate un poco che vi guardi . . . e che vi esamini bene . . . perché la mia vista è *turbulenta* . . . e mi abbisognerebbe, un paio di occhiali di cristallo di Rocca di Boemia, grandi quattordici volte più della Luna, per poter vedere, e assicurar-mi, che voi, siete proprio voi . . . il signor Marcobetto . . .
Macb. Suvvia, adunque . . .
Figh. Ah! che vi fosse venuta la tarantella, per quattordici giorni, e una settimana e mezzo, quando vi è venuto nella mente, il tristo e *malsgur-ato* pensiero, di mandarmi in questo posto indiavolato! . . Oh povero me! Che sconvolgimento nella mia povera macchina corporale!
Macb. Ma che ti avvenne?
Figh. Lasciatemi prendere una libbra, e tre once e mezzo di fiato, e poi vi dirò la mia dolente e moribunda istoria! . . . . Auuufff! . . Ma prima di tutto . . . dica . . . signor Martobetto . . . la sarebbe una cosa molto ben fatta quella di ritirarsi almeno un quaranta miglia lontano da questi brutti posti? . . perché, a dire la verità . . . questa per me, è una posizione troppo indigesta e pericolosa, perché io credo che questo posto qui è abitato da un numero infinito di spiriti *cornuti!*
Ban. Gli hai tu veduti?
Figh. Altro che *venduti!* . . Li ho anche sentiti . . . provati . . . esperimen-

tati! . . E il fiocco della mia beretta . . . che è stato alla prova, se ne ricorderà almeno per due mila anni di quegli *spigoli* mal *spigolati!*

Macb. Ma infine cos'è stato?

Figh. Adesso ve lo dirò subito . . . subietto . . . subiola. Appena sono arrivato qui, mi pareva di sentire un *rumoribus fracassoribus* indiavolato! . . Urli da Cane . . . da Gatto . . . da Leone . . . da Pantera . . . da Orso . . . da Leopardo . . . insomma urli di tutte le bestie, maschi e femmine, dell'Arca di Noè. Tuoni da una parte, terremoto dall'altra . . . e sì che io chredo di essere un uomo di sproposito . . . ma quando ho sentito tutto quel bordello . . . ho detto fra me e me . . . Fighetto, fatti coraggio, e torna indietro! Difatti ero lì per avviarmi . . . quando . . . sento: "Patatach!" un pugno così forte sulle spalle, che mi è parso, una Bomba Prussiana! Non mi ero neanche rimesso di questo primo colpo che "Planfete!" mi è arrivato un garofano di cinque dita nella faccia, che mi credevo che mi andassero tutti i denti in gola, fino giù in fondo al taffanario! . . E lì, pronto un altro, per formare il terzetto; mi regala un calcio nel preterico, che mi ha sfragellato la cucitura delle braghe, lasciandomi scappare . . . arma, munizione, e bagagli! . . Alzo gli occhi per vedere chi ma faceva tutti questi belli e gentilissimi complimenti . . . e vedo quattro brutti musi Diavoleschi, della razza degl'uomini mal maritati, che senza vergogna avevano i corni dritti in testa . . . E lì detto e fatto . . . senza neanche domandare compermesso . . . mi prendono . . . due per parte . . . poi si mettono a quattrocento novanta passi di distanza . . . e poi: "Ponfete!" e su per aria, e poi giù, "Pinfete!" il primo quindici alla battuta! "Vada!" e andavo tanto in alto, che assomigliavo un pallone volante! . . Guardate un po' . . . a quelle brutte faccie, gli è venuto il capriccio di fare una partita al pallone; e per pallone, si sono serviti del mio corpo! Quando sono stati stanchi di giuocare, mi hanno lasciato cadere per terra . . . e sghignazzando come tanti matti, sono spariti.

Macb. Povero Fighetto!

Figh. E povero il mio taffanario!! . . Dunque, dica, Signor Morto-becco! Se voi volete che io resti al vostro servizio . . . fatemi il piacere, andiamo via subito, subito . . . scappiamo, come scappano i tiraborse . . . quando vedono i sbirri che gli camminano addietro per agguantarli. Andiamo altrimenti, io vi licenzio . . . e v'impianto!

Macb. Io voglio per poco ancora qui trattenermi. Tu precedimi alla Città, fra poco io ti raggiungerò. Va!

Figh. Cosa dite? . . andar via da per me? . . Cuccù?! . .

Macb. Taci, qualc'uno si avanza. *Tuono e Lampo* Ma, quale sinistra luce appare?!

Figh. Ah! povero me! . . Se mai fossero i quattro giuocatori da pallone, che venissero per finire la partita? . . Io la mia parte l'ho già fatta, adesso tocca a lor signori; Sotto a chi tocca! E scappa, Fighetto, scappa! *Via*

Scena IV

    Tuoni e Lampi. Pronte le Streghe.
Compariscono le Tre Streghe, Una con Corona in mano.
Macb. Quali orridi ceffi! . . Chi saranno costoro?!
Ban. Chi siete voi? Di questo mondo, o d'altra regione?
Macb. Or via parlate!
1ª Stre. Salve! . . o Macbetto, di Glamis Sire!
2ª Stre. Salve! . . o Macbetto, di Caudor Sire!
3ª Stre. Salve! . . o Macbetto, di Scozia Re!
Macb. Tremando Come!?
Ban. Macbetto! . . e che . . . tremare ti fanno così lieti auguri?
Macb. Io tremare! . . e perché? . . *da sé* Io Re di Scozia!
Ban. Creature fantastiche . . . favellate a me pure . . . e se non vi è ascoso,
    svelate il mio avvenire.
1ª Stre. Salve!
2ª Stre. Salve!
3ª Stre. Salve!
1ª Stre. Meno sarai di Macbetto, e pur maggiore!
2ª Stre. Non quanto lui, ma più di lui felice!
3ª Stre. Non Re—ma di Monarchi genitore!
Tutte. Macbeth e Banco, vivano! . . Banco e Macbeth, vivano! *Via per*
    l'aria
Macb. Banco! . . udisti!? Saranno i figli tuoi Sovrani.
Ban. E tu, Re prima di loro.
Macb. Avranno predetto il vero?
Ban. Chi mai può saperlo! . . Sono arcani assai, quei loro detti.
Macb. Io nulla credo!

Scena V

    Messaggiero Reale e detti
Macb. Reale Messaggiero, a che ne vieni?
Mess. Ad incontrarti. Prode Macbetto, nobile vanto, e onore di
    Scozia! . . Vieni, t'affretta a ricevere il meritato premio de'tuoi marziali
    sudori. Duncano, magnanimo e generoso, il nostro e tuo Re. Sire ti
    elesse di Caudore.
Macb. E sia vero?! Ma quel Sire ancora vi regge!
Mess. No. Scoperto traditore fu percosso dalla legge, . . . e sotto il ceppo
    egli spirò.
Ban. da sé Dunque l'Averno il vero predisse!
Macb. da sé Due Vaticini sono già compiti! . . Il terzo mi promette il
    trono di Scozia! Alla corona che mi offre il destino, la mano rapace
    giammai non alzerò! . . Ma per giungervi fa d'uopo un delitto!
Ban. E perché, o Macbeth, a tale annunzio, rimani muto, e pensoso?
Macb. Io! che dici? . . Io sono lieto . . . e perché non dovrei esserlo?
Mess. Duce! . . attendo i tuoi cenni.

Macb. Precedimi. Ma no . . . sono con te *da sé* Oh! quanti . . . e quali
pensieri mi scorrono la mente! La mia testa è divenuta un vulcano! . . rapido, e bollente mi scorre il sangue per le vene! . . non so
quel che mi faccia! . . ho l'inferno nell'anima! . . *Via e il Messaggiero
con lui*

Ban. Oh come costui si empie d'orgoglio, nella folle speranza di premere
un Trono! . . L'esaltata sua immaginazione lo accieca . . . lo trasporta
. . . e gli sembra già di avere sull'altera sua fronte, la Corona di
Scozia! . . Ma nell'insano tuo delirio, ben folle sei o Macbeth! . . Insen-
sato, . . e non comprendi che l'Averno inganna, ci illude . . . e quando
credi di essere giunto all'apice della desiata fantastica grandezza in cui
egli ti spinge . . . ti abbandona, e ti precipita in quell'Abisso che seppe
malignamente scavarti. *Via*

Sipario e Fine dell'Atto Primo

ATTO SECONDO

Grande Atrio nel Castello di Glamis

Scena I

Lady Macbeth, leggendo una lettera—ha un fazzoletto
Lady. Nel dì della vittoria, io le incontrai nella temuta Selva. Stupito io
n'era per le udite cose; quando i Nunzi, del Re, mi salutarono Sire di
Caudore . . . vaticinio uscito dalle veggenti stesse che predissero un
serto al capo mio. Banco, attestare lo può, era presente. Racchiudi in
cuore questo segreto. Addio! . . Spirito ambizioso tu sei Macbetto . . .
tu aneli alla grandezza, ma per giungervi ti è d'uopo divenire mal-
vagio! . . Pieno di perigli è il passo alla potenza! . . e male per colui che
il piede dubitoso vi pone, e retrocede! . . Oh, vieni! . . affrettati! . . io
saprò accendere quel freddo, e timido tuo cuore! . . io benchè donna,
t'infonderò il coraggio . . . io ti spingerò tuo malgrado sulla via . . .
fosse pur quella del delitto! . . purché ti conduca a quel soglio che le
Profetesse ti hanno promesso . . . e che il mio cuore ancora ardentem-
ente anela!

Scena II

Fighetto e detta
Figh. Buon giorno, signora, Madama Daldy!
Lady. Che vuoi?
Figh. Sua Maestà il Re di Scozia, il signor Duncano . . . dopo d'aver
camminato tutta la giornata per andare alla caccia verrà qui al Castello,
per riposarsi e dormire. Dunque, la prego di prepararle un buon

letto . . . Se non mi sono dimenticato qualche cosa . . . credo di avere
detto tutto.

Lady. Sarebbe vero! . . Egli Duncano! . . E Macbeth è seco?

Figh. Il signor Mortobecco . . . è proprio quello che lo accompagna.

Lady. Tutto adunque sia pronto onde accoglierlo con quella splendide-
zza che a un Rege è dovuta. Va sollecito.

Figh. Mi metto le gambe in tasca, e cammino come un gambero cotto. *Via*

Lady. Duncano sarà qui! . . qui passerà la notte? Ora, a voi infernali
ministri, che al delitto l'universo spingete, infiammate il gelido cuore
di Macbeth! E tu, larva tremenda dell'ambizione, ministra mai sempre
di stragi e di vendette, arma la sua destra di un acuto pugnale, e fra
gli orrori della prossima notte, fa che ferisca . . . uccida colui, la di cui
morte può solo condurlo alla grandezza, ed al trono.

Scena III

Macbeth e detta

Macb. Oh, Donna mia!

Lady. Caudore! Oh vieni . . . vieni che io ti rasciughi la fronte dal nobile
sudore di cui sei coperto. *l'abbraccia, e gli asciuga la fronte* Macbetto!

Macb. Oh, mia sposa!

Lady. M'inganno io forse! . . tu sei ottuso . . . inquieto . . .

Macb. Tutt'altro! Fra poco avremo ospite in nostra casa il Re.

Lady. E che perciò? . . Ti reca forse affanno un tale arrivo?

Macb. No! . . Stanco dalla caccia, e lungi dalla Capitale, nel mio Castello
chiese ricetto, e di tanto onore ne vo' superbo! Or dimmi . . . leggesti
il foglio che ieri ti ho spedito?

Lady. Lo lessi. Le Profetesse ti predicevano allora un Soglio . . . ora la
fortuna te lo offre.

Macb. In quale maniera?

Lady. Il Re qui giunge a pernottare nel tuo Castello . . . egli è l'unico
ostacolo che si frappone alla tua grandezza. Un colpo . . . ed il Vaticinio è avverato.

Macb. Intendo! Ma sento che io non ne sarò mai capace! Additami un'altra via, forse saprò tentarla. Ma sopra colui, che largo di tanti doni, e
onori sopra di me cosparge e dippiù ancora la casa mia colla Reale
sua presenza onora, io non alzerò giammai la traditrice mia mano!

Lady. Soffoca adunque la tua importuna ambizione, resta nella polvere
qual vile insetto, poiché non hai l'ardire d'innalzarti! Sommesso china
l'orgogliosa tua fronte ne sognarti di ergerla mai, se non hai il coraggio
di svellerti dalla schiavitù!

Macb. Ah! . . taci! . . per pietà . . . taci!

Lady. La sorte mi destinava a teco dividere l'onore di essere un dì Regina
di Scozia! . . ma la tua codardia, destina entrambi ad essere schiavi
per sempre!

Macb. Cessa! . . non più! Mia sposa hai vinto! I detti tuoi m'infiammano
il sangue, e mi cangiano il cuore!

Lady. Oh, suprema gioia! . . In questi detti riconosco il prode, l'augusto Macbetto!
Da lontano, odesi la Musica—la quale avanzandosi a poco a poco, annunzia l'arrivo del Re. Durante questo dialogo suona sempre.
Macb. Il Re si avanza . . .
Lady. Andiamo giulivi ad incontrarlo. Questo è l'istante in cui si richiede tutta la tua fermezza, questo punto tutto decide. Non vacilli il tuo braccio! . . un colpo, un colpo! . . E la Scozia tutta, sarà soggetta a' tuoi cenni.
Macb. Ma . . . se mai fallisse il colpo!?
Lady. Non fallirà, se tu non tremi. Suvvia . . . non più dubbi . . . ogni tardanza potria recare grandi sospetti. Seguimi . . . allegro sia il nostro volto, onde nessuno si accorga de' nostri pensieri. Andiamo.
Viano dalla parte ove arriva il Re

Scena IV

> *La Musica, entra in scena e si ferma nel Fondo—il Re, accompagnato da Macbeth, e Lady, trapassa la scena—Lo seguono, Banco, e Malcolmo-Macduffo e Fleanzio—molti Nobili lo seguono, la Musica pure si allontana. (Mettere il Pugnale a Macbeth)*

Scena V

> *Banco e Macduffo*
Ban. Lo hai veduto, amico? . . hai osservato com'egli era tetro, e malinconico? Egli correva ad incontrare il Re . . . ma in luogo della gioia che dovrebbe provare, perché Duncano gli comparte di farsi ospite in sua casa, il di lui occhio è cupo . . . ed incontrandoci non ci vide nemmeno.
Macd. Che Macbeth, fosse dispiacente di ricevere un tanto onore?
Ban. Non voglio crederlo. Anzi riconoscente essergli dovrebbe. Duncano, fu ognora il suo benefattore . . . a lui è debitore di tutta la sua grandezza . . . fu sempre leale e fedele . . . e credo che non ismentirà giammai dalla sua fama. Ma . . . dacché attraversò quella fatale selva . . . dacché udì da quelle misteriose donne il suo avvenire che gli promette un trono . . . egli non è più lo stesso . . . intrattabile e superbo, è divenuto con chicchessia. Tale metamorfosi . . . così io giudico . . . non può essere in lui prodotta che dall'orgoglio di divenire Sovrano! Nulla di male, io però sospetto . . . ma, avrei desiderato che il Re non fosse venuto a passare la notte in questo Castello di Glamis, e perciò resi te pure partecipe de' miei . . . forse inocui sospetti . . . onde potessi dissuaderlo, coll'ascendente che su lui tieni.
Macd. Io lo tentai, ma invano—egli lo ama, lo appella il sostegno della sua Corona. Non volli insistere d'avvantaggio, temendo ch'egli potesse attribuire i miei detti ad invidia per Macbeth.

Ban. L'ora è già tarda; il Re col figlio saranno diggià al riposo. Ritiriamoci noi pure, ma vegliamo alla di lui sicurezza. *Viano. Notte.*

Scena VI

Macbeth con pugnale

Macb. esce guardingo La notte, è nel suo pieno buio . . . tutto è silenzio. Or morta sulla metà del mondo è la natura. Io solo veglio armato di acuto pugnale a guisa dell'assassino che come fantasma si striscia fra le ombre in traccia della sua vittima. Gioite o Streghe . . . i vostri misteri or si compiono! E tu o terra, a' passi miei sta muta! Si vada! . . *Retrocede* Ma che! . . Sembra che un'ignota mano mi respinga . . . ed un'orrenda voce mi dica: "Assassino ti allontana!" Ma invano tentate o ideali fantasmi di opporvi . . . io deggio oltrepassare quel varco . . . quella è la via che mi conduce alla grandezza! *Odesi uno squillo di Campanella* È deciso . . . sì . . . quel bronzo m'invito! . . Non udirlo, Duncano! È squillo di morte, che nel Cielo ti chiama, o nell'Inferno! *Via nella Stanza Reale*

Scena VII

Lady Macbeth sola—guardando d.d.

Lady. Osservando dov'è entrato Macbeth Alla fine vinse il terrore, ed è entrato! . .

Voce. di dentro—lamenterole quasi spenta Oh! . . Dio! . .

Lady. Qual cupo gemito! . . Ah! tutto è compito!

Scena VIII

Macbeth, spaventato con pugnale insanguinato: e Detta

Macb. Furie d'Averno, gioite! . . la vittima è sacrificata! . . Le mie mani, come il mio pugnale, sono lordi di sangue! . . E l'oceano intero, non potrebbe queste mani a me lavare! Lady! . . Non udisti come io . . . un mormorio cupo . . . sibillante?

Lady. Io altro non udii, che lo stridere rauco del Gufo!

Macb. Ma ben'io . . . ben'io l'intesi! . . ed il sangue sento gelarmi per lo spavento!

Lady. E che! . . a metà dell'opra vacilli . . . tremi come un codardo . . . ti arresti sul più bello dell'impresa?! . . Dov'è il prode Macbetto? . . Va! . . sei indegno del nome di Glamis, e di Caudore! . . altro non sei che un'anima debole . . . un'imbelle fanciullo!

Macb. Dimmi . . . chi dorme nell'attigua stanza?

Lady. Il Regale figlio.

Macb. Di colà parvemi udire . . .

Lady. Suvvia, scuotiti una volta . . . e seguimi . . .

Macb. E dove?

Lady. A dar fine all'impresa.

Macb. Altro sangue forse!
Lady. È necessario.
Macb. Io non lo posso.
Lady. No?! . .quel pugnale, nella stanza ove riposa il figlio del Re, gettarlo è d'uopo . . . vo' che l'accusa sopra di lui ricada. Vieni. *lo spinge nella Stanza. Viano.*

Scena IX

   Banco
Ban. Che mi fossi ingannato! . . Parvemi udir delle voci, ed un muover di passi . . . ma qui nessuno si vede . . . tutto è tenebre e silenzio. Ma . . . non m'inganna l'orecchio . . . sì . . . qualcuno si avanza . . .

Scena X

   Macduffo
Macd. Qui tu pure, o Banco?
Ban. Avevo appena al sonno chiusi gli occhi, che fui scosso da un cupo gemito . . . e pareami che un . . . prolungato: "Oh, Dio!" ferisse il mio orecchio. Balzo dal letto . . . attentamente ascolto . . . ma quella voce si spense . . . e non udii più nulla . . . credetti che la mia immaginazione mi avesse ingannato. Tornai a coricarmi, ma un subito mormorio di voci confuse, me fece balzare nuovamente, ed alla più terribile agitazione qui mi aggiro onde accertarmi del funesto mio sospetto.
Macd. Presso a poco, a me pure accadde lo stesso; ma ora, che faremo?
Ban. Io direi di svegliare il Re.
Macd. A quest'ora?
Ban. Ei già lo disse, di svegliarlo per tempo.
Macd. Ma è ancora notte . . .
Ban. Non importa; le faremo nota l'agitazione che avevamo per la preziosa sua vita, ed egli vorrà perdonare.

Scena XI

   Lady.
Lady. di dentro Oh, orrore! . . orrore! . . Oh Dio! soccorso! . . gente accorrete! . .
Ban. Lady Macbeth!
Macd. Ella chiede soccorso . . . Che mai sarà?
Lady. con i Servi—fuori. Ah! . . quale sciagura! . .
Ban. Lady . . . che avvenne?
Lady. Un caso atroce! Ma ditemi, o Signori, . . a che vi aggirate in queste ore notturne?
Ban. Udimmo dei gemiti, e ci fecero temere della vita del Re, . . e siamo tosto accorsi, se fa d'uopo, in suo soccorso.
Lady. Troppo tardi! . . troppo tardi! . . Noi pure fummo svegli da un

rapido concitato rumore di passi, e da voci lamentevoli che uscivano dalla stanza del Re! . . entrammo . . . e . . . orrore! . . orrore! . .

Ban. Ma giusto Iddio, parlate . . . che fu di Duncano?!

Lady. La dentro! contemplate voi stessi! . . io dire nol posso! . .

Ban. ad un servo Precedimi. *Viano, eppoi di dentro* Correte! . . ola, correte! . . Oh delitto nefando! . . oh, tradimento! . . *fuori* Oh, infamia! oh, noi perduti! . . Là! . . là! . . mirate! è morto assassinato il Re Duncano!

Macd. Ma chi fu mai l'empio! . . ove si cela?

Lady. Macbetto gli è dietro con uno stuolo de' suoi più fidi servi . . . e forse non potrà fuggire.

Ban. Egli!? Ma dunque il colpevole, l'esacrando assassino chi fu?

Lady. Non è che mero sospetto: . . Innorridite! . . apparecchiatevi ad udire un misfatto che fa fremere il Cielo . . . e la Natura . . . e l'Averno istesso!

Ban. Grande Iddio! parlate . . . chi fu quell'empio?

Lady. Malcolmo!

Ban. e uniti esclamano: Suo figlio!!!

Macd.

Lady. Egli stesso!

Ban. Ma come lo sapeste?

Lady. Il pugnale insanguinato che trovasi nella sua stanza, . . e la sua improvvisa fuga, lo palesa chiaramente.

Ban. Non posso crederlo! Egli fu sempre docile, amoroso figlio . . . la sua bell'anima inclinata sempre alla virtù, non è capace di un delitto così atroce! Altri forse per ambiziose mire avrebbe potuto . . . Ma chiunque sia, tremi il colpevole! . . e la nostra, e la divina vendetta saprà raggiungerlo . . . atterrarlo . . . calpestarlo! Vieni, o Macduffo, . . corriamo a squarciare le tenebre che avvolgono questo terribile misfatto! E tu, Dio giusto! Dio possente! . . che penetri ne' cuori . . . tu ne assisti! . . in te solo fidiamo—da te cerchiamo lume, consiglio, aita! Sprigiona l'ira tua formidabile, . . e colpisci l'empio che con sacrilega mano osò versare il sangue del più giusto, e clemente Monarca! *da sé* Gran Dio! . . quale pensiero! Le veggenti Maliarde gli predissero il Trono di Scozia! Qui nemici al Re non ve ne sono. Il solo nemico, è l'ambizione di Macbetto! . . ed egli solo può . . .

Macd. A che pensi, Banco?

Ban. Nulla . . . nulla! . . *da sé* Dio tolga il mio funesto presagio! Andiamo. *Viano.*

Lady. Ite . . . correte! Oh stolti! . . cercate pure di delucidare il mistero . . . ma egli è travolto nelle tenebre, il di cui velo è incomprensibile! E tu, Banco, che incauto osasti intravedere il tuo sospetto . . . tu, devi tremare! Lascia che la Scozia sua Regina mi chiami . . . e poi lo giuro . . . o la vile mannaia . . . od un pugnale, ti faranno per sempre tacere.

Via e Sipario.
Fine dell'Atto Secondo

Atto Terzo

Magnifica Sala, con Trono nel mezzo

Scena I

Macbeth, da Re. Entra furente. Lady da Regina.
Macb. Entra furente. Lasciami! . . lasciami! . .
Lady. Perché mi sfuggi, o sposo? Perché fisso ognora in mesti pensieri?
   Il fatto è irreparabile! Le maliarde hanno profetizzato il vero, e Re tu
   sei! Di Duncano il figlio per l'improvvisa sua fuga in Inghilterra, parricida fu detto. Tu fosti eletto Re in sua vece, e già ne impugni il
   temuto scettro. Tutto qui sorride a' tuoi voti . . . eppure mesto sempre
   ti vedo ed inquieto.
Macb. Ed a ragione! Poiché le spirtali donne, profetizzarono che Banco
   sarà padre di Regi! Dunque i suoi figli regneranno? Duncano per
   costoro avrò io dunque ucciso?!
Lady. Egli, e suo figlio vivono è vero!
Macb. Ma vita immortale non hanno! Ah! Forza è che scorra un altro
   sangue, o donna! Si, egli cadrà, se non è pur anco caduto!
Lady. Dici tu il vero?
Macb. Ne diedi un cenno a Riccardo.
Lady. Riccardo è fedele, né mancò mai a' suoi impegni. Eccoti anco da
   questo lato felice.
Macb. Felice!? Ah! . . se tu potessi scendere nel fondo di questo mio
   cuore, e leggervi i miei tormenti, a mille a mille ti cadrebbero le lagrime dagl'occhi! I patimenti del mio spirito sono acuti, intollerabili!
   Lo spavento mi strazia l'animo, ed i rimorsi m'incalzano! Voglio fuggire i vivi! . . e mi trovo coi morti! Le ombre per atterrirmi prendono
   figure visibili, e spaventose! Orridi giorni! . . funeste notti . . . miseramente io passo! Se talvolta pregare io voglio . . . una voce terribile mi
   grida: "Va maledetto!" Questa è la mia vita!
Lady. Questo è l'effetto delle anime deboli! Or via Macbetto, scaccia dalla
   tua mente queste vane follie, questi vili timori lasciali al volgo.
Macb. Ben dici. Ma come te, non posso assicurare né vincere i rimorsi,
   che incessanti mi tormentano!
Lady. Cesseranno, non dubitarne. Abbandonati ciecamente al piacere,
   ed ogni traccia di tristezza svanirà dal tuo cuore!
Macb. Farò forza a me stesso! Odo dei passi . . . qualcun' si avanza.

Scena II

Riccardo e Detti

Ricc. *Sul limitare.* Sire!

Macb. Riccardo! Ah!!! . . tu di sangue hai brutto il volto!

Ricc. È di Banco!

Macb. Il vero ascolto?

Ricc. Si. Nella traversata del Parco, alla prima torre del suo Castello, fu assalito e pugnalato.

Macb. E Fleanzio . . . suo figlio?

Ricc. Ne sfuggí! . . e nell'oscurità della notte, non vidi per dove . . .

Macb. Cielo! Sulle sue traccie movi guardingo, e sia egli pure vittima del tuo pugnale.

Ricc. Farò il possibile.

Macb. Va; sarai largamente ricompensato de' tuoi fedeli servigi. Ora, mi lascia.

Ricc. *S'inchina e Via.*

Macb. Banco estinto! Egli! . . egli che vinse in battaglia i più valorosi, e superbi nemici . . . dovette perire sotto il pugnale di un vile prezzolato sicario! . . e per mio comando! Ah! . . son ben empio!

Lady. Macbetto! . . suvvia dimentica il passato!

Macb. Vorrei . . . ma nol posso! Oh, mia sposa! . . stammi sempre d'appresso, . . ho bisogno di troppo de' tuoi consigli, per vincere la mia debolezza.

Voci. *interne* "Morte all'assassino! . . morte!"

Macb. Che è ciò? Quale tumulto?

Lady. Corro al balcone di Piazza ad osservare.

Via veloce

Macb. Che il Cielo volesse punirmi della morte di Banco!

Voci. *come sopra* "Morte all'assassino! . . morte!"

Scena III

Riccardo ansante e Detto

Ricc. Ah! . . Sire! . . Sire! . . salvatemi per pietà!

Macb. Tu Riccardo! . . Parla che avvenne?

Ricc. Informato il popolo da Fleanzio, che io fui l'uccisore di suo padre . . . tutta Edimburgo è in sommossa, ed ogni labbro grida, e chiede la mia morte . . . arrivai in tempo appena di fuggire, per pormi in salvo. Il Palazzo del Re, è sacro, inviolabile . . . e qui tutto io spero dalla clemenza del mio Sovrano.

Macb. Sciagurato! Palesasti forse che io . . .

Ricc. Non ebbi tempo di parlare . . .

Macb. Ma il popolo vedendoti a qui venire, potrebbe sospettare . . .

Ricc. E chi sarà tanto ardito di sospettare della M:V:? Ah! . . Sire! . . per i tanti servigi che la mia mano vi ha prestati . . . deh! . . non abbandonate un vostro fedele . . . salvatelo dalle furie di quei forsennati! Pensate che i gradini del Trono li avete saliti mercé il mio braccio . . . e questa mia mano ministra inesorabile delle vostre vendette . . . non ancora lavata, ma tutt'ora fumante del sangue di tante infelici nobili famiglie ... or ora si è intrisa in quello di Banco ... e ...

Macb. Taci ... qualcuno potria udirti. Salvati in quella stanza; apparentemente ti farò chiudere in un carcere; domani sarai posto in libertà, e munito de' miei doni ti recherai fuori del mio Regno, per viver altrove.

Ricc. Maestà! .. quante grazie ...

Macb. Ritirati tosto.

Ricc. S'inchina e Via

Macb. Vittima del mio oro è costui ma se cade nelle mani del popolo, col prestigio di salvare la vita, potrebbe svelare i miei arcani. No! .. non sia! Sei caduto nella rete, non mi fuggirai ... Chi è di là!

Scena IV

Armigero e Detto

Macb. Te appunto, o Clerch, la di cui fedeltà mi è nota, e da questa assicurato, or ti affido una importante missione. Prendi teco dieci soldati, entra in quella stanza, vi troverai un'uomo; .. per la via sotterranea lo condurrete nel fondo di torre vicino al fiume. Questa notte poi lo farai segretamente morire. Domani getterai il cadavere nella sottoposta onda, e spargerai la voce che l'uccisore di Banco per isfuggire il supplizio, da sé stesso si è ucciso. Obbedisci ... la tua vita mi sarà garante della tua fedeltà, e del tuo silenzio!

Armig. Via inchinandosi

Scena V

Macduffo e Detto

Macd. Perdonate, o Sire, se m'innoltro a voi, senza essere chiamato; ma il motivo che qui m'adduce è di sommo rilievo, e ogni indugio potrebbe essere fatale. Questa notte fu commesso un orribile misfatto: il valoroso Banco, nel recarsi al suo Castello, fu empiamente trucidato; uno degli assassini riconosciuto perfettamente fu teste veduto entrare nella vostra Reggia. Sire! In nome della giustamente sdegnata popolazione, vengo, perché consegnato tosto mi sia il colpevole, onde subisca il meritato castigo.

Macb. Fui avvisato dalle mie Guardie che poc'anzi un uomo entrò precipitoso, forse per trovare uno scampo. Egli è già in carcere. Fate noto al popolo, che la vita dell'estinto Duce mi era troppo cara, perché non pensi tosto a vendicarlo; .. e se sarà il vero colpevole, subirà una tremenda punizione.

Macd. Perdonate, Sire, il mio ardire, se faccio riflettere alla M:V: che spetta ai Giudici l'indagare, e scoprire la verità, ed infliggere la punizione.

Macb. E se volessi io stesso farmi severo Giudice di questo ribaldo ... se volessi io stesso vendicare la morte del mio amico senza ricorrere agli interpreti della Legge ... che avreste a dirmi del mio operato?

Macd. Legge sacra è ogni vostro detto, e consiglio; . . nè io sarò tanto ardito da fare obbiezzione al volere di V:M: Ma temete del popolo il bisbiglio e lo sdegno; furente voleva irrompere nella vostra Reggia . . . a stento lo trattenni, promettendogli che presto vedrà la sua testa cadere per mano del Carnefice. Che dirà la sfrenata plebe, se vede che il castigo non sia eseguito conforme alle Leggi? Oh! . . guai! . . se sorgesse mostruoso gigante! . . si alzerebbe onde reclamare i suoi diritti!

Macb. E chi sarà tanto ardito da censurare le azioni del suo sovrano? . .

Macd. Il popolo, vi ripeto, o Sire! Egli è un Giudice formidabile, e stende il suo giudizio sul Monarca, egualmente come sul più vile degli uomini.

Macb. Il popolo è mio suddito; . . ed io non mi abbasserò giammai a divenire suo schiavo. Io solo comando, . . e guai a colui che osasse opporsi a' voleri miei! Guai! . . cada la testa del primo che ardisse contraddirmi! Andate . . . e fate nota la mia decisa volontà.

Macd. da sè Despota infame! Ora il mio sospetto si è cangiato in piena certezza.

Macb. A che pensate, o Macduffo?

Macd. Ad obbedirvi, o Sire. E tosto vado ad eseguire i venerandi ordini vostri. Ma prima vi prego, per quanto havvi di più sacro, non lasciate impunito tale misfatto. Se non temete l'ira del popolo che qualche volta è pur formidabile . . . temete quella di Dio che reclamerebbe vendetta! La sdegnata sua ombra, minacciosa si aggirerebbe fra le vostre soglie per turbare i giorni vostri . . . l'avrete presente nei sonni . . . nelle veglie . . . finché in preda a' più strazianti rimorsi . . . al più cupo spavento, invocherete, ma invano la calma ai combattuti vostri spiriti . . . e non troverete sollievo alla vostra disperazione. *Via*

Macb. Quale ardire! Ma purtroppo egli disse il vero! . . e già lo spavento che mi predisse . . . mi circonda . . . mi accerchia il cuore! Oserebbe forse costui, aizzarmi contro l'insolente plebe? . . Ah! . . prima che ciò accada, altri sicari sapranno, non te solo, ma tutta la tua stirpe annient-are e distruggere! Ma perché, o crudo destino, se tiranno mi volevi . . . perché serbarmi ora a questo vile timore! . . Oh, orrore! . . oh, fiera agonia di morte! . .

Scena VII

Lady e Detto

Lady. Il popolare tumulto è cessato. Ma che vedo!? Quale sinistra luce ti balena in volto! . . Macbetto, mio sposo, . . favella . . . che hai? . . per-ché così contrafatto? . . che mai ti avvenne? . . deh! . . parla . . .

Macb. Nulla! . . nulla! . . Un'improvvisa indisposizione . . . ma tutt'ora è passata. Vieni . . . ritiriamoci da questo luogo . . .

Scena VIII

L'Ombra di Banco, avvolta in bianco lenzuolo e Detti

Macb. da un tremito Che vedo!!! . . l'insanguinato spettro di Banco!!! No! . . non m'inganno! . . è desso!!

Lady. Che dici?

Macb. È desso! . . lo raffiguro! . . Oh! . . non dirmi . . . ch'io fui il tuo assassino . . . Non scuotermi incontro quelle chiome cruenti di sangue!

Lady. Macbetto! . . sei tu un uomo!?

Macb. Si . . . lo sono! . . ed anche dir mi posso audace, se ho il coraggio di fissare imperterrito lo sguardo sopra una cosa, che recherebbe spavento al demone istesso!

Ombra. Sale sui gradini del Trono

Macb. Non lo vedi Tu? Là! . . là! . . ritto! . . nol ravvisi? Ma ben'io . . . si . . . lo ravviso! . . Oh, orrore! . . vedilo! . . egli si asside sul mio trono!!!

Lady. Sposo! . . tu sei demente!

Macb. Allo Spettro—Convulso Oh! . . poiché il capo scrollare ti è concesso . . . favella! . . puote il sepolcro rendere gli uccisi!?

Ombra. Via e Macbeth lo segue collo sguardo

Lady. Macbetto! . . delira la tua mente . . .

Macb. Delirante Questi miei occhi l'anno veduto! . . egli era là! . . là! . . ritto . . . minaccioso! . .

Scena IX

  L'Ombra riappare e Detti

Ombra. Riappare a Macbetto

Macb. Eccolo! . . riappare!!! . . nol vedi?! . .

Lady. Nulla io vedo . . .

Macb. Nel massimo Delirio Va! . . spirito d'abisso! . . lasciami in pace! Spalanca una fossa, o terra . . . e l'ingoia! Fiammeggiano quelle ossa! . . quel sangue fumante mi balza nel volto! . . quello sguardo a me rivolto mi traffigge il cuore! . . Diventa pur Tigre! . . un Leone minaccioso mi abbranca! . . Macbetto tremare non vedrai! . . conoscere potrai se io provo timore! . . Ma fuggi! . . deh, fuggi tremendo fantasma!

Ombra. Via e Macbeth seguendolo collo sguardo

Macb. Ah! . . la vita riprendo!

Lady. Vergogna, o Signore!

Macb. Ombra. tremenda . . . sangue mi chiedi? . . si! . . sangue avrai . . . lo giuro! Alle Profetesse ritornare io voglio, e da esse il velame del futuro io squarcierò! Da esse, apprendere desio quello che da me esige questo spettro crudele, e quale essere debba il mio fatale destino! *Via*

Lady. Va, creature imbelle! Soltanto il tuo insano timore, ti crea dei vani fantasmi! . . Oh, stolto! . . il delitto è consumato . . . e colui che scende nella tomba, non può uscirvi mai più! *Via*

Sipario
Fine dell'Atto Terzo

ATTO QUARTO

Orrida oscura Caverna, che poi si trasforma in Bolgia Infernale. Nel mezzo una Caldaia. All'alzarsi del Sipario, Forti scroscii di Tuoni. Lampi—il fuoco è acceso sotto alla Caldaia. Le Streghe l'attorniano.

Scena I

Le Tre Streghe, indi Diavoli.

1ª Stre. Tre volte miagola la Gatta in collera!

2ª Stre. Tre volte l'Upupa lamenta ed ulula!

3ª Stre. Tre volte l'Istrice guaisce al vento! *Tuoni—Lampi*

1ª Stre. Questo è il tremendo istante! Suvvia! . . sollecite giriamo la pentola . . . entro mesciamo i possenti intingoli. Sirocchie! . . all'opra! . . l'acqua già fuma, e schiumeggia! . . *tutte attorno* Tu, Rospo venefico che suggi l'Aconito. Tu Lepre. Tu, Radica tagliata al crepuscolo, . . va cuoci e gorgoglia nel vaso infernale!

2ª Stre. Tu lingua di Vipera. Tu, pelo di Nottola. Tu, sangue di Scimmia. Tu, dente di Buffalo, . . va, bolli, e ti avvoltola nel brodo infernale!

3ª Stre. Tu, dito di pargolo strozzato nel nascere. Tu, labbro di un tartaro. Tu, cuore di un'Eretico. Tu, seme Umano, . . va dentro e consolida la Polpa infernale! *Tuoni*

1ª Stre. E voi Spiriti, negri e candidi . . . rossi e cirulei; venite, e rimescete! . . *Tuoni e Lampi, Compariscono i Diavoli* Voi, che mescere ben sapete, Rimescete!

Tutte. Rimescete! . . Rimescete! . . *Gran Ballabile di Streghe e di Satanelli*

1ª Stre. Fermatevi. Qualcuno a questa parte s'innoltra.

2ª Stre. Chi mai sarà quest'audace?

1ª Stre. Macbetto, noi qui attendiamo.

2ª Stre. Si, ma non è desso . . . è il suo Scudiero.

3ª Stre. Dobbiamo strozzarlo? . . e farlo bollire nella gran Pentola infernale?

1ª Stre. Oh, no! Egli è un grazioso pazzarello . . . ci divertiremo un poco e quindi spaventandolo lo faremo fuggire. A Trosojna ne daremo la cura. Noi ci ritiriamo ad osservare ogni cosa. Olà! *Tuono* Trosojna, all'opra! *Tuono; e Viano tutte tre.*

Scena II

Fighetto solo, si avanza tremando.

Figh. Ah! povero Fighetto! . . che brutto posto che è mai questo . . . io resto istupinito! . . La mi pare, l'Anticamera dell'inferno! . . Guarda com'è oscuro; . . Fammi un poco il piacere! . . guardate, che cosa ci deve venire in testa al mio padrone Malgobetto, di voler venire in questi spregiatissimi appartamenti della casa del Diavolo; abitati, solo dai Pipistrelli . . . dai Ragni . . . dagli Scarafacci . . . e da tutte quelle altre brutte bestie, che io non conosco! Ma quella più grossa, è quella cosa di volere che io venga avanti da per me . . . e per forza, mi vi ha fatto venire. *Guarda attorno* Non si vede proprio nessuno . . . e io sarei curioso di guardare dentro in quella pignatta . . . se ci fosse mo un'qualche Vitello—oppure un Bue! . . perché mi sento una fame superlativa—distruttiva che non ne posso più! E se delle volte fosse robba del Diavolo! . . Oh questa sarebbe proprio graziosa, se mangiando tutto io, ci toccasse di fare vigilia! Oh ma a me, quanto si tratta di mangiare, mi passa la paura e sfiderei . . . Minosse, Radamanto, Satana, e Belzebù! . . Allè! . . facciamosi coraggio, e guardiamo che cosa c'è dentro. *Facendo lazzi, vi appressa.* Uu'mm! . . che odore! . . E un odore, che fra tutti gli odori, non vi è odore, che assomigli a questo odore! . . mi fa venir sulla saliva come le palle di cannone . . . *Si appressa*

Scena III

Stregha truccata e Detto

Stre. *Con voce sdentata* Benvenuto, mio bel forestiere!

Figh. *Si volge spaventato* Aiuto! . . misericordia!

Stre. Non spaventarti, che io non voglio farti nessun male. Anzi, tu mi piaci, . . e se fossi certa che tu corrispondessi all'amor mio, . . saprei amarti sinceramente, e forse concederti la mia mano di sposa.

Figh. Eeeh . . . che cosa hai detto? . . Un bel maschiotto della mia sorte . . . ha da sposare te?! . .

Stre. E perché no?

Figh. Fammi il piacere! . . così vecchia . . . senza denti—che bisognerebbe masticarti il brodo, per darti da mangiare! . .

Stre. Oh non lo sono poi tanto! . . Ho appena compiti i cento anni . . .

Figh. Misericordia! . . Ci scometto che i cento anni, tu li hai compiti quaranta volte! . . Sei più vecchia tu, che Matusalemme, ch'era il papà-grande d'Adamo! . .

Stre. E poi, sono ancora robusta, e verginella; capace di farti padre di una dozzina di figli.

Figh. Una dozzina di figli? . . alla larga! . . Tu, daresti troppo da lavorare al fornaio, a farci il pane per tutti! . . E poi . . . e poi . . . senti la mia cara svirgenella, . . io sono persuaso che non ti manchi altro che di covare l'uovo del Basilisco per compire l'opera. E poi, per finirla, bisogna tu sappi, che io non voglio maritarmi.

Stre. Perché?

Figh. Perché?! . . Perché la donna; basta che sia una donna, è sempre una calamita; E poi insomma per finirla . . . ipso-facto . . . io sono uno di quegli uomini che non desidero di fare delle conoscenze nuove!

Stre. Guardami bene . . . credo di essere anche bella . . .

Figh. Altro che! . . quattordici volte bella! . . ma la bellezza d'una donna, è come una presa di tabacco sopra una rosa . . . dopo la prima fiutata, si starnuta un paio di volte . . . e poi addio! . . la rosa diventa appassita, svanisce di colore . . . perde le foglie . . . e ci resta . . . dimmelo tu, cosa ci resta . . . E le tue bellezze . . . va là . . . senza ch'io te lo dica, si vedono anche senza lume, anche a un'ora dopo mezzanotte!

Stre. Cosa dici? . .

Figh. Dicci . . . che sei brutta fino per due metri, sotto dall'ombellicolo della pancia.

Stre. Senti, mio caro! . . Giacché la sorte ti ha condotto nella mia casa, te ne faccio padrone. Vieni, che voglio darti un tenero ed amoroso bacio.

Figh. Fammi il piacere . . . ritirati più lontano che puoi . . . oh brutta vecchia bavosa, invece di voler baciare me, bacia tua sorella! . . Passa via! . . passa via! . . *Nel respingerla, sparisce la Cuffia e resta la testa calva.* Misericordia! . . cosa vedo! . . oh, che spettaccolo! . . guarda . . . guarda! È pelata, come il culo d'una scimmia . . .

Stre. Via . . . non far meco lo sdegnoso . . .

Figh. Ma . . . chi sei tu? . .

Stre. Sono la padrona di questi luoghi.

Figh. Va pur là, che hai un bell'appartamento . . .

Stre. Questa non è che la cucina. Senti . . . intanto che si cuociono le vivande . . . Vieni meco, ti farò vedere appartamenti magnifici—dopo pranzeremo insieme.

Figh. E dimmi un poco comare! . . hai qualche cosa di buono da mangiare?

Stre. Tutto ciò che potrai desiderare.

Figh. *da sé* È meglio andare colle buone, perchè mi dii da mangiare.

Stre. Vuoi dunque venire?

Figh. Andiamo pure.

Stre. Dammi braccio . . . mio caro.

Figh. Si, io ti darò braccio, basta che tu stii voltata in là, perché ti puzza il fiato in modo che non ti si può stare vicino! . . mi sembri un letamaio! . . Basta, vieni pur qui! *Nel prenderle il braccio, questo sparisce. Guarda.* Che razza d'un negozio è questo?

Stre. Via . . . prendimi quest'altro.

Figh. Prendiamo pur quest'altro. *Sparisce anche l'altro. Guarda.* Ma dimmi, vecchia . . . come è questa faccenda? Dimmi un poco, come farai a grattarti la Rogna, adesso che sei senza braccia? . .

Stre. Quando li voglio, gli faccio comparire ancora.

Figh. Ah! . . adesso, ho capito tutto . . . dì la verità—tu, sei una strega . . . e vorresti tirarmi in trappola. Oh, ma te lo darò io . . . brutta canaglia d'una vecchiaccia! . . adesso ti strangolo . . . *Fa per prendergli i Collo, e la testa, Sparisce. Guarda attorno, e per terra.* Uumh! . . anche la testa è sparita! Dove l'avrà mai messa? Nello stomaco forse? . . ah! adesso ho capito, sicuro che l'ha messa nella gobba!? . . Voglio un poco guardarci . . . *Si trasforma in un Vaso di Fiori* Oooooh! . . questa è anche più bella! . . La Vecchia è diventata un vaso di Fiori! . . Senti, come mandano odore . . . la mi sembra la quint'essenza di tutti i Trentasette odori d'un Orinale da Ospedale! . . Fatti coraggio, Fighetto, . . adesso di questi fiori! . . ne faccio un bel mazzo da portare alla mia amante

. . . e dopo, in te sola confido, ci canto quella canzone: "Daghela avanti un passo!" . . . *Fa per prendere i Fiori—e si trasforma in un Piccolo Diavolo.* Uuuh! . . un Diavolo!!! . . scappa . . . scappa! . . *p.p. e si ferma* Ma cosa, . . un uomo della mia qualità, deve aver paura di quel Diavoletto lì?! Adesso anzi voglio vendicarmi con te, anche per quelle brutte canaglie, che si sono serviti di me, per giuocare al pallone . . . *Per prenderlo—Il Diavolo si allunga. Retrocede.* Misericordia! . . quarda come è lungo, sembra una Giraffa! . . Dissù, per parlare con te, ci vuole una scala lunga almeno, quattordici piuoli, non è vero?

Diav. No! . . *Si accorcia o restringe.*

Figh. Oh, un'altra! . . questa è arcimagnifica! . . È fatto come le braghe del Signor Lorenzo, che si allargano, e si restringono! . . Oh! . . mo' guarda, cosa sono questi due affari che hai piantati in testa?!

Diav. L'arma del matrimonio!

Figh. Acqua fresca . . . Sonch'io che tanti maritati . . . sono costretti a portare il capello duro! . . Io che ho la beretta, mi salterebbero fuori . . . no, no! non mi marito io . . . auf 'caldi!!! . . Ma sai che io sono stanco di perdere il mio tempo con te! adesso ti abbranco per l'osso del collo . . . e te lo torcio, come si torce un pollo! . . *Il Diavolo si allunga e l'insegue.* Aiuto! . . aiuto! . . coraggio . . . scappa, Fighetto, scappa! . . *Viano.*

Scena IV

Macbeth da Re, senza corona e Dette.

Macb. Che fate voi, misteriose donne? . .

1ª Stre. Un'opra senza nome.

Macb. Per quest'opra infernale io vi scongiuro! Che io sappia il mio destino! . .

1ª Stre. Dalle incognite posse udir lo brami, cui fedeli ministre obbediamo, . . ovvero da noi?

Macb. Se l'oscuro enigma del futuro mi possono chiarire, avvenga ciò che l'Averno vuole, . . io non lo temo! Evocatele pure! . .

1ª Stre. Dalle oscure profonde voragini, e dalle alte dimore, spiriti erranti, salite, scendete! . . al cenno nostro obbidienti accorrete! . . *Fulmine . . . e sorge da Terra—Un Capo coperto—d'Elmo!*

Macb. Dimmi, o Spirito . . .

1ª Stre. Egli ti ha già letto nel cuore. Taci e n'odi le voci segrete.

Appar. O Macbeth! . . Macbeth! . . Da Macduffo ti guarda prudente!

Macb. Ah! . . tu nel seno mi accresci il già concepito sospetto! Solo un accento . . . un motto solo . . . *L'Apparizione—Sparisce.*

1ª Stre. Richieste non vuole. Eccone un altro di lui più possente. *Fulmine! . . Sorge un Fanciullo insanguinato.*

Macb. Fantastico fanciullo! . . Spirito lordo di sangue! . . dimmi . . .

1ª Stre. Taci e n'odi le occulte parole.

Appar. O Macbeth! . . Macbeth! . . Esser puoi sanguinario e feroce; Nessun nato da donna ti nuoce! . . *Sparisce.*

Macb. Che intesi! . . Nessun nato da donna mi nuoce!? . . Ora, Macduffo, la vita tua perdono! . . Ma, no! . . no! . . morrai! Sul Regale mio petto doppio usbergo sarà la tua morte. *Fulmine! . . Sorge dal mezzo un Fanciullo Coronato; che porta un'Arboscello.*

Macb. Che vedo! . . Un Fanciullo col Serto dei Re! . . Parla . . .

1ª Stre. Taci ed odi.

Appar. Sta d'animo forte! Glorioso, invincibile sarai, Finché il Bosco di Birna muoversi vedrai E venire contro te! . . *Sparisce.*

Macb. Sublime contento! Quale lieto augurio! . . E quando mai s'intese che Selva alcuna siasi mossa per magico potere? Ora ditemi: Potrà la progenie di Banco, un tempo salire al mio Trono?

1ª Stre. Non cercarlo, e sia meglio per te!

Macb. Lo voglio! . . lo voglio! . . Altrimenti vi farà parlare la mia spada! . .

1ª Stre. Ti accheta . . e sarai pago! . . *Suono sotterraneo di Cornamusa.*

Macb. Parlate! . . Che avviene? . .

1ª Stre. Silenzio, Macbetto! Apparite! . .

Tutte. Apparite! . .

1ª Stre. Poscia qual nebbia di nuovo sparite! . . *Si apre uno Sfondo dal Quale passano Otto Re, uno dopo l'altro. Da ultimo, viene Banco, con uno Specchio in mano. Viano.*

Macb. *Al primo* Fuggi! . . fuggi, o Regale fantasma! . . la tua triplice Corona, è folgore che mi abbaglia, e atterrisce! *Al secondo* E tu pur fuggi spaventosa immagine che di Bende hai cinto il crine! *Agli Altri.* Ed altri ancora né sorgono!? . . Un terzo! . . Un quarto! . . Un quinto! . . Oh, mio terrore! . . Un sesto! . . Un settimo! . . Che veggo! . . l'ultimo tiene fra le mani uno specchio! . . ed in quello vi si additano altri Regi! . . E chi me li addita? . . Oh, orrore! egli è Banco che sorridendo, trionfa dopo di me!

Scena V

Spiriti, Ballerini e Detti. Gli Spiriti, intrecciano una Danza—girando intorno a Macbeth. Finita la Danza via tutti, meno Macbeth.

Macb. *Rinviene* Ove son'io? Che vidi? Che ascoltai? Oh! . . sia ne'secoli maledetta quest'ora in sempiterno! . . Dunque, i figli di Banco regnare dovranno dopo di me, sul soglio mio!? Ah, no! . . non lo potranno! . . io sradicare saprò fino dalle profonde radici questa escranda progenie! Ma che mi perdo io mai in vani deliri?! . Suvvia, Macbetto, il tuo potere affermare devi coll'opre, . . e non con vani sortilegi! Vada in fiamme, ed in polver cada l'alto Castello di Banco . . . e la superba Rocca di Macduffo, . . figli . . . sposa . . . tutti a filo di spada . . . e scorra quel sangue a me fatale! E quanti nobili in se la Scozia aduna, ed a me ribelli; vile plebe di Grandi, vi trascinerò nel fango! Tremi la terra che preme il mio piede . . . che l'ira mia, la mia vendetta, ovunque si diffonderà! . . e tra le fiamme, e cenere muta rimarrà sepolta la Scozia! *Via.*

Scena VI

Le Tre Streghe. Tuoni.
1ª *Stre.* Egli è partito in preda a tutte le furie che suscitare gli seppe l'Averno intiero! *Forte scroscio di Tuono.* Che vuol dire ciò!? . .
2ª *Stre.* Giunge il nostro Gran Maestro.

Scena VII

Ostragamus e Dette.
Ostra. Oh, voi figlie dell'Erebo, che dello Stige bevete la negra onda, e vi cibate dei pomi infernali che tossico spirano, eppure sempre vivete! Voi, che nelle vostre vene sangue non scorre, . . voi, che co'serpenti dormite, e ravvolgete, e ne succhiate il latte . . . ministre dell'Erebo monarca, con voi mi allegro; soddisfatto appieno io sono del vostro operato! Macbetto è nostro! . . Ma la vittoria per meglio assicurare, d'uopo abbiamo, d'aiuto maggiore. L'Averno tutto in nostro favore invochiamo, e certi saremo ch'egli non ci sfuggirà mai dai nostri artigli! . . Ritiratevi. *Le Streghe Viano.* Oh, voi . . . Dei terribili, angioli ribelli dal cielo scacciati . . . abitatori delle profonde tenebre . . . ministri di rabbia . . . odio e vendetta, tutti v'invoco! . . Uscite! . . spargete orrore, lutto, e desolazione, ed infondete nel cuore di Macbetto, i venefici vostri strali! . . tirannico furore gli signoreggi il cuore! . . e tutti i mali che sanno le Furie inventare per mezzo suo trasportate in Iscozia! *Via con fiamma. Tuoni—fulmini—Urli—La Caldaia si trasforma in orribile Drago alato-Sassi in Diavoli—e Serpenti—e Mostri—La caverna diventa un'intiera Bolgia Infernale Bengala.*

Sipario
Fine dell'Atto Quarto.

Atto Quinto

Luogo deserto, ai Confini della Scozia, e dell'Inghilterra. Nel fondo vedesi la Foresta di Birnam.

Scena I

Profughi Scozzesi, d'ambo i Sessi. Macduffo, in disparte. Fleanzio. Malcolmo, e Soldati Inglesi.
1ª *Prof.* Patria oppressa! Il dolce nome di madre, no! . . avere più non puoi! . . che dispersi sono i tuoi figli! . . Tutti noi—ed altri ancora pi-

angono chi lo sposo—chi la prole—chi i congiunti! . . e nessuno ognor rimane che dia un pianto a chi soffre, ed a chi muore! . .

Macd. Oh! . . figli! . . figli miei! . . da quel tiranno tutti uccisi voi foste! . . ed insieme con voi la madre sventurata! . . La mia paterna mano, non potè farvi scudo, contro gli empi sicari che vi trassero ad'immatura morte! Perché fuggiasco, occulto, mi chiamavate invano! . . Ma la celeste vendetta invoco, che all'empio mi tragga in faccia, e vendicati appieno sarete! . .

Flean. Ed io, misero! . . che di Banco l'amato genitore, . . vidi di Macbetto i sicari infami assalirlo, e trucidarlo—e sopra di me ancora scagliato avrebbero i micidiali loro colpi furibondi, se l'oscurità della notte non mi avesse favorita la fuga!

Malc. Giusto è il vostro dolore, ora però inutile! . . Le vostre lacrime per sensibili che siano, non ponno ridonare la vita a' vostri cari; ma bensì il vostro ardire può vendicare la loro morte! . . Lasciate il dolore, e di fermezza armatevi! Prima di essere Grande, fui astretto all'altrui barbarie! Sopportai la pena dell'esilio benché innocente, . . e fui accusato parricida! Orsù! . . alla vendetta si pensi, giacché il momento è vicino. Udite: Questa è la Foresta di Birnam—ognuno di voi strappi un ramoscello da quelle piante, e se lo ponga innanzi, . . e con questo accorgimento guerriero, inganneremo così i nostri nemici, onde non si avveggano che siamo soldati. Ad un mio cenno, ognuno, prenda le armi, e non le deponga finché, non sia compito il totale esterminio de' nostri nemici, e del vile oppressore della nostra patria. Malcolmo, il figlio dell'estino Re Duncano, vi guida alla vendetta—coraggiosi seguitemi, . . e l'empio Macbetto riconosca in noi il Giudizio di Dio! . .

Macd. Il tuo consiglio, o Reale Principe, tutti noi siamo pronti ad eseguire. Fratelli! Seguiamo l'esempio di questo giovine Eroe, . . egli è il nostro Duce—il nostro Re! Pugniamo con coraggio, e giuriamo di non desistere dalla pugna che vincitori, o estinti!

Tutti. Lo giuriamo!

Macd. Macbetto, trema! Se il brando mio ti raggiunge, l'Averno istesso, in cui molto ti affidi, non potrebbe salvarti!

Malc. Questo giorno deciderà della nostra patria, e di noi! . . Andiamo! Nel Castello di Glamis, fu assassinato il Re mio padre! . . là dimora l'empio tiranno—e là, trovi ancora Macbetto la sua punizione! . . All'armi! . . all'armi! . . alla vendetta! *Viano tutti*

Mutazione di Scena.
Magnifica Sala—nel Gran Castello di Macbeth.

Scena II

Dama e Medico.

Dama. Deh! . . per pietà! . . non frapponete indugio! . . la Regina trovasi nel più deplorabile stato! . .

Medi. Ma che avenne?

Dama. La frenesia che da sei mesi l'assale, . . oggi è giunta all'eccesso! Il suo delirio desta spavento, . . raccapriccio, e terrore, domina in noi tutte . . . e nessuna delle sue Cento Dame ardisce accostarglisi . . . Arcane parole, le sfuggono talora—non conosce più alcuno. Parla di spettri! . . di streghe! . . Ahi! . . misera! I suoi capegli grondano sudore! . . Fredde agghiacciate sono le sue membra . . e pesante il passo!

Medi. Disgraziata! Il suo delirio è prodotto da qualche trista sensazione dell'anima, e l'Arte non ha rimedi per tali accessi! Però, tutto mi adoprerò per suo favore; ma temo inutile ogni mio studio! Dite . . . di che parlava nel sonno suo?

Dama. Ridirlo non debbo ad'uomo vivente. Oh, eccola! . .

Scena III

Lady Macbeth in bianco—capegli sparsi: e Detti.

Medi. Oh come, come gli occhi spalanca!

Dama. Eppure nulla vede! . .

Medi. Perchè frega la mano?

Dama. Crede lavarsi.

Lady. In scena, correndo a destra si ferma sul limitare, e si guarda la mano. Una macchia! *Frenetica.* Via ti dico, o maledetta! *moderata* Una! . . Due! . . Questa è l'ora! . . *crescendo a poco a poco.* Tremi tu? . . Non'osi entrare!? . . Un guerriero . . così codardo!? *con forza* Oh vergogna! . . Orsù, ti affretta . . .

Medi. Che dice?

Dama. Zitto!

Lady. Naturale Di Fiffe il Sire . . . sposo e padre, or' ora non era? *elevata.* Che ne avvenne? *crescendo* Questa mano!!! Questo sangue!!! *Delirando* Oimè!!!

Medi. I panni, indossa della notte!

Lady. Or via, ti sbratta!!! *crescendo* Duncano è spento! . . Banco, non è più! . *Furente.* Dalla tomba i morti più non sorgono! Macbetto, vieni! . . Non ti accusi il tuo pallore!!! *Via rapidamente.*

Medi. Seguiamola. *Via con la Dama dov'è uscita Lady.*

Scena IV

Macbeth con spada sguainata

Macb. Furente. Perfidi! Agli Inglesi contro me vi unite?! . . Stolti! Cadde di Norvegia il Re, al lampeggiare della mia spada e voi tutti pur cadrete!!! Le Infernali potenze presaghe, hanno profetato: Esser puoi sanguinario, e feroce; nessun nato da donna ti nuoce! . . No! . . non temo di voi, né dell'imbelle fanciullo che vi conduce! Raffermarmi sul Trono questo assalto mi deve, o sbalzarmi per sempre! Ma prima, il furente mio acciaro mieterà mille, e mille vittime—ed un torrente di sangue diverrà la Scozia al fulminare del mio brando! Eppure! . . un segreto terrore di me s'impadronisce! . . il cuore mi agghiaccia, ed il sangue, ed una voce interna sembra che mi annunzi il mio tristo

fine! . . Ben venga! . . impavido lo attendo! . . Ma prima del mio morire, tremi l'Universo intero del furore di Macbetto!

Voci. di dento È morta! . . è morta!

Macb. Quai gemiti!?

Scena V

Dama e Detto.

Dama. Ah! Sire! . . quale ria sventura! . .

Macb. Che fù? . . Perché quel pianto?

Dama. È morta la Regina! . .

Macb. E che importa!? Meglio sarebbe che nata non fosse! . . Or non mi
troverei in tale stato! . . Andate.

Dama. S'inchina e Via.

Scena VI

Capitano e Detto

Cap. Ah! Sire! . . Sire! . . Quale innaspettato prodigio!!!

Macb. Che fù? È risuscitata la Regina!?

Cap. Ah, no! Nuovo portento! . . la Foresta di Birnam si muove, . . e
sembra venire contro di noi!

Macb. Scherzi tu forse?!

Cap. No, Sire! . . il vero ti narro! Alcuno lo disse . . . ed io, ad'affermare
se era vero . . . corsi—e vidi!

Macb. Ah! . . presagio infernale! . . tu mi hai deluso!!!

Voci. Interne. All'armi! . . tradimento! . . all'armi! . .

Macb. Che ascolto! . . Quali voci.? Va, corri, raduna i miei fidi, i disponiti
alla più disperata difesa.

Cap. Volo ad'obbedirti. *Via inchinandosi.*

Macb. Coraggio, Macbetto! . . si voli alla vittoria, od alla morte! . . Tre-
mate, nemici miei! . . Macbetto saprà fulminarvi col solo suo sguardo!
Rapidamente Via.

Scena VII

*Mutazione di Scena—si Cambia in vasta pianura—nel fondo vedesi il castello
di Macbeth. Irrompono sulla Scena i soldati Inglesi, tutti coperti, colle frondi
in mano da gettare a terra—indi.*

Malcolmo e Macduffo, con spada.

Malc. Via le frondi—e mano alle armi! Seguitemi all'armi! . . all'armi!
Via.

Tutti. All'armi! . . all'armi! . . *Sortono gli Scozzesi, e si azzuffano cogli Inglesi.
Combattimento Generale, colla rotta degli Scozzesi.*

Scena VIII

Macbeth con spada e Detti.
Macb. Oh! . . Infausto giorno! . .

Scena IX

Macduffo armato e Detti.
Macd. Ti ho raggiunto alfine, assassino de' figli miei!
Macb. Macduffo! . . a che vieni?
Macd. A che ne vengo, mi chiedi? e non te lo dice lo spavento che provi
alla mia vista? Le vittime da te trucidate, gridano aspra vendetta ed
io vengo a compirla.
Macb. E chiedi?
Macd. La tua morte, chiedo.
Macb. Invano lo speri! . . Fatato io sono! . . Non puoi traffigermi tu . . .
da una donna nato!
Macd. Stolto! . . Nato io non sono! . . Ma tolto fui dal materno seno.
Macb. Misero me! Che ascolto!? Già lo dissero le possenti invocate infer-
nali voci! Macbeth! . . Macbeth! . . Da Macduffo ti guarda prudente!
Non cale! . . a caro prezzo venderò la mia vita! Se sfuggisti i pugnali
de' miei sicari nell'eccidio della tua famiglia, e se per tua mano morire
io deggio, questa spada che stringo in pugno, prima si bagnerà del
tuo sangue! . . In guardia!
Si battono accanitamente.
Macd. Mori, iniquo! . . *lo ferisce e Macbeth cade.* Sposa! figli! . . vendicati
or siete! . . innulta non è la vostra morte!
Macb. Dio possente! . . Son perduto! . .

Scena X

Malcolmo, Fleanzio, e Detti.
Malc. Ove si asconde l'iniquo usurpatore?
Macd. Eccolo steso al suolo.
Flea. Oh, Banco! . . mio genitore—vendicato or tu sei! . .
Macb. Che vedo! Fleanzio! . . di Banco il figlio! . . ringrazia quel Dio che
ti protegge, e che io bestemmio—che i pugnali fuggisti de' miei
sgherri! . . Le Maliarde profetizzarono che la tua stirpe dopo me Re-
gnasse! . . Regni!!! Ma del padre tuo intanto, amara, inconsolabile ne
piangi la morte! Oh, rrrabbia, che mi strazia! Demoni! Furie infernali! . . prendetemi! . . son vostro! . . son vostro! *Facendo un Capogiro,*
rovescia, a terra, Sorgono Due Demoni e lo portano. Via.
Malc. Tergi ora il pianto, o afflitta Scozia il tuo tiranno è spento!
Tutti. Viva Malcolmo, Re di Scozia!
Malc. Scozzesi! . . Se io ritorno a rivedere la mia patria, lo debbo a voi,
alla vostra lealtà. Mercè il valor vostro, io vengo a stringere quello
scettro che impugnava l'Augusto mio genitore. Riconoscente, vi giuro

di essere più che Sovrano, amoroso padre! spenta è la tirannia, . . e risorga maestosa a circondare il mio Trono, la Giustizia, e la clemenza!

Sipario
Fine dell'Atto Quinto e del Dramma Tragico
Ridotto per Marionette da Cagnoli Alfredo.

Notes

INTRODUCTION

1. Many Italian terms relating to the field of theater of animation have resonances and distinctions of meaning which are lost in translation. For this reason, some Italian terms will be used, but an explanation will be found in the glossary. All footnote translations of passages quoted in the text are by the writer.

2. "a letter of Private Advice, addressed to the Lord Mayor of London on 14 July 1573 which authorized, as in the past and since time immemorial, the Italian *burattinai* to establish in the City their 'strange-motions,'" Yorick (Pietro Coccoluto Ferrigni), *La storia dei burattini* (Florence: Tip. Fieramosca, 1884), p. 287.

3. Dora Eusebietti, *Piccola storia dei burattini e delle maschere* (Turin: S.E.I., 1966), p. 140.

4. The small format thirteen-page manuscript was found in a German monastery in 1710, and was published in 1781. It consists of a memorial version of parts of the original, mixed with scenes of low comedy. The findings of Ingrid Hiller are summarized by Nino Amico, "Shakespeare coi pupi," *Quaderni di teatro* 13 (1981), pp. 96–101.

5. "The old dispute about whether or not Shakespeare had personal knowledge of northern Italy because of the precise references to places and customs in his works (the well of San Gregorio in Milan in *Two Gentlemen of Verona*, Bellario as a name from Padua, the evening mass at Verona, the details of Juliet's funeral in *Romeo and Juliet*, the memories of the Rialto exchange, and the ferry which links Venice with the mainland in *The Merchant of Venice*, to quote only a few) could find a reasonable solution in the certain fact that the great English dramatist had met Italian *burattinai* (he very often makes reference in his works to the wooden characters) in the places which he himself frequented, such as the Elephant in Bankside, then the quarter of the theaters. It is very likely that he had drawn from the shows of these operators that knowledge of the topography and customs of our country which has so amazed and exercised the scholars of Shakespearean works." Renato Bergonzini, Cesare Maletti, Beppe Zagaglia, *Burattini e Burattinai* (Modena: Mundici e Zanetti, 1980), p. 32.

6. *Two Gentlemen of Verona*, 2.1.101; *A Midsummer Night's Dream*, 3.2.288; *The Taming of the Shrew*, 1.2.79, and 4.3.103; *Hamlet*, 3.2.257; *King Lear* 2.2.39; *Antony and Cleopatra*, 5.2.208.

7. "In 1573 the first Italian puppet theater was established in London, which must have often had in its audience William Shakespeare, so ready to mention *marionette* in so many passages in his works; while right at the end of the century (1599), the first English *burattinaio* appeared, a certain Captain Pod." Giuseppe Fanciulli, "Marionette e Burattini," Rivista italiana del dramma 6 (1938), p. 339.

8. "Only the puppet-players were advantaged by this state of affairs: it seems

that the *marionette* were tolerated (like bullfights!) as harmless spectacles. Certain *marionettisti* from Norwich who were famed for their ability were invited to come to London. The vogue for the *teste di legno* did not cease with the reestablishment of the monarchy, in fact, in October 1662 the *marionette* were called to court to entertain Charles II and his family, according to Samuel Pepys. The live actors were jealous and worried and did everything they could so that the *marionettisti* did not take the lion's share." Eusebietti, p. 141. See also Fanciulli, p. 340.

9. Mario Praz, *The Flaming Heart* (New York: Doubleday, 1958), p. 148.

10. For example a number of echoes of Castiglione's *The Book of the Courtier* can be found in Shakespeare's writing. In *Hamlet*, Polonius's advice to Laertes about behavior (1.3.72) is reminiscent of Castiglione (book 2, section 27). Both Hamlet and Prince Harry (in *I Henry IV*) are courtiers of the type delineated by Castiglione (which in the case of Hamlet is a change made by Shakespeare to the warrior hero of his sources, Saxo and Belleforest). The tone of *Much Ado about Nothing* and *The Two Gentlemen of Verona* resembles the courtly game and witty debate which Castiglione describes. The central concepts of the Renaissance revival of Neoplatonism that had originated in Italy with Ficino can be detected in Shakespeare's writing, especially in Hamlet's words about the nature of humanity (2.2.304) and those of Cassio in *Othello* (2.3.257). From the humanist revival of interest in Pythagorean cosmology came the idea of the "music of the spheres" as a figure for universal harmony. According to Ficino, only Pythagoras could hear this music because of the purity of his life and Lorenzo echoes this belief in *The Merchant of Venice* (5.1.60). The Platonic belief in the restorative effect of music is present in Shakespeare's *Twelfth Night* (2.4.1,4), *Pericles* (12,86; and 21,219), and *King Lear* (4.7.26). A number of Shakespeare's sources were Italian, such as *Gl'ingannati*, *I Suppositi*, *Il Decamerone*, and *Hecatommithi*. See Muriel Bradbrook, *Shakespeare in his Context: The constellated globe* (New Jersey: Barnes and Noble, 1989); S. K. Heninger Jr., *Touches of Sweet Harmony: Pythagorean Cosmology and Renaissance Poetics* (California: Huntingdon Library, 1974); Kenneth Muir, *The Sources of Shakespeare's Plays* (London: Methuen, 1977).

11. For example: Murray Levith, *Shakespeare's Italian Settings and Plays* (Basingstoke: Macmillan, 1989); Mario Praz, *The Flaming Heart* (New York: Doubleday, 1958); Felix Raab, *The English Face of Machiavelli* (London: Routledge & Kegan Paul, 1964); Arthur Lytton Sells, *The Italian Influence in English Poetry* (London: Allen & Unwin, 1955).

12. Agostino Lombardo, "Shakespeare in Italy," *The Disciplines of Criticism* (London: Yale University Press, 1968), pp. 531–80; S. Nulli, *Shakespeare in Italia* (Milan: Hoepli, 1918) and "Shakespeare sulla scena italiana," *Il marzocco*, 23 April 1916; Mario Corona, *La fortuna di Shakespeare a Milano 1800–1825* (Bari: Adriatica, 1970); Anna Busi, *Otello in Italia 1777–1972* (Bari: Adriatica, 1973).

13. Hilary Gatti, *Shakespeare nei teatri milanesi dell'Ottocento* (Bari: Adriatica, 1968).

14. Eusebietti, p. 300.

15. Ferrigni, *Storia dei burattini.*

16. Charles Magnin, *L'histoire des marionnettes en Europe* (Paris: n.p., 1852–62).

17. Alessandro Cervellati, *Fagiolino & C: Storia dei burattini e burattinai bolognesi* (Bologna: Cappelli, 1964).

18. Roberto Leydi and Renata Mezzanotte, *Marionette e burattini* (Milan: Collana del "Gallo Grande," 1958); Maria Signorelli, *L'opera dei burattini* (Rome: I.G.T., 1951).

19. Giuseppe Pitré, *Usi e costumi, credenze e pregiudizi del popolo siciliano* (Palermo: Pedone Lauriel, 1889) and other titles.

20. Beginning with Antonio Pasqualino, "L'opera dei pupi," *Cronache parlamentari siciliane* (Palermo: 1966).

21. *Teatro di figura* is an all-encompassing term now firmly established in the Italian language that includes all forms of theater that employ animated objects, shadows, or puppets of any type. It applies equally to traditional and innovative techniques. Within the context of this study, it is used as a collective term for the three types of theater, using *marionette, burattini,* or *pupi.*

22. This approach is found in Edward Gordon Craig, "The Actor and the Uber-marionette," *The Mask* 1 (1908), pp. 3–15; Doretta Cecchi, *Attori di legno: la marionetta italiana fra '600 e '900* (Rome: Fratelli Palombi, 1988); and Serge Kaplan, *Marionette,* trans. Laura Savaglio (Rome: Lucarini, 1986).

23. It receives a brief mention in Doretta Cecchi, *Attori di legno: la marionetta italiana tra '600 e '900.*

24. Even though the burattinaio did not use a written text that would have required approval from the censor, his improvised comments could lead to imprisonment or flogging. Censorship was imposed by both the civil authorities and the church and at times extended to a total ban. The subject of censorship is outside the scope of this work but is dealt with in some detail by Michael Byrom who points out that "The system of censorship and the granting of theatrical licences was very strict throughout Italy, and there are reports even from the 17th century, of people with puppet shows getting into trouble through not observing the regulations. . . . Under a law of 1680, there were even rules governing the dress of the puppets, including a stipulation requiring the painting of blue knickers on all the figures in the *corps de ballet!" Punch in the Italian Puppet Theater* (London: Centaur, 1983), p. 72.

Chapter 1. Performances with *Marionette*

1. According to Doretta Cecchi "Io attore di legno," *In punta di mani* (Ravenna: Longo, 1991), p. 265.

2. "If we observe the history of the *marionettisti* we see them act instead within the system of hegemony, according to the rules of a theater which is relevant to the ideology and the behavioral models of the class which enjoys it and which determines, shapes, connotes and also controls it. When the *marionette* break the rules, they do not in fact pose the risk of the eruption of a culture which is 'other' and disputative, rather they participate consciously in the game of the contradictions within the ruling system, as does the 'major' theater." Roberto Leydi, *Burattini, marionette, pupi* (Milan: Silvana, 1980), p. 16.

3. *I balli plastici* was a program of five short performances choreographed by Gilbert Clavel and Fortunato Depero that was presented at the Teatro dei Piccoli in Rome.

4. See chapter 4, n. 4.

5. *The Mask* 3–4 (1908), p. 71.

6. "One notes an Othello and a Desdemona in elegant eighteenth century costumes," Alessandro Brissoni, *Storia delle teste di legno* (n.p.: Forma ed espressione, 1973).

7. Roberto Leydi, *Burattini, marionette e pupi,* p. 73; Doretta Cecchi, *Attori di legno: la marionetta italiana tra '600 e '900,* p. 20.

8. Gatti, *Shakespeare nei teatri milanesi dell'Ottocento.*

9. Agostino Lombardo, "Shakespeare and Italian Criticism," trans. Anthony Mortimer, *The Disciplines of Criticism,* ed. Peter Demetz, Thomas Greene, and Lowry Nelson, Jr., (London: Yale University Press, 1968), p. 560.

10. Doretta Cecchi reaches the same conclusion in *Attori di legno: la marionetta italiana tra '600 e '900,* p. 36.

11. "Folchetto once heard a *Macbeth* with Facanapa, loyal Scot, 'in which authentic Shakespearean passages were alternated with witticisms of the celebrated and lamented Reccardini,'" Giancarlo Pretini, *Facanapa e gli altri* (Udine: Trapezio, 1987), p. 141.

12. Gatti, *Shakespeare nei teatri milanesi dell'Ottocento.*

13. "Traces of his passing are found, in company with Andrea Menotti, at the Teatro Nazionale in Udine in 1876, from the 30th of September until the 26th of October. These were his shows: *Robert the Devil, Romeo and Juliet, Facanapa Custodian of the Women, The Beauty and the Beast* (dance), *The Giant Pantafaragaramus* (dance); plus other classic pieces from the repertoire of that time." Pretini, p. 321.

14. "It is known that the Mazzatorta family began to give marionette performances in 1850. Established as a touring company, its activity was carried out in the Lombardy area, mainly in the territory of Milan and the neighboring provinces. The theater remained in the hands of the Mazzatorta for a century, being kept alive by the various members who succeeded one another with the passing generations. The company was dissolved in 1950, the family being reduced by then to only two brothers. They were years of serious crisis for everyone, *marionettisti* and *burattinai.* There was very strong competition from the cinema and the arrival of television was not far away, which dealt the final blow to a type of spectacle which had for some time been losing its public and which no longer offered any prospects to the young. With the cessation of activity, the gradual dispersion of the material followed, as happened with many other companies. It was only thanks to the fact that the material constituted a treasured inheritance for the last two Mazzatorta that something was saved." Pino Capellini, *Un secolo di marionette: la famiglia Mazzatorta 1850–1950* (Bergamo: Quaderni del vicolo, 1982), p. 16.

15. Quoted in Danila Dal Pos, *Burattinai e marionettisti a Castelfranco e nella Marca Trevigiana* (Venice: Corbo e Fiore, 1984), p. 20. Repertoire listed on p. 123.

16. Dal Pos, p. 26.

17. "the portrayal of the traditional masks such as Brighella, Gerolamo, Gianduja and Famiola, in roles in classic texts, altered the stage structure with a completely arbitrary freedom." Gianni and Cosetta Colla, *Il popolo di legno* (Milan: Imago, 1982), p. 24.

18. "From the very outset the theater was an enormous success: Podrecca had divined, correctly, that a revival of marionette theater should be based first and foremost on musical foundations; indeed, he maintained that 'marionettes are made from the same stuff as music, from the rhythm of art and life that emanates from it. . . . And because they are operated by singing strings like musical cords, marionettes are almost musical instruments; they are interwoven with music, with a melodious and symphonic essence'." *In Punta di Mani,* ed. Centro Teatro di Figura (Ravenna: Longo Editore, 1991), p. 72.

19. "it seems absurd, inconceivable, that the Italian stage became acquainted for the first time with this great Shakespearean statement, this fundamental

work in the history of human thought, by means of a work of a theater of *marionette*," Leonardo Bragaglia, *Shakespeare in Italia* (Rome: Trevi, 1973), p. 186.

20. "The performance of *The Tempest* . . . altogether worthy of the very difficult undertaking. The staging was a delight to the eyes and a valuable guide to the imagination. The reading of the poetry which had been entrusted to excellent actors and actresses of the theater and silent screen was an admirable collaboration on the part of all in the enchantment of the fairy tale. Vera Vergani was a Miranda of truly exquisite artlessness and sweetness, Soava Gallone gave to her voice which had to speak the part of Ariel the immateriality of a light and fickle breath; Cesare Dondini spoke the part of the gentle and wise Prospero with that humanity which is fitting for this unforgettable character of Shakespearean theater, and everyone, an admirable Caliban, Calò, Piacentini, Brozzolari, each with a sure and precise understanding of their part, contributed to the fascination of the finished product which made yesterday evening's spectacle a great credit to Vittorio Podrecca and one of the most important events of recent theatrical history. Maestro Cantarini, a musician of lively intelligence, had composed for the Shakespearean tragedy some beautifully constructed and fluently inspired orchestral interludes and vocal passages which have undeniably contributed much to the joyful outcome of the spectacle." Review by Fausto Maria Martini in *La Tribuna*, 21.1.1921, quoted in G. and L. Vergani and M. Signorelli, *Podrecca e il Teatro dei Piccoli* (Pordenone: Casamassima, 1979), pp. 73–74.

21. "The special effects and the mechanical contrivances of a highly refined simplicity gave us delightful effects. Caliban really was a horrible monster, Ariel actually flew! And what a storm and what a tranquil vision of the pacified sea at the return!" quoted in Bragaglia, p. 187.

22. "There is one thing which has to be said, that he did not act only Hamlet as a character, but naturally he did Laertes, he did Polonius, he did the ghost, he did the king, he did Hamlet, he did everything: Guildenstern, Fortinbras, all of them." Raffaele Pallavicini, quoted in Italo Sordi, "Burattini, marionette, pupi: la tradizione italiana" in Pëtr Bogatyrëv, *Il teatro delle marionette* (Brescia: Grafo, 1980), p. 33.

23. *Cantico di Natale* from *A Christmas Carol* by Charles Dickens, stage adaptation in five scenes by Giorgio Latis (Milan: Filadelfia, 1971).

24. Conducted by the writer, following an interview in Milan on 5 June 1992.

25. "For me, the marionette is the perfect theatrical machine, because it can do, within limits, everything which an actor will never be able to do. It is, in fact, the theatrical instrument par excellence. It liberates the imagination. It is the means by which one can invent endlessly." From an interview quoted in the company's program for the 1988/89 season, p. 29.

26. Music by Gia De Donato, scenery by Franco Brai, sound by Federico Crespi.

27. Music by Nicolò Castiglioni, parts spoken by actors of the Angelicum.

CHAPTER 2. PERFORMANCES WITH *PUPI*

1. "The *pupi* from Palermo measure about eighty centimeters in height and have jointed knees; in addition to the main rod, which passes through the head to attach to the chest, they have another for the movement of the right arm, to which is fastened a string which, passing through the clenched fist, allows the

sword to be drawn and sheathed. The animators operate them from the sides of the stage, standing on the same level on which the *pupi* move. The *pupi* from Catania however are almost the size of a man, one meter twenty, they have rigid knees and as well as the main rod they have one for the movement of the right arm, the clenched fist of which always holds the sword. They are animated from above from an operating bridge positioned behind the backdrop. The *pupi* from Naples, about one meter in height, differ from those from Sicily in that they do not have a rod to the right hand, which is open, but a string; the sword is attached to the palm of the hand, the legs have jointed knees like the *pupi* from Palermo and they are animated from an operating bridge, like the *pupi* from Catania." Antonio Pasqualino, "Il teatro delle marionette nell'Italia meridionale," *Burattini, marionette, pupi* (Milan: Silvana, 1980), p. 232.

2. "*Pupi* which allow bloody special effects are very curious: for example there are figures which split in two after a terrible downward stroke of a sword, or armor which breaks into pieces, at the same time uncorking a small bottle of red ink inserted in the thorax, which floods the white shirt of the warrior with 'blood'. . . ." Petr Bogatyrëv, *Il teatro delle marionette* (Brescia: Grafo, 1980), p. 30.

3. From Antonino Uccello, "Due tragedie di Shakespeare nel repertorio dell'opra," *Galleria* 15 (1965), pp. 191–94.

4. Uccello, p. 189.

5. To be presented tomorrow evening—Grand evening from Verona of Romeo and Juliet—War between the Montagues and Capulets—Romeo kills Paris—Romeo pretends to be an ambassador and introduces himself to Capulet—Nocturnal love of Romeo and Juliet—Death of Tybalt killed by Romeo—Death of Romeo and Juliet.

6. The typical *cartello* in Palermo was a painting in tempera on a canvas approximately 150 centimeters by 200 centimeters which depicted scenes from the spectacle and was hung outside the theater as an advertisement.

7. To be presented tomorrow evening—Othello the Moor of Venice—Basirocco's dream—Terrible battle between Turks and Christians—Othello is freed and armed—Othello kills Basirocco and destroys the Turks—Betrayal of Cassio—Terrible duel of Othello and Iago—Death of Iago and Cassio—Othello is banished—Othello suffocates Desdemona at night but feels remorse and kills himself with a dagger.

8. "Assisted by Antonio Pasqualino, he staged a *Richard III*, reviewed by Guido Salvini as 'a show of a remarkable artistic level' (March 1950)." Maria Signorelli, "Pupari, pittori, scultori dell'opera dei pupi in Sicilia," *Quaderni di Teatro* 13 (1981), p. 129.

9. From Nino Amico, "Shakespeare coi pupi," *Quaderni di teatro* 13 (1981), pp. 96–105.

10. "the results on an experimental level (the classics with *pupi*) have been more than positive. A spectacle of substance has emerged, of a full three hours duration, which has taxed the *pupari* and *parlanti* more than usual." *Giornale del Sud,* 2 June 1981.

11. "a *Coriolanus* (from Shakespeare) performed several years ago by the Associazione amici dei pupi." Antonio Pasqualino, "Tradizione e innovazione nell'opera dei pupi contemporanea," *Quaderni di Teatro* 13 (1981) p. 11.

CHAPTER 3. PERFORMANCES WITH *BURATTINI*

1. "It can in fact be stated that most of the comedies or '*tutte da ridere*' derive from ancient plots or even from Shakespearean productions: such as *The Two*

Doctors in which is revived the spirit of Plautus's *Menaechmi* (a motif which was taken up by Shakespeare for *The Comedy of Errors*) and *Brisabella or the Wife of Fagiolino* or even *The Dowry of Two Million* which recalls *The Taming of the Shrew* of Shakespeare. On the other hand, the great English poet is not neglected either by our *burattini* or by those overseas: also in France and in Belgium the repertoire includes *Hamlet, Othello, Romeo and Juliet,* and even *A Midsummer Night's Dream, Macbeth,* and *Julius Caesar.*" Alessandro Cervellati, *Fagiolino & C.,* p. 282.

2. Cervellati, p. 286.

3. Cervellati, p. 286.

4. Ed. by Natale Tommasi, Milan, 1891.

5. "At the end of last century he drew comedies and drama for *burattini* from the theatrical series published by many editors. Everything which he produced met with the approval of the *burattinai* of the Po valley area, but especially popular was his version of *Hamlet* which, despite unavoidable reductions, kept intact the spectacular key moments of the drama: the famous monologue, the dialogue between Hamlet and Ophelia and between the prince and his mother." Renato Bergonzini, *Burattini e Burattinai,* p. 34.

6. "With regard to *Hamlet* acted by the *burattini* of Angelo Cuccoli, the writer Antonio Bruers, who had attended the performance, wrote nothing less than these very words in his *La Voce di Bologna:* 'If the booth of the *burattini* gave rise in Goethe to the sublimity of *Faust,* it revealed Shakespeare to me, that is, the understanding that the power of his drama consists in the fact that his intellectual heights are rooted in the most elementary humanity, so that his works, which the highest minds do not manage to consume, are also dramas for the popular arena which the masses live and understand.'" Cervellati, p. 284, note 4.

7. Valeria Mazzolli, "Attività nel campo del teatro d'animazione di Giordano Mazzavillani" (unpublished thesis, Dipartimento musica e spettacolo, Facoltà di lettere e filosofia, Università di Bologna, 1976/77).

8. "in the *Hamlet* performed by the *burattinaio,* Ponti, one could hear phrases of this nature, directed by Sandrone to Claudio, king of Denmark: [a difficult to translate but clearly irreverent curse, perhaps 'O holy crown, a pox upon you'] and other such refined comments." Cervellati, p. 284, note 4.

9. "rightly considered one of the greatest *burattinai* who had ever existed. A bust is dedicated to him in the Teatro Adriani in Mantua." Leydi and Mezzanotte, *Marionette e burattini,* p. 516, note 13.

10. Bergonzini, p. 113.

11. Loosely translated as "Let's go and see what's up. Look at this omelette! (indicating the dead) What a pity it can't be eaten!" The humor is based on Arlecchino viewing even a tragic finale and a pile of corpses in terms of gastronomic imagery.

12. To be or not to be? To eat or not to eat? To sing or not to sing? To beat or to be beaten? To give someone a beating and go to prison or to be beaten and remain a gentleman? To steal and stuff myself with tasty morsels or cool my heels at home and remain with an empty belly and die a good death? By Jove! This is the problem. When I think about death I get gooseflesh. To think that even I will one day be without a nose and that instead of these two ?sparkling ?slitty eyes, I will have two deep, dark holes, deep, brr . . . I would buy a meal for someone who could tell me whether or not one eats and drinks in the afterlife. If one is always hungry, I'll stay here because, after death, I don't want to die of hunger. Oh, here is the beautiful Ophelia! Oh, my darling! She seems an angel! Except that she hasn't any wings! But one could attach them to her.

13. "Pina brought into the little theater a wholly feminine impetus. Discreet, attentive, as orderly as an ant, with her the *baracca* seemed to be covered with rosebuds. She was the custodian of the *teste di legno*, who groomed, cleaned, checked, and scolded on a daily basis. She was the tailor who designed, cut out, and sewed new jackets and gowns in bright colors and cloaks as black as coal. She was the cashier who, with housewifely grip, ensured minimum takings enough at least to cover the expenses of transport and the daily food. And it was always she, who, with violent tugs, brought me back down to earth from the world of dreams in which I invariably became immersed in order to exercise the imagination. Pina, or rather the rational part, the calculating mind of the *baracca*. An irreplaceable and indispensable part. One works better as a couple: there are two heads to think, two hearts which beat on the same wave, four hands which move under the stimulus of a single command, two souls which merge. Family harmony and serenity translate in the *baracca* into perfect synchronization of movements and total agreement on how to animate the *teste di legno*. The communion of ideals, affections, and feelings is the unifying fluid of a life like ours, always exposed to the risks and the trials of a craft which moves in the world of unforeseen events and the imponderable." Roberto Alborghetti, *Una vita da burattinaio* (Bergamo: Cesare Ferrari, 1986), p. 86.

14. Translation by Ferdinando Carlesi in the series *I Classici Azzurri*.

15. "The mesh of the plot had to be widened to allow him to enter and to shape the comedy as he pleased. But this forced entry must not alter the originality of the work." Alborghetti, p. 88.

16. At the Dipartimento musica e spettacolo, Facoltà di lettere e filosofia dell'Università di Bologna.

17. Valeria Mazzoli, "Attività nel campo del teatro d'animazione di Giordano Mazzavillani" (unpublished thesis, Facoltà di lettere e filosofia, Università di Bologna, 1976/77).

18. "He was very well known in Bologna and perhaps even more so in all the cities of northern and central Italy, where he gave an enormous number of performances with brilliant success. He spoke many dialects and was capable of sustaining an entire show alone, playing all the parts and the masks, except for the female characters, which task was entrusted to his wife, Maria." Cervellati, p. 247.

19. Mazzoli, p. 141.

Chapter 5. Analysis of a Production

1. "how beautiful this ancient Neapolitan dialect is, so Latin, with its full words, not truncated, with its musicality, its sweetness, the exceptional flexibility and the ability to bring to life magical, mysterious events and creatures which no modern language possesses any longer!" *The Tempest*, trans. Eduardo De Filippo (Turin: Einaudi, 1984), p. 187.

2. "Bent over the stage, with curved spine, seeing only a perpendicular view of the 'actors' to whom we give life and movement, every show is an extraordinary effort. Between us and the *marionetta* which we move is created a relationship of total exchange, a magical liaison of emotions which only the applause and the amazement of the public manages to break . . . until the next show. Until the next enchantment." Maurizio Dotti, quoted in an interview with Remo Binosi.

3. "The poetic power of Eduardo De Filippo in restoring, by means of the

richness of the Neapolitan language, the 'popular' dimension of a text which by now has been examined and reexamined in the light of philosophical and intellectual interpretations, appeared to be a more intense and more solid meeting point with the theater of *marionette,* which makes the world of the imagination tangible by means of magic and scenic enchantments." Eugenio Monti Colla, quoted in the program for the performance at the Venice Biennale.

4. *Viva Milano,* 7–13/11/85.

5. Described in Jiří Veltruskỳ, "Puppetry and acting," *Semiotica* 47 (1983), p. 119.

CHAPTER 6. SHAKESPEARE WITH STRINGS: HOW THE BARD HAS FARED IN *TEATRO DI FIGURA*

1. First staged in Rouen in 1888 under the title *Les Polonais.*

2. Henryk Jurkowski, "Transcodification of the sign systems of puppetry," *Semiotica* 47 (1983), p. 138.

3. Such ritual laughter accompanies new life in both fertility and agricultural rites. Vladimir Propp, *Theory and History of Folklore,* trans. Ariadna Y. Martin and Richard P. Martin, *Theory and History of Literature* 5 (Manchester: Manchester University Press, 1984).

4. Antonio Pasqualino, "Marionettes and glove puppets: Two theatrical systems of Southern Italy," *Semiotica* 47 (1983), p. 224.

5. There was often a small opening in the covering of the lower portion of the *baracca* through which the *burattinaio* could observe the audience.

6. The role of teatro di figura in the diffusion of Italian is examined by Doretta Cecchi, *Attori di Legno: la marionetta italiana tra '600 e '900,* p. 23.

7. Discussed at length by Agostino Lombardo, "Shakespeare and Italian Criticism," trans. Anthony Mortimer, *The Disciplines of Criticism,* ed. Peter Demetz, Thomas Greene, and Lowry Nelson Jr. (London: Yale University Press, 1968), pp. 531–80.

8. Marvin Carlson, *The Italian Shakespearians* (Washington: Folger, 1985), p. 15.

9. Carlson, pp. 15–19.

10. Pëtr Bogatyrëv, *Il teatro delle marionette.*

11. Veltruskỳ, p. 79.

12. Veltruskỳ, p. 102.

13. Thomas A. Green and W. J. Pepicello, "Semiotic interrelationships in the puppet play," *Semiotica* 47 (1983), p. 157.

14. Green and Pepicello, p. 159.

Glossary

(Where appropriate, the plural is given in parentheses.)

baracca. The booth used for performances with *burattini*. Made of a wooden frame with a canvas covering, it can be disassembled. The opening for the stage is at a height that allows the operator and his equipment to be concealed beneath it. At the front of the opening is a ledge about twenty centimeters in depth which provides a surface for the placing of any properties and the collapse of dead or disabled *burattini*.

burattino (burattini). A half-figure puppet without legs which is moved from below by the hand of the operator that is inserted into the body as if into a glove.

burattino a bastone. A type of *burattino* that has a sculpted body or torso as well as the head and cannot, therefore, be worn on the hand of the *burattinaio* and is instead supported by means of a wooden rod.

burattinaio (burattinai). The person who prepares performances with *burattini* and both operates them with the hands and speaks their dialogue.

cartello. A large painted canvas that showed scenes from a performance with *pupi* and was hung outside the theater as an advertisement for the show. It usually depicted eight scenes and in the case of a serialized spectacle, a card was attached to indicate which episode would be presented that evening.

copione (copioni). The text for a performance by *marionette, burattini*, or *pupi*. It is usually handwritten in large lettering to facilitate its reading during the performance. It also contains instructions regarding lighting, props, scene changes and cuts to the text. The *copione* for a performance by *burattini* or *pupi* is usually not a full text but a brief outline for dialogue which the operator improvised or supplied from memory.

marionetta (marionette). A full-length figure, usually wooden, that is animated from above by means of strings or rods. Small counterweights are attached to the wrists and soles of the feet to facilitate the animation. The average height is eighty centimeters and the weight approximately seven kilograms. *Marionette* are also known as *pupazzi* in Rome, and as *fantoccini* in Tuscany.

225

marionettista (marionettisti). The person who prepares and mounts performances with *marionette* and animates the *marionette* during the show by means of their strings.

opra dei pupi. The term that describes the unique theatrical genre which centers on the *pupi*.

parlatore (parlatori). The unseen speaker of the dialogue of the *pupi*.

ponte di manovra. The bridge that runs across the stage, with an access ladder at each end, from which the *marionettisti* operate the *marionette*. Elaborate productions may have more than one bridge to increase the depth of stage on which the *marionette* may appear.

pupo (pupi). A *marionetta* from Naples or Sicily which is distinguished by its larger size, costume of armor and specialized repertoire of chivalric legends.

puparo (pupari). The person who operates, and may also construct, the *pupi*, but does not always speak the parts.

teatro di figura. An all-encompassing term now firmly established in the Italian language which includes all forms of theater in which material images of humans, animals, or spirits are created, displayed, or manipulated in narrative or dramatic performance. It applies equally to traditional and innovative techniques.

teste di legno. The term used by *burattinai* to refer to their *burattini* (literally "wooden heads").

Bibliography

Alberti, Carmelo. *Il teatro dei pupi e lo spettacolo popolare siciliano.* Milan: Mursia, 1977.

Alborghetti, Piero. *Una vita da burattinaio: Con Benedetto Ravasio nel mondo della baracca.* Bergamo: Cesare Ferrari, 1986.

Allegri, Luigi. *Per una storia del teatro come spettacolo: il teatro di burattini e di marionette.* Edited by Arturo Carlo Quintavalle. Quaderni di Storia dell'Arte, 10. Parma: Università di Parma, Centro studi e archivio della comunicazione, 1978.

Amico, Nino. "Shakespeare coi pupi." *Quaderni di teatro* 13 (1981): 96–101.

Antonelli, Calfus Lucilla. *Gerolamo e il suo teatro.* Milan: Comoedia, 1925.

Apollonio, M., and E. Monti. *Storia e arte della compagnia Carlo Colla e figli.* Milan: Fiscambi, 1966.

Baird, Bill. *Le marionette, storia di uno spettacolo.* Trans. by Anna Raschi Espagnet. Milan: Mondadori, 1967.

Baty, Gaston, and René Chavance. *Breve storia del teatro.* Turin: Einaudi, 1951.

Bello, Marisa and Stefano de Matteis. "Un burattinaio e la sua storia." *Scena* 3–4 (1977): 15–19.

Bergonzini, Renato; Cesare Maletti; and Beppe Zagaglia. *Burattini e Burattinai.* Modena: Mundici e Zanetti, 1980.

Bogatyrëv, Pëtr. *Il teatro delle marionette.* Brescia: Grafo, 1980.

———. "The interconnection of two similar semiotic systems: The puppet theater and the theater of living actors." *Semiotica* 47 (1983): 47–68.

Bragaglia, Leonardo. *Shakespeare in Italia.* Rome: Trevi Editore, 1973.

Brissoni, Alessandro. *Storia delle teste di legno.* n.p.: Forma ed espressione, 1973.

I burattini dei Ferrari. Catalogue of show at Cervia. Cervia: Centro Teatro di Figura, 1986.

Burattini, marionette e pupi. Catalogue of show at Palazzo Reale, Milan. Milan: Silvana, 1980.

Burattini e marionette italiani. Catalogue of show at Museo Teatrale alla Scala. Milan: Museo Teatrale alla Scala, 1957.

Busi, Anna. *Otello in Italia 1777–1972.* Bari: Adriatica, 1973.

Byrom, Michael. *Punch and Judy: Its origin and evolution.* Aberdeen: Centaur, 1972.

———. *Punch in the Italian Puppet Theatre.* London: Centaur, 1983.

Capellini, Pino. *Un secolo di marionette: la famiglia Mazzatorta 1850–1950.* Bergamo: Quaderni del vicolo, 1982.

———. *Baracca e burattini: Il teatro popolare dei burattini nei territori e nelle tradizioni lombarde.* Bergamo: Grafica Gutenberg Gorle, 1977.

Carlson, Marvin. *The Italian Shakespearians.* Washington: Folger, 1985.

Cavallone Anzi, Anna. *Shakespeare nei teatri milanesi del Novecento (1904–78).* Bari: Adriatica, 1980.

Cecchi, Doretta. *Attori di legno: la marionetta italiana fra '600 e '900.* Rome: Fratelli Palombi, 1988.

———. "Una magia animata dai fili." *Historia* 412 (1992): 70–77.

Centro Teatro di Figura Cervia, ed. *In punta di mani: Figura da burattino, mappa del teatro italiano di maschere, pupi e burattini.* Ravenna: Angelo Longo, 1991.

Cervellati, Alessandro. *Le maschere e la loro storia.* Bologna: n.p., 1954.

———. *Storia delle maschere.* Bologna: Il Resto del Carlino, 1955.

———. *Fagiolino e C: Storia dei burattini e burattinai bolognesi.* Bologna: Cappelli, 1964.

Chiopris, G. *Amleto ovvero, Arlecchino principe di Danimarca.* Trieste: Trieste e Fiume, n.d.

Colla, Gianni and Cosetta Colla. *Il popolo di legno.* Milan: Imago, 1982.

Corona, Mario. *La fortuna di Shakespeare a Milano (1800–1825).* Bari: Adriatica, 1970.

Craig, Edward Gordon. *Il mio teatro.* Milan: Feltrinelli, 1980.

———. *On the art of the theatre.* London: n.p., 1957.

———. "The actor and the Uber-marionette." *The Mask* 1 (1908): 3–15.

Cuticchio, Mimmo. *Storia e testmonianza di una famiglia di pupari.* Palermo: S.T. Ass, 1978.

Dall'Acqua, Isabella Quattromini. *La realtà della fantasia ovvero, il Museo Giordano Ferrari.* Fidenza: Comune di Fidenza, 1981.

Dal Pos, Danila. *Burattinai e marionettisti a Castelfranco e nella Marca Trevigiana.* Venice: Corbo e Fiore, 1984.

De Nigris, Fulvio. *Otello Sarzi burattinaio annunciato.* Bologna: Patron, 1986.

Enciclopedia dello spettacolo. Rome: Le Maschere, 1958.

Eusebietti, Dora. *Piccola storia dei burattini e delle maschere.* Turin, S.E.I., 1966.

Fanciulli, Giuseppe. "Marionette e Burattini." *Rivista italiana del dramma* 2 (1938).

Ferrari, Italo and Francesca Castellino. *Baracca e burattini.* Turin: S.E.I., 1936.

Ferrigni, Pietro Coccoluto (Yorick). *La storia dei burattini.* Florence: Tip. Fieramosca, 1884.

Gatti, Hilary. *Shakespeare nei teatri milanesi dell'Ottocento.* Bari: Adriatica, 1968.

Giancane, Daniele. *Le marionette di Canosa: alla ricerca di una cultura.* Bari: Levante, 1965.

Green, Thomas A., and W. J. Pepicello. "Semiotic interrelationships in the puppet play." *Semiotica* 47 (1983): 147–61.

Gurr, Andrew. *The Shakespearean Stage, 1574–1642.* Cambridge: Cambridge University Press, 1980.

Jurkowski, Henryk. "Transcodification of the sign systems of puppetry." *Semiotica* 47 (1983): 123–146.

Kaplan, Serge. *Marionette.* Trans. by Laura Savaglio. Rome: Lucarini, 1986.

Kennard, Joseph. *Masks and Marionettes.* Washington: Kennikat Press, 1935.

Kobler, Cyril. *Marionette.* Rome: n.p., 1986.

Levith, Murray. *Shakespeare's Italian Settings and Plays*. Basingstoke: Macmillan, 1989.

Leydi, Roberto and Renata Mezzanotte. *Marionette e burattini*. Milan: Collana del 'Gallo Grande', 1958.

Li Gotti, Ettore. *Il teatro dei pupi*. Florence: Sansoni, 1957.

Lombardo, Agostino. *Strehler e Shakespeare*. Rome: Bulzoni, 1992.

———. "Shakespeare and Italian Criticism." Trans. by Anthony Mortimer. *The Disciplines of Criticism*. Edited by Peter Demetz, Thomas Greene, and Lowry Nelson Jr. London: Yale University Press, 1968.

Magnin, Charles. *L'histoire des marionnettes en Europe*. Paris: n.p., 1852–62.

Marotti, F. *Amleto o dell'oxymoron*. Rome: Bulzoni, 1966.

Marta, Guido. "Una tradizione che si rinnova: le marionette di Podrecca." *Emporium* 72 (1930): 241–47.

Mazzoli, Valeria. "Attività nel campo del teatro dell'animazione di Giordano Mazzavillani." Thesis, Dipartimento musica e spettacolo, Facoltà di Lettere e Filosofia dell'Università di Bologna, 1976/77.

Modignani, A. Litta. *Dizionario biografico e bibliografico dei burattinai, marionettisti e pupari della tradizione italiana*. Bologna: Clueb, 1985.

Monti, Eugenio. *Il Gerolamo: C'era una volta un teatro di marionette*. Milan: Strenna dell'Istituto Ortopedico Gaetano Pini, 1975.

Nulli, S. "Shakespeare sulla scena italiana." *Il marzocco*, 23 April 1916.

———. *Shakespeare in Italia*. Milan: Hoepli, 1918.

Obrazcov, Sergej. *Il mestiere di burattinaio*. Rome: n.p., 1986.

Pandolfini Barberi, Antonio. *Burattini e burattinai bolognesi*. Bologna: Zanichelli, 1923.

Pasqualino, Antonio. *L'opera dei pupi*. Palermo: Sellerio, 1978.

———. *L'opera dei pupi*. Palermo: Sellerio, 1990.

———. *I pupi siciliani*. Palermo, STASS, n.d.

———. "Marionettes and glove puppets: Two theatrical systems of Southern Italy." *Semiotica* 47 (1983): 219–280.

———. and J. Vibaek. *Eroi, mostri e maschere: Il repertorio tradizionale nel teatro di animazione italiano*. Catalogue of show at Magazzeno del Sale, Cervia. Florence: Artificio, 1990.

Pasqualino, Fortunato. *Teatro con i pupi siciliani*. Palermo: Cavallotto, 1980.

———. and Olsen, Barbara. *L'arte dei pupi: Teatro popolare siciliano*. Milan: Rusconi, 1983.

Petrai, Giuseppe. *Maschere e Burattini*. Rome: Perino, 1885.

Petrolino, Ettore. "I burattini di Italo Ferrari." *Scenario* 4 (1936): 163.

Praz, Mario. *The Flaming Heart*. New York: Doubleday, 1958.

Pretini, Giancarlo. *Facanapa e gli altri*. Udine: Trapezio, 1987.

Raab, Felix. *The English Face of Machiavelli*. London: Routledge & Kegan Paul, 1964.

Racca, Carlo. *Burattini e Marionette*. Turin: Paravia, n.d.

Rasi, Luigi. "I Burattini." *La Lettura* (1913): 165.

Rigoli, Aurelio. *Eroi di Sicilia*. Palermo: Gidue, 1983.

Sangiorgi, Sergio. *I burattini, maschere, storia e atti unici.* Bologna: Ponte nuovo editrice, 1980.

Sells, Arthur Lytton. *The Italian Influence in English Poetry.* London: Allen & Unwin, 1955.

Shakespeare, William. *La Tempesta.* Trans. by Eduardo De Filippo. Turin: Einaudi, 1984.

Signorelli, Maria. *Burattini e marionette in Italia dal Cinquecento ai giorni nostri; testimonianze storiche, artistiche e letterarie.* Rome: Fratelli Palombi, 1980.

Speaight, George. *The history of the English puppet theatre.* 2d ed. London: Hale, 1990.

Suppo, Rodolfo; Manuela Cerri; and Gian Mesturino. *Il museo della marionetta di Torino.* Turin: Priuli & Verlucca, 1989.

Il teatrino Rissone. Catalogue of show at Teatro del Falcone, Genova. Modena: Panini, 1985.

Uccello, Antonino. "Due tragedie di Shakespeare nel repertorio dell'Opra." *Galleria* 15 (1965): 187–98.

Veltruskỳ, Jiří. "Puppetry and acting." *Semiotica* 47 (1983): 69–122.

Vergani, G. and L. and M. Signorelli. *Podrecca e il Teatro dei Piccoli.* Pordenone: Casamassima, 1979.

Volpi, Luigi. *Usi, costumi e tradizioni bergamasche: la maschera di Gioppino e il suo teatro.* Bergamo: Edizioni del 'Giopi', 1937.

von Kleist, Heinrich. *Il teatro delle marionette.* Genoa: Il Melangolo, 1982.

Index